The Sou... ...ific

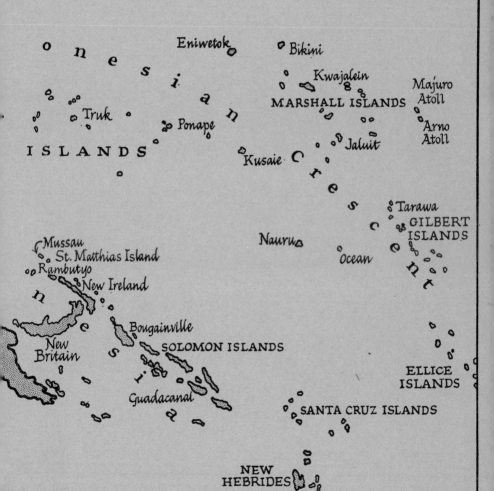

Saipan

o n e s i a n

Eniwetok   Bikini

Kwajalein   Majuro
Atoll
MARSHALL ISLANDS
Truk   Arno
Ponape   Atoll

I S L A N D S   Jaluit

Kusaie   C r e s

Tarawa
GILBERT
ISLANDS
Nauru
Ocean   c

Mussau   e
St. Matthias Island
Rambutyo   n
New Ireland

n   Bougainville   t
New   SOLOMON ISLANDS
Britain   ELLICE
i   ISLANDS
s
Guadacanal   SANTA CRUZ ISLANDS
a

NEW
HEBRIDES

BLACK ROBE AND GRASS SKIRT

BLACK ROBE

& Grass Skirt

by PHILIP R. *and* PAULINE M. TOOMIN

HORIZON PRESS

NEW YORK

1963

To Everett McKinley Dirksen, the Junior Senator from Illinois, without whose advice and unflagging interest this book would never have been written.

CONTENTS

CHAPTER 1

FROM PATIO TO PARADISE

It happened seemingly by accident, yet to those who, like myself, see the hand of fate in all human activity, it had a primal cause not difficult to determine. Years before, I had remarked to the Senator that I could not possibly accept a post in Washington; nevertheless if something glamorous developed, say in the neighborhood of Paris, or even Bali, requiring the deft hand of a trouble-shooter, I might be had for the asking.

Three years passed before this chance conversation was translated into action. Meanwhile, ambassadors, cabinet members and federal judges had been appointed by the score. I had every reason to believe that I was and would continue to remain the forgotten man. Each day I had sat in my office feeling sorry for my government: How much it was suffering from an incredible waste of talent by keeping me cooped up in the practice of law for my few clients, when I could be making decisions to confound the lives of millions. It was small comfort to me that this job was being ably done by others. In fact, I vented my disappointment in criticizing them, carping in accordance with an old American principle: Let George do it—but make him suffer for it.

Suddenly one summer day a call came from Harold Rainville, the Senator's irrepressible man Friday. "Phil," he said, "a really glamorous post has opened, and we think you can fill it. Requires good legal background. It is Associate Justice of the High Court of the Pacific Trust Territory. You would have to live in the Truk Islands for two years, and travel and hold court in the various districts."

"But, Harold," I said, "I speak a very poor Trukese, and besides, I doubt that my wife would consent to give up canasta and live like a pioneer."

"That's easy," he said. "Just tell her she can spend the holidays shopping in Hong Kong and Tokyo. No woman can resist that."

So it proved. After a few more details from Rainville, I was easily convinced that I was the man for the job. I set out to sell it to my wife. This, I knew from long years of diplomacy, could be achieved best by an oblique approach, and so one evening I said in what I thought was a disarming tone, "Honey, how would you like to take a trip to Hong Kong with a little of Tokyo thrown in?"

"I would only go," quoth she, "if I could stay long enough to see all there is to be seen, not as we usually do—try to cover the world in three weeks."

"Fine," I said, "I have just accepted a judicial appointment close enough to Hong Kong (3000 miles) to give you your wish. Now all we have to do is rent the house, dispose of the children and your mother to the highest bidder, and off we go."

I had to explain a little more than that, but in the end I won a half-consent; it was all I needed for the moment. I reported to Rainville that I was willing but that it would be necessary to have certain items of information to satisfy the Associate Justice's wife. She was, for example, interested in such mundane things as where and how we would live, and whether laundries and cleaners were available, not to mention drugstores, beauty parlors and, particularly, doctors.

Rainville simply handed me a questionnaire to complete, with the remark that everything would be explained to our satisfaction if and when Washington decided it wanted me.

I found little trouble with the questions. Of course, they were designed to help the examining authority determine whether the applicant's education and experience qualified him. In addition, inasmuch as the Pacific Trust Territory is within our country's security framework, the Navy had been given the responsibility of clearing appointees. This meant giving information about my past association with organizations of whatever character; over the years, in my interest in political, social and economic controversy, I had espoused numerous causes and joined many organizations.

When I delivered the completed questionnaire to the Senator's office, I was advised to await action from the Department of the Interior, under whose administrative wing I would labor. Months passed. There was no news from anyone. I came to regret all our research on life in the Marianas, the Carolines and the Marshalls, in which Trust Territory is located. We had read and re-read the annual monographs in the *Britannica;* we had noted the distances, the routes of travel through the area. It had become a family joke that we would never get closer to a tropical paradise than our patio.

Then one day my telephone operator announced a call from Washington and it was an official of the Department of the Interior: I was acceptable to the Department if I could come. He suggested meeting him at the airport that week end, asking specifically that my wife come too. He said we would have no difficulty in recognizing him, he would be the biggest man to step off the Washington plane, 6'3" in height and over an eighth of a ton in weight.

There was no need to guess that Sunday morning. The giant strode towards us. He turned out to be unfailingly courteous, humorous and tactful—the ideal career man. He lived in Virginia, he came from Kentucky, answered easily all the typical feminine questions about housing, shopping, transportation, and doctors, and he did not attempt to gild any lilies. It was clear that we would have to do without some of the amenities of civilization but we might be reconciled to their absence by the interesting, purposeful life we would lead, participating in a project of national importance, training the islanders in the traditions of American justice. He stressed that we would be making a major contribution to our country's program there.

As we and such personal effects as we considered essential would have to be transported some 8000 miles, and as we would be unable to come and go at will he left us with the injunction to think it over carefully. I agreed to report our conclusion within a week.

Then the board of directors duly convened and considered the matter. Daughter, having arranged to spend a year studying French civilization (and men) at the Sorbonne, was enthusiastic over the prospect of visiting another part of the world when she completed her schooling. Son, who was half through his Marine Corps enlistment, was not very elated at the prospect of more discipline in the shape of a judge in the family, but was won over with our promise to visit Marine battlegrounds in the area. The two parental members of the board succumbed to the lure of palm trees waving in the gentle breeze, beaches of soft white sand, and a cool drink on a shaded veranda at sundown, all within ten minutes of the daily work routine. We knew there were few recreational facilities on the islands— our social life would consist chiefly of contact with our neighbors—so we concluded that the worst we could expect would be a pleasant interlude in our frenetic suburban existence, and a lengthening of our life-span by an untold number of years.

Added to this dream of a relaxed life in the tropics was the really vital curiosity we felt about the native peoples among whom we would live and about their achievement in the arts of civilization. We wondered how we would fit into the life of administered government. We would soon know.

We told the government we were ready and before long received detailed information on the kind of housing and facilities available to us. We started to assemble and pack clothing, china, glassware, linens, delicacies, miscellaneous equipment—all, hopefully, to make the anticipated sub-standard living conditions more tolerable.

The day came for the final trip to Washington for the ceremony of induction into office. It took place in the presence of the employees of the Division of Territories, in the Office of the Secretary of the Department of the Interior, whom we found to be an unassuming and amiable gentleman, of average build, quite conversant with the problems of administering the islands, and keenly interested in the welfare of the employees delegated to carry out our government's duties there.

The ceremony and the customary photographing took about a half hour, after which my wife and I joined the Secretary in a receiving line to greet the assembled staff and accept their congratulations. Then an official took us around to the various offices to meet staff members in their lairs and, observing that most of them were enjoying the morning coffee break, I ventured the remark that now I knew how the bureaucrats worked in Washington. To which my guide rejoined that it was no longer seemly to criticize bureaucrats, I was now one of them.

Officials of the Department furnished me with mimeographed material and printed pamphlets on the history of
the islands, their civilization and customs, and the kind of
cases I would have to adjudge. From this material I
learned that the area of my jurisdiction would be some
three million square miles, mostly water, divided into some
six districts containing ninety-six inhabited atolls and islands with a total area of 687 square miles. The six districts
were known as the Marshalls, Ponape, Truk, Yap, Palau and
Rota, and contained in all a population of some 65,000 natives plus other inhabitants.

Most of the islands and atolls are generally included
within that huge section of the Pacific Ocean known as
Micronesia, and in the historic island groups known as the
Marshalls, the Carolines and the Marianas—held by the
United States under trusteeship from the United Nations,
although they could have been kept by right of conquest
and seizure from Japan in 1944. Japan had seized the islands from Germany at the outbreak of World War I in
1914 and had occupied them until 1935 as trustee under a
League of Nations mandate. Back in 1899 Germany had
acquired the islands by purchase from Spain whose claim
of discovery went back to the early 16th Century. It
seemed likely, therefore, that a considerable admixture of
legal principles from diverse traditions would have developed under the circumstances. I found that this was indeed
the case.

To avoid confusion, however, in applying appropriate
law to a given situation a special code of laws was adopted
at the time the trusteeship was accepted by the United
States in 1947. This was the code of laws I was sworn to
apply and enforce. I was to find that it had been translated
into the principal native tongue in each of the six districts
and was rapidly becoming well understood. Basically it at-

tempted to establish, as the framework of the island legal system, the English common law in force in the United States in 1776 as interpreted by our American Courts. Since land is the most precious resource in island culture, one important qualification appeared in this code of laws: except where otherwise provided by the written code, in each district the customs of ownership, use, possession and inheritance of land were to be given controlling effect. Because customs varied somewhat from district to district, it could be guessed that there would be more to the trial of cases involving land rights than could be learned from books. And so it proved, as will be shown later on in our story.

We returned to our home near Chicago, and after a few days received word that the S.S. Contest would shortly be ready for our voyage from San Francisco to Guam.

CHAPTER 2

THE ONLY WOMAN

It might have been the sight of my husband rather tired and limp, getting off a hot commuter's train on a summer evening, or the imminence of my 49th birthday with no glorious adventure to boast of, or maybe the romantic spirit within us that dreams of an island of our own in the sun. In any case, I was receptive, and though at first we treated it lightly, in fact as something of a joke, I couldn't wait to dash for the atlas. It took my new specs plus a magnifying glass, but there it was—a tiny dot on the map 8500 miles from Glencoe, Illinois and it looked mighty glamorous and alluring to me. I began immediately to dream of leisure and servants and time to read and, who knows, even to paint or write. Palm trees and white sands—Paradise indeed.

The events leading up to our voyage across the Pacific were hardly noteworthy. I recall only the beginnings of a few qualms that one couldn't turn back the clock and endure what one could at twenty. We began to have turbulent seas from the time we sailed under the Golden Gate Bridge, and for three solid weeks our little freighter (it was not so little either) tossed and bobbed up and down like a cork. Our captain, a veteran sailor, said it was one of his roughest crossings, and seemed quite worried about our cargo lashed together with chains to the deck which was heavily laden with all kinds of equipment bound for Midway Island and Eniwetok. Twice we had to turn and go with the storm so that the deck crews could secure things more tightly. In any event, we made it, but before our arrival in Guam we both realized what a great distance we were putting between us and our dear ones at home. Only those who have crossed it can appreciate the vastness of that great heaving ocean or feel the utter loneliness of not passing any other ship in the night.

It took three weeks to make the trip with two stopovers, one at Honolulu and another at Midway Island. After Honolulu we headed northwest for Midway and even rougher seas. No one had told me we would not be in southern waters on leaving Hawaii, and I had envisioned sun-bathing on this cruise, instead of which I was becoming battered and bruised. One funny thing I noticed was the attitude of the ship's officers. I'm sure they expected both of us to be confined to our stateroom, there were odds that I'd never make mess, but I was determined to show them I was a good sailor and I never missed a meal. Our most interesting study and sport, when the weather permitted sitting on deck, was to watch the "Gooney Birds." These birds of the albatross family are grayish-black with white wings which spread about seven feet. Their home is on Midway, where many attempts to get rid of them have failed because they are so numerous; but because Midway is a flat barren island the male bird flies away at certain times in search of food and may stay on such a foray for weeks on end.

I first noticed them a day or two out of Honolulu. There were only a few, first soaring alongside, then behind us, settling on the water only long enough to feed on the sumptuous meals thrown overboard twice daily. They certainly liked our food; each day our convoy grew, never resting, flying all the way for six full days, going home to mama who was nesting and about to bring forth more little birds, who in a few months would go forth searching for another ship and food to bring back. When we finally came ashore at Midway, the "Gooneys" were everywhere, by the thousands, in the middle of the road, on the porch steps; every available spot where an egg was laid became a home. The females were sitting, and already little ones were peeping out at us as we walked with great care so as not to step on one. Sometimes a proud mother would stand up to stretch and let us see her newest offspring.

They were very comical in their antics, particularly during the courting season. The male picks his light of love, bows to the lady and then emits a clacking noise. This goes on quite excitedly, and finally both perform a sort of stepping, pecking, bowing to each other, very much like a square dance. Sometimes a foursome dances together, not always a mixed foursome. Sometimes four males. They are very clumsy on the ground and seem to be aware of it. As gracefully as they soar through the air, they come down like an airplane in an awkward landing, flopping over and picking themselves up, looking about indignantly, as if to say, "Who pushed me?"

We were amazed at how our skipper ever found this island, so tiny, a mere speck on the ocean, not over a mile square. And yet on this minute dot in the vastness, I found in the officers' club, where we were hospitably welcomed, Miss Joni Bell, a teacher who had lived in my small Mississippi home town of Marks, and who remembered my family and even me as a small child.

She made it possible for us to be housed in the V.I.P. Suite of the B.O.Q. (Bachelor Officers' Quarters) when it became known that the ship's facilities had been turned off while we were tied to the dock. This meant that I, accustomed to my private bath and creature comforts, had to come down the gangplank and walk a long city block to the Officers' Head (toilet) during the time we were in port. On the occasions that I used it my husband had to come along and stand guard outside, I being the only woman around the dock. Looking back now, I can imagine how frightened some unsuspecting officers, not knowing the S.S. *Contest* carried a lady passenger, would have been to meet me.

From Midway to Guam our voyage was made more pleasant. We shared good music from the hi-fi sets of some of the officers, and enjoyed an evening of bridge with the first mate and the purser.

We steamed, literally steamed, into Guam at about noon. It was lunch time. We had to wait an hour for the pilot boat to come out and bring us into port. We passed the world's largest dry dock in the harbor, about ten stories tall and big enough to accommodate two battleships at one time. We had not been in tropical waters very long. Now for the first time we were in and out of summer-like squalls. By the time we docked at Apra Harbor it was wet and sticky, and the sun was beating down as it does only after a rain. I had wanted to make an impressive entrance but, although we had been prepared for the heat, I am afraid that by the time we cleared the ship I was rather wilted. We had reached headquarters for Trust Territory and would soon know the people and the kind of life in store for us.

Guam, the metropolis of the Marianas, with a population of about 100,000 is about as large as Chicago. It is sixteen air-hours from Honolulu and eight from Manila, and fast becoming stateside in its appearance and customs. We were driven, in rather heavy traffic down a wide boulevard in Agana, the chief city, and Judge Furber, the Chief Justice of Trust Territory, and Mr. Gilmartin, the Deputy Commissioner, who had met us, pointed out the things of interest. It looked much like a city of used car lots and barber shops,

but I discovered later that it had many nice shops and restaurants, luckily all air-conditioned. Some people in Micronesia call Agana the salad bowl, not because the Guamanians
raised any lettuce or tomatoes, but because the Navy brings
them in as do the "reefer" ships, such as the one that had
brought us. The supermarkets are beautiful, also air-conditioned, and offer delicacies from all over the world at a
somewhat higher cost than we pay at home.

I saw the faces of the gentlemen who met us fall when
they saw us gathering our baggage, which included a typewriter and a guitar case, eleven pieces in all. It was not until
we knew them much better that we understood their looks;
the man who had preceded my husband had been a great
entertainer with the guitar, in fact it was a question whether
he excelled more in singing hill-billy songs than in judging.

We were taken straightaway to the Tropics Hotel, the
one and only in Agana, and unlike any I have ever seen before or since. We drove up to a low, white, one story building, with a quite attractive exterior, and upon entering the
lobby found it cool with electric fans blowing upon Japanese
chimes and creating a tinkling sound. Palm fronds and native handicraft tacked to the walls gave the place a South
Pacific flavor.

The lobby was furnished in rattan furniture, with an upright piano and small desk. There was also a large scale
which I later found useful for weighing luggage in transit
between the islands. Behind the lobby was a large dining
room and lunch counter where one could get a snack, a full
meal, or just a beer. The proprietor also had a magazine
rack, displaying a sign above, which read, "Be Honorable,
Pay."

We were shown to our room. It resembled a small cell. It
contained twin beds on opposite walls, a desk and chair, a
chest of drawers, a wash basin (running water, of course),

and nothing else, no other chairs, nothing on which to put our pieces of baggage. But it wasn't until we returned late that night that I discovered, to my almost disbelief, that the room partition went only halfway up to the ceiling on the corridor side, and as we made ready for bed, realized with horror the lack of privacy. From the halls came the sounds of other occupants throughout the night—a symphony of coughs, groans, grunts and snores. I could only lie there thinking of George Orwell's *Animal Farm,* which I had read recently, and I had great difficulty in controlling a hysterical giggle.

The outside walls of the rooms were screened, but had removable wooden panels used only during a typhoon. Early every morning a tropical shower would awaken me, the heavy downpour lasting just long enough to splatter my face and head and give me a chill, the only time I was ever cold on Guam.

The hotel is so designed that the lobby is in the center, and the bedrooms down a hallway on either side. There is only one bathroom for men and one for women. Naturally, we were on the wrong side for me, so that on each occasion I had to cross the lobby. It was not long before I lost my sensitivity enough to cross over in my robe. Later I found a Hawaiian *mumu* more desirable to wear from room to bathroom, especially when one met a familiar face or our inimitable innkeeper, Dick Dornfeld, who often wandered about in a sort of Fu Manchu kimono and loved to stop and chat.

Our indoctrination period on Guam was short. We arrived on Tuesday and departed the following Monday. We spent the evenings meeting my husband's new colleagues, whom I found to be most cordial and hospitable, as they were throughout the whole Trust Territory. There were several dinners for us, culminating on our last night, with a large one given by the High Commissioner, who stood up at about 9:30 P.M. and announced that since several of the party (meaning us) had to be up by 4:30 A.M. for the plane to Truk, the party should adjourn. That was one night I shall always remember. My mind was full of thoughts about the next day's trip and concern about our destination, and I slept not a wink.

On schedule, we were at the Naval Air Strip at dawn and then began the weighing in. Now I realized the advantage of having a big scale in the hotel. Normally, one is allowed just thirty pounds for the flight into the districts. Besides our luggage, we had acquired a set of Japanese china, and taken from our trunks two pillows, four sheets, four pillow cases and half a dozen towels—all I had in order to set up housekeeping until our household effects would be shipped down by surface from Guam. They were with us on the *S.S. Contest*, but we discovered that we had just missed the supply ship bound for Truk; what I didn't know was that the next one would not come to us for two full months.

At the air strip we discovered that because of us and an overflow of people wishing to return to the Marshalls and Ponape, they were running a special flight just to Truk, the first lap of the trip. I could see the little amphibious planes on the field, but it was not until we boarded that my stomach turned over. Those planes are equipped to carry fifteen passengers but this one was missing seven seats; in their place were all of our belongings, plus those of the other passengers, thirty dozen fresh eggs, and a rooster. I was to learn later that fresh eggs are a delicacy, and until said rooster was properly introduced to the hens in the agriculture station, we would have a shortage. Before we were settled in our seats, someone came on board with the mail sacks, and then more re-arranging took place beneath the ropes which secured our cargo. It was now raining in torrents, but daylight had come. It was shortly after 7:30 that we had to lean forward in our seats (we occupied the back row) for the engineer to open a small door and start a motor running. This, plus both other engines, did the trick. By the time we were taking off into the soup, I had already said a prayer and thought: if only I could be back, even if bored, in my pretty little ranch house in Glencoe. Gil Thomas, our pilot that day, sensed my discomfort and assured me I was at least as safe.

The noise was terrific. You couldn't carry on a conversation with the person right next to you, so for the next four hours I leaned my aching head on my husband's shoulder and he held my hand for re-assurance. I was not exactly the brave pioneer woman my friends at home had envied.

After what seemed the longest flight ever, someone poked me to look out of the window—and there it was: the barrier reef which encloses the huge lagoon and, dotted within, the dozens of islands which make up the Truk District. They rose high and imposing out of the blue waters. From the air, the deep sapphire of the ocean changed to a light green over the reef, and inside the lagoon were lovely shades of turquoise, aquamarine and green, depending on the depth of the waters and the coral which lay beneath them. It was breathtakingly beautiful. The excitement inside my body now mounted to the roar of the plane's engines. We were descending rapidly, and I could now detect some war relics half sunken in the harbor, great rusting hulks of barges and other craft.

All of a sudden, without circling or pattern, Gil came down like the bomber pilot he used to be, and boom, we were on the air strip at Moen, the island where Administration headquarters were based, and where we were to live. Miss Griffin, the court reporter who made the trip with us, had wanted me to step off the plane in hat, gloves, and my best, but thank goodness I used what little good judgment I possessed and in no wise did I look like a model out of *Vogue*. That would have been a mistake in view of the informal dress of those awaiting our arrival. We were there. A sea of faces greeted us. Someone handed me a beautiful orchid. And a completely new and different life began for me.

CHAPTER 3

INTRODUCTION TO THE TROPICS

A loud siren blasted into the night. It was 6:30 A.M. The siren notified the natives in the nearby villages who work in the District Center that they had one hour to get there. It also served for any American personnel who might have overslept. During most of the year in the islands, there is as much daylight as night, without dawn or twilight. When the telephone operator (on duty all night) set the siren off it was still dark, but within a very few minutes the sun was up over the hills and the best part of the day had arrived for the cool early dew-dipped island, glistening in its freshness.

Moen Island, seven or eight square miles, is quite beautiful. Its lowlands along the water rise to a plateau and culminate in two tall peaks from twelve to fifteen hundred feet high. The highest, Mount Tonochon, looks like a top hat. Of the villages which dot the water's edge there is one also named Moen, which in Trukese means "man." A few miles away across the water is the island of Fefan, which means "woman." The American base on Moen nestles in a high valley between the two mountains, and on the heights one can see the waters of the lagoon in two directions.

When the weather is good, as it is most of the time, the trade winds blowing from the east make life quite comfortable. Winds coming from the west are a storm warning; perhaps a typhoon is brewing. The normal temperature by day rarely exceeds eighty-five degrees; at night it drops to about seventy-five, but because of the humidity one imagines it is much hotter.

The island is an artist's paradise, though very difficult to capture the ever-changing colors dramatically affected by cloud formations and the position of the sun.

In the center of the district stand the Truk Hotel, the hospital, the administration building, the courthouse, the constabulary and jail, the post office, and the commissary. Though quite unlike San Francisco, it has something in common with that city by virtue of the hills where the American families lived. There was Intellectual Hill where most of the teachers resided; Telegraph Hill, so named because it was near the Radio Station; and Nob Hill, where we lived, got its name in the early Navy days because the officers' homes were there. In this section were the so-called better quonsets, distinguished by wooden floors. We did not at first like the house assigned to us mainly because it did not have a good view of the harbor and had a concrete floor, but before we left I was more than satisfied with it and would not have moved if I could. Its concrete floor turned out to be much easier to keep clean, and it was cooler and showed less signs of wear than the others.

We spent the ten days before our house was redecorated and ready in the Truk Hotel, where I was busy becoming acquainted, scouting for a maid, and getting used to the weather, to the customs and to the shortages. Everyone was very kind and by the time we moved, our new friends had supplied us with pots, pans, glasses, silver, electric iron and other things to help us until the next supply ship from Guam would bring our belongings. By this time we were all on a first name basis—all but my husband, whom everyone, including me, called "Judge." But in the privacy of our home I would prefix it with the word "some." This was our private

joke since he had had to pass a very rigid truck-driver's test
in order to drive the pick-up truck we were to use for recreational purposes. Some truck-driver, some Judge! I never
thought he was that good a driver!

We were automatically elected to membership in the
Community Club to which almost everyone belongs. Its
clubrooms are in the hotel and it maintains a modern library,
including the best sellers that appear on the *New York
Times* listings. It sponsors movies twice weekly, bingo
every other week, and gives a dinner dance each month—
always a gala occasion, with two or three couples, whose
names were drawn alphabetically, responsible for the food,
decorations and entertainment. Dancing was naturally to a
juke box or a piano of ancient vintage, but the dances were
usually clever, for the time available for planning permitted
the hosts to display great ingenuity.

Our house was attractive, and amazingly enough, cool
after the sun went down. Our large living room, about
twenty by thirty feet, was attached to an open screened
porch extending out another ten or twelve feet. The porch
was divided by an open book shelf and planter stand which
provided much needed space for books and records and for
the shells which we began to collect immediately. On each
side of the living room was a good sized bedroom. Behind
the living room on one side was a hallway off which were
the bathroom and laundry room, and on the other, the
kitchen, with adequate counter and storage space, equipped
with a middle-aged Frigidaire, and a tired, beaten-up bach-
elor-size electric stove. The front of the house lent itself
beautifully to entertaining which, I had been forewarned in
the States, was the chief recreation.

The crew of painters, all young native men, were having
a fine time slopping paint all over the concrete floor, the last
thing to be painted. The house was empty so no drop-cloths

were needed. I quickly won their friendship by dividing a package of cigarettes among them daily to encourage completion of the job. The Trukese are never in a hurry, but I had not yet slowed myself down to their pace.

The Government supplies each family with essential furniture, chairs, beds and tables made of rattan, most of it looking very much alike, but none of it in the best condition —partly because of the weather but mainly because of human nature. There were ring marks on all the tables, it took a full day for a boy to scour and clean the little stove, after which I found one burner completely out, and months passed before it was replaced. The beds looked as if they had been rained on. I certainly hoped so. Thank goodness I had taken mattress covers. The screens were old and rusty, with holes big enough for things to crawl through. Upon inspecting what was to be our domain for the next two years, I made a long list of not too unreasonable "musts." First of all, all openings were to be closed; next, boards were to go under sagging mattresses. Actually, there were new mattresses in the warehouse but because of a scrimpy budget it was the policy to let them stay unused, subject to mildew, until such time as money appropriated for this district became available.

The chest drawers were so warped that they would not close or open until I had them planed down. While my husband was at his job the first few weeks I worked hard, trying to improve things with the paint and wallpaper I had brought with me, and when I finished I thought we had one of the most attractive places on the island.

All the houses were equipped with hot closets, containing a combination of hot coils and ordinary light globes. In mine, I kept my clothing, shoes, writing paper, luggage, leather bound books and records. Nothing we took with us was ruined by mildew, but many of my dresses were very faded both by the frequent washing and the light burning constantly in the closets.

One of the cabinets in the kitchen was also fitted with a coil—supposedly to keep items such as crackers, flour, coffee, rice and the like. Once a cracker can was opened, the crackers had to be eaten immediately or put into the refrigerator, the only place safe from tiny ants and cockroaches. In my ice box I kept sugar, flour, coffee, crackers, cookies, jellies, condiments, etc. Naturally, it was always filled to capacity and as we had to buy in small quantities we had to shop daily.

Our garden or "property," was a disgrace when we took over. No one had lived in our house for some months and the few bushes and tangled grass looked more than wild. We had oleander, hibiscus, a gardenia bush, caladium, crotons, and some scraggly periwinkle.

The first thing I did was to hire a yard boy, who spoke only one English word. Yes. He said "yes" to everything. Through my maid who acted as interpreter we planned an elaborate garden and, because the rainy season was due soon, he worked arduously and lovingly. We didn't really need him every day but because of his devotion to me (he refused to work for my neighbor) and the going rate of a dollar a day, plus breakfast and lunch, I kept him by the week. His name was something which sounded like Cassius and like Cassius he was lean and hungry. He came from one of the far-away islands and slightly resembled an oversized good-natured monkey, sitting on his haunches all day cutting grass with a large machete. He seemed never to rest, and when he began to build a low wall of coral rocks around the plots we had picked for our vegetables, he seemed like a small boy playing with blocks. He ended up with two small enclosures surrounded by a miniature China wall, inside of which he planted all my stateside seeds: lettuce, parsley,

corn and eggplant. On returning home one day I was
shocked and angry to see that he had mutilated several large
bushes by cutting branches from them three and four feet
tall and planting them around the house. Despite my displeasure he looked quite pleased and nodded "yes" to all
my scoldings. Imagine my complete surprise a few days
later when the rains came and with them a blooming of
everything, including those stocks which by this time had
lost all their leaves. They really took root and were quite
lush when I left, and I could not tell which bush the cuttings
had come from. This, in contrast, is what happened to our
seeds: Within three or four days after planting, they had
germinated. It was a thrill to see them grow almost by
inches. But when they were up about four inches, I was simply devastated the next morning to see that the tops were
chewed off and the following day, lo, there was nothing left.

This was on account of the numerous African snails which
litter the ground after each rain. During the dry season they
lie dormant under the ground and after a rain, come out by
the thousands. They are a hungry horde. After a few weeks
of fighting these pests, we gave up and concentrated on the
indigenous fruits, papayas, pineapple and bananas, all of
which grew on the slope in front of our house.

I lost Cassius because of an unfortunate circumstance. One
day he did not come to work, and after the weekend passed
and he did not show up on Monday, I had my maid Chieko,
who lived in the same village, find out why. She reported
that he was very sick with sore feet and was unable to stand.
"He very bad, Missus," she said. "But he no go hospital."
When my husband came home for lunch, we decided to
take her with us to find him and bring him to the doctor.
She had frightened me when she said he might be stricken
with the yaws, a disease the American medical staff have

almost wiped out. It took a lot of coaxing; only when she told him his baby might get it too, did he reluctantly let us take him. Fortunately, it was not that dreaded disease, but somehow the hospital was more frightening to him than his pain for he never came back to work, and Chieko thought he had returned to his home island. She replaced him with Senano, a likeable boy who stayed with us until we left. I couldn't quite blame Cassius for his fear of the hospital after my few brief encounters there. When we first came to the islands I tried to work in the hospital office, but found that I was really not needed there. The crowd of native women holding their sick children was a depressing sight against the background of the unsanitary and drab hospital furnishings and equipment.

One Sunday when everyone else was off on a picnic to one of the other islands, I gave my finger a jagged cut on a tin of English biscuits. My husband and I applied first aid to no avail, the bleeding would not stop, and we were fast running out of our supply of bandages. It took some time to commandeer wheels to take us down to the hospital. We found a girl in the office who knocked on the door of a room marked "private" and awakened the native medical practitioner on call. He sleepily put on his trousers and introduced himself as something sounding like Dr. Barton. He was a Palauan with long hair and sideburns that met his beard in front. After one good look at his unkempt appearance I thought I would rather bleed to death. However, in very good English, he asked if I would faint at the sight of blood —all the while my bandage was dripping—and then said to the girl, "Take her to surgery." I must admit the doctor was quite antiseptic. The operating room was air-conditioned, and he put on rubber gloves and carefully unwrapped what he must have thought a near-amputation, to find only to his great disappointment and my relief it had stopped by itself. However, he dusted on a little sulfa powder and bandaged me up rather prettily.

Another time I went to the hospital to see Dr. Ruark the American doctor, and quite a good one too, for my ears. He said they needed a washing and sent me into a treatment room. I soon discovered that he didn't intend to do it himself, but had sent in a young native interne of sorts. At first I was very angry, since Dr. Ruark was not that busy, and at home I usually went to a nose and throat specialist, who was happy to do it for five dollars. On Truk it only cost twenty-five cents and I guess my experience was worth the other $4.75. The young interne began to put into the sterilizer all kinds of lethal looking instruments lying about the room. He said it would take thirty minutes and that I should wait. All the while I was fuming, so I said I'd be back in ten minutes. The Court House was next door so I hurried over and indignantly told the judge, who said: "How can he hurt you, just washing out your ears? Save the doctor for something more serious." I began to see the humor in it then and returned, though I made very sure he didn't intend to use all those things he had put in to cook. We chatted a bit, and all the while I noticed the little room was getting crowded with a good many Trukese. I still don't know who all the spectators were, or why they were there. Either they just happened to be visiting in the hospital and were curious, or my young native wanted to show them how unafraid an American lady was at being treated.

Actually, the native practitioners are fine doctors, considering their limited formal training, at most three years at the medical school conducted by the British at Suva in the Fiji Islands. Dr. Michi, a very able native surgeon on Truk took over as the head of the hospital there after Dr. Ruark left, and native practitioners regularly staffed the hospitals in all the other districts. This made it possible for the two American doctors to divide their time among all the districts.

Perhaps one of the most rewarding experiences was the fellowship of the American colony, but it was disappointing not to have more social contact with the natives. Actually they just were not ready for it, especially the women. Some of the younger natives (and these were few) who had been away to school on Guam or at Honolulu could meet one socially, but the others were too shy and gave us no opportunity to meet them. Only the teachers and the educational department were able to arrange evenings together with native students, but our social gatherings were entirely American. On our travels, however, we met and were able to talk with many natives from the other districts, and so we gained more information about their living conditions.

CHAPTER 4

THE JUDGE IN THE MARSHALLS

On Guam the first week was given over to my indoctrination: meetings with staff members, reading the material on the activities conducted by the territorial government and, to a lesser extent, examining the facilities maintained there by the government and making some contact with the men in charge of the various operations.

The principal office of Trust Territory Government was in a one-story structure behind the Tropics Hotel, close enough to permit the staff to use the dining room's rear entrance for coffee and coke breaks. The building was partly air-conditioned, with private offices for the High Commissioner, the Deputy Commissioner, the Attorney General and about six other officials, and a large general office and several smaller offices housing about forty other employees. There was also a mail and shipping room, and a radio and communications station which maintained constant contact with the six administrative districts and with weather stations and shipping in the territory.

The departments were executive and administrative, legal and public safety, education, finance, personnel, and the political, social and economic staff.

Near the government headquarters was a small building for the construction and maintenance department, and beyond that, a meeting hall able to accommodate several hundred persons. These structures and the hotel were part of the government compound which stretched along a thousand feet of the highway leading to the Naval Air Station, and in which there were more than a dozen dwellings for staff members and their families. One of the buildings, of barracks type, housed unmarried male employees. All these attractive units were rented to staff members at moderate cost.

The government also maintained homes for the High Commissioner and his deputy far outside the compound, and a large supply warehouse and yards not far from the commercial docks in Apra Harbor. Slightly over 100 employees in all carried on the governmental operations of Trust Territory Government on Guam. Other operations had their principal centers on other island districts: Public Defender, the Judiciary and Communications Departments on Truk, the Public Health and Agriculture Departments on Ponape, and the Dental Department in the Marshalls.

The chief executive and the repository of legislative power under the code was the High Commissioner. During my tenure he was a career man, Delmas K. Nucker, who had served the United States in foreign lands for many years. He was not the kind of executive to find satisfaction in sitting at a desk and reading reports from his far-flung domain. He was constantly traveling all over the territory, consulting local officials and making decisions on the spot, and traveled extensively to Washington and New York, particularly when committees of the United Nations held hearings on administration of trust territories. Nobody knew the conditions of each district as he did. Possessed of great energy and a friendly, disarming manner, Mr. Nucker was esteemed by the native peoples for his democratic approach and genuine interest in their well-being.

The Deputy Commissioner, Mr. Gilmartin, was a lawyer

who had been out in the islands only a short time before my
arrival. Before I left he was appointed judge of the United
States District Court on Guam, and was succeeded in his
office by the Attorney General, Joe Putnam, who having lived in the district centers and traveled extensively
throughout, gave me an hour's valuable briefing on the administration of justice in the territory, and the kind of legal
problem I would have to meet. A native of California and a
career man, Joe was a studious and legal officer of high cali-
ber. He and his charming wife lived in a comfortable house
next door to the main office building, so he was always available long after hours for any emergency.

In addition to holding short meetings with the three top
executives, I was privileged to confer with John De Young,
the staff anthropologist, who gave me valuable background
material from his storehouse of cultural information.

But the most informative and best informed person in
Trust Territory about its history, its aspirations and problems
in all fields, as well as the hardest working and most capable
civil servant I encountered, turned out to be my superior,
Judge Edward P. Furber. A native of New England and a
graduate of Harvard Law School, Judge Furber had left his
Boston law practice to serve in the Navy after Pearl Harbor.
At the war's end he was in Hawaii as an officer in the Judge
Advocate Division and available for setting up the legal system under which the Navy would administer the newly-
conquered Marshalls, Carolines and Marianas. With two
other officers, Judge Furber drafted the Code of Laws which
is still in force after a dozen years with remarkably few
significant changes.

When the administration of the islands passed to the
Department of the Interior in 1952, Judge Furber became
the first Chief Justice, a most fortuitous choice for the United
States. With good natured efficiency he runs a department

of over a hundred Micronesian judges and clerks of courts, who exercise great influence. This requires a sure instinct in the selection of nominees, and the rare cases of misplaced confidence which have come to light, so far as my information goes, argues well for Ed Furber's judgment of men.

Besides a general review of personalities and problems, he gave me little information at the outset. He very wisely said I would learn mainly through experience and the sooner I started acquiring it the sooner we would make a dent in the litigation which had piled up in the absence of an associate justice. He arranged to have me spend a week or so getting acclimated at Truk, while he flew to the Marshalls for a civil court session. I would be able to read all of the High Court opinions in cases originating in the various districts, and thus become familiar with the precedents. I was to join the judge at Majuro, the capital of the Marshalls, and from there we would go to Arno Atoll nearby for our first joint session.

I stayed on Truk just long enough to get my wife settled in our newly decorated quonset dwelling, spending my days studying the mimeographed decisions of the judges who had preceded me.

The day came for my journey to the Marshalls, which was to keep me from my home base on Truk some three weeks. The light bag I packed contained the first essential of the judicial office, a long black robe. I also carried the one-volume Code of Trust Territory Laws, which I had been studying religiously on the long sea voyage to Guam. This quite unique Code consists of a combination of Constitution and Bill of Rights, similar to ours, and the laws to carry them into effect. Only 139 pages, it represents a skillful attempt to penetrate a primitive society with American concepts of civil government, law and institutions.

At first a sharp-eyed native pointed to a tiny speck in the

clouds, and then the plane came down out of the hazy blue, looming ever larger until its butterfly wings seemed to flap down on to the coral runway. With a last burst of speed it taxied to the end of the runway, then made a turnabout up to the makeshift terminal where many of the base personnel and numerous natives were assembled. The platform was moved to the side of the plane, its door opened and the passengers deplaned. After shaking their heads to the agriculture officer's questions about the transport of forbidden plants into the district, they strode through the brilliant sunshine to the coolness of the open-air terminal waiting room.

Here I met my companions for the trip to Ponape and the Marshalls, the pilot and co-pilot, the navigator and flight engineer; also Horace Leavitt, ex-Army officer and now head of the Public Works Department of the Territory, and Joe Driskell, ex-Marine Sergeant and now head of the Territory's Department of Public Safety. It was easy to like both men, veterans of the Pacific campaign and well informed about the history and problems of the islands.

The plane was kept on the ground about an hour while the cargo of mail and express was removed, and fuel taken aboard. Meanwhile my wife and I were taking final leave of one another, she to remain in our new home on Moen Island while I journeyed to distant parts. We arranged for such communication as the situation afforded, by radio dispatch to the district center in the Marshalls, and I agreed to return promptly in the event of any real emergency. I dutifully promised not to tickle the pilot on take-off or landing, and not to jump from the plane until it had come to a full stop. I could see her tears behind the brave front, and realized how trying a moment it was for my wife as she contemplated her lonely life ahead until my return. It was not unexpected, but the real thing seemed harsher than the imagined.

After a jovial leave-taking from the residents, and with their promise to take care of my wife in my absence, I mounted the steps into the plane with the other half-dozen passengers, and off we took over the reef. Soon we made a graceful turn to the right on our way to Ponape, some 500 miles to the southeast.

We rose up to our planned altitude of 7000 feet. The water below looked calm and gray, and as we flew for hours without sight of anything but vast spaces of water and the spectacular panoply of clouds in the tropical heavens, our isolation came home to me.

In less than three hours of uneventful cruising we sighted signs of land straight ahead. First I noticed the low coral reef surrounded by sand bars sinking into the green waters and rising on the landward side to the dignity of small, heavily wooded islands. Then we dropped to about 2000 feet and the high plateau land of Ponape appeared, with the table mountain of Sokehs looming austere and forbidding on our starboard side. One of my companions told me that we would land in the lagoon about three miles from the harbor of Kolonia, the district center, and would be taken there by the picket boat which met all flights. This was my first water landing and I was curious to see how the little Grumman Albatross acted in the water. After many such trips I was to develop intense admiration for these hardy little planes, despite their noise and lack of comfort. Later I wondered whether they had been selected for transport of Trust Territory personnel and their families as much for the latter reasons as the former, upon the sound premise that people would prefer to sit at home rather than travel on planes from which creature comforts had been removed.

Soon we were down to several hundred feet, skimming over a treacherous field of submerged coral rock, and just as we passed over clear deep water the pilot hovered for a few

seconds before the first dip. We hit the water sharply and
our speed churned up waves and spray high enough to obscure vision from the cabin windows. When our speed slack-
ened and the spray subsided, I could see that we were down
in the harbor, taxiing away from the mountainous islands
behind us. I noted a sign I was to look for on all future trips
with welcome relief, the friendly picket boat standing off to
port, watching us make the turn towards the sea-strip, and
following us in to our berth like a respectful dog.

As we approached the sea-strip built by the Japanese and
carefully preserved from injury by the airmen who had plastered the harbor during World War II, our little craft let
down its wheels, found the submerged runway leading to
the strip, and waddled up its ramp onto the concrete platform. The strip jutted out into the water from mountainous
Langer Island, in whose side the Japanese had stored tons of
supplies and an ocean of gasoline and oil. The strip extended
about a thousand feet and was wide enough to hold two
planes like ours, alongside each other.

The motors stopped, the landing platform was pushed
alongside by smiling natives in western dress, and we
walked out into the murky atmosphere of a typical Ponapean rain-squall. On hand to greet me was Ekener. the
Clerk of Courts, and his assistant, Francisco, who escorted
me to the picket boat waiting alongside the strip. The long-
shoremen transferred our bags and the cargo to the picket
boat and we were on our way to Kolonia.

The harbor is well protected by mountainous walls on
both sides and a high rise island across its mouth; the channel, marked by buoys, is so shallow in spots that even boats
of low draft like ours had to slacken speed and proceed cau-
tiously through the last mile of the trip. We pulled up at the
dock, transferred to waiting jeeps and in minutes I had a

room in the small four-room cottage known as the Women's Hotel.

I went to bed early that night and had the opportunity to read some of the history of the Marshalls I had taken from the library at Truk and the pamphlets I had borrowed from John De Young on Guam. I learned that the district consisted of some twenty-nine low-lying coral atolls and five low sandy islands, containing some seventy-four square miles of land inhabited by about 12,000 people and scattered over some 375,000 square miles of ocean.

The principal crops appeared to be coconut, breadfruit, arrowroot, pandanus, taro and bananas. An ample supply of fish from the bountiful ocean and rice imported from the United States supplement the meager native diet.

Early the next morning I walked down to the dock with the plane crew, Leavitt and Driskell and several Marshallese returning to their home island. After the checkup by pilot and mechanic and a final sweep of the take-off channel by the picket boat to eliminate floating debris from our path, we were ready for the take-off. The waters of the lagoon were so smooth that one of the amateur experts on the picket boat feared we might be unable to rise for lack of the impetus supplied by choppy waves. This time, at least, there was no problem. The picket boat pulled away from the pier, took up its station about a mile down channel awaiting our take-off, and we sidled down the ramp into the bay. Our wheels were retracted into slots along the body and the pontoons took over. We taxied to the head of the channel where we sighted the outer reef a few miles ahead, and were soon churning the waters into a furious spray. In no time we were air-borne and over the reef.

With the loosening of seat belts we relaxed and took up the escape literature which most of us carried for the five or so monotonous hours over the placid waters. We were soon lulled into the intermittent sleep which overcomes air passengers on an uneventful flight and we droned on past midday with no change in speed, direction or height and not a word from the pilot. Who could have imagined the peril which would appear within the hour?

It came just as we prepared to land at Uliga Airport, one of the airstrips which had been pulverized by the Navy pilots making their nightly sorties from the Gilberts, after Tarawa. The story was told of how they had named these island targets after favorite girl friends, and kept up a running cross-fire over their radios about the loving attention they were going to give Rita and Laura that night. The Japanese never caught on. Today the event is preserved in the change of name of these islands to the make-believe ones used by the pilots.

About five miles ahead we could see Majuro Atoll, a group of low-lying coral islands extending in a huge circle enclosing the blue waters of the lagoon. The islands lay along the circumference of the circle right on the reef so that on one side of the narrow strip of land was the ocean, and on the other the lagoon. Majuro Island lay along the western boundary of the circle and at least ten miles across to the east the Uliga air strip could be seen seeming to start at the edge of the lagoon, with tall palms on both sides of the strip.

Landing signals were given and into the passenger compartment strode George Manic, the navigator. The flight engineer checked our seat belts and returned to the cockpit. The navigator remained in the compartment and, sinking into a seat, fastened his own belt. I was seated on the starboard side and had put aside my reading material as is my custom in order to concentrate on the approach and landing. We were now traveling at a height of about 500 feet. The

wheels came down, the flaps inclined slightly to brake the
excess speed, the strip loomed up dead ahead. We were
preparing the final descent when suddenly I heard shouts
from Leavitt and Driskell to the men in the cockpit, "Your
gear is up," and saw them straining forward and tugging
frantically at their seat belts. Their faces were frozen with
alarm. Before I could apprehend the danger, the navigator
dashed forward through the plane to the open door of the
cockpit shouting, as he ran, the same warning to the pilot.
The plane was now within seconds of touching down without wheels, but somehow the pilot was able at the very
last to pull up and let down the landing gear and, seemingly
without disturbance, came on down and bounced to a
rough landing on the coral runway.

While we taxied up to the terminal and deplaned, the
navigator was still muttering to himself; the passengers
were white-faced and shaken. Later the pilot explained
that he had first let down his wheels but had retracted
them when he saw a fuel truck driving across the strip,
apparently unaware of our approach. This failed to satisfy
at least one of the crew members as well as the two passengers whose warning had alerted the navigator, and the
fact that the wheels came down immediately after the
alert tended to convince us that this could have become one
of the statistics of air catastrophe.

Awaiting us at the terminal were Judge Furber, and the
court reporter, Miss Griffin; also several officials from the
District Government. As the approach to the strip is hidden
from the terminal, none of them had any suspicion of what
had happened.

Also awaiting my arrival was the dignified clerk of courts
of the Marshalls District, Raymond deBrum, whose qualities I was to admire in the months to come. Of stocky build
and less than average height, his face tempered by a half-

century of wind, wave and sun, Raymond represented the westernized Micronesian at his best.

Like most Marshallese, he wore cotton trousers, colorful *aloha* shirt and Japanese type sandals. In excellent English, he welcomed me to the Marshalls. He was the chief interpreter in trials before the High Court and also served as advisor in controversies likely to reach the courts. Of noble birth, and entitled to sit in the House of Nobles in the Marshall Islands Congress, Raymond's descent traced from his Portuguese grandfather, who with another, bought the Likiep Atoll in the 1880's from its native chieftain, took a Marshallese wife and settled permanently in this island paradise some 300 miles north of Majuro.

As we drove from the airport in one of the government pick-up trucks, Raymond indicated points of interest. An unpretentious one-story structure of salvage lumber was the post-office, and a row of quonset-type corrugated-iron buildings turned out to be the district hospital. The Catholic Mission and School, conducted from a pretentious two-story wooden structure, a massive water tank, and a series of warehouses appeared along the road leading to the administration building. This also was of quonset type, surmounted by a high vaulted ceiling, the interior dark and cool; a sleeping dog was lying across the threshold.

The administrative staff of some twenty people seemed relaxed, two-thirds of them chocolate-skinned Marshallese, and the rest American, some quite obviously of Hawaiian-Chinese-Japanese ancestry. None of the officials had private offices and even the district administrator and his assistant, wearing shorts, being seated at desks available to any caller. I found this informality typical of Trust Territory government, encouraging friendly association between officials and natives. In no time I had met everybody and received best wishes for a successful court sitting.

Our next stop was the court house. It was a weather-beaten, dingy, old quonset which was certainly consistent in construction and appearance with the several score of native dwellings that composed the nearby shanty town. The judges' chambers consisted of a small office with two desks and two uncomfortable swivel chairs of ancient lineage, a wall cabinet housing supplies, and a set of law books called *American Jurisprudence,* an electric refrigerator corroded and rusty but still usable, and the court clerk's typewriter and desk. In fact this was the office used by Raymond and the judges of the lower courts when the High Court was not present.

From the open doorway of the chambers I watched a Marshallese mother a few steps away bathing her naked infant from a small basin in front of her home. Another woman had made a fire outside of the family cook house, and a pot was boiling on the open flame. Every private act was open to a neighbor's scrutiny.

In the court house I met the presiding judge of the Marshall Islands District Court, Kabua Kabua, a high chief of much intelligence and industry. Like the Japanese government before us, our government had learned that it was sound to select men from the chiefly line as judges and magistrates. Kabua was an *iroij* (native king), with his position as paramount chief recognized on atolls far distant from his residence on Uliga. His English was excellent and his zeal to comprehend the principles of American justice exemplary. Not yet fifty and father of thirteen, he could trace his ancestry back at least ten generations, naming both direct and collateral heirs in the blood line.

After a few pleasant remarks with Kabua, I left the courthouse for the sparse accommodations at the district hotel, where I had been assigned the room adjoining Judge Furber's; a common bathroom served us both. The furnishings were of the plainest—bed, easy chair, dresser, writing table and chair, and a wardrobe attached to the wall in which an electric heating fixture and globe burned continuously. This was the hot locker where clothing and shoes were kept to avoid mildew. After our experience on Truk, I was not shocked to discover that usable water was in short supply here also; this was the dry season and as little rain had come to replenish the storage tanks, water from the taps would be available one hour in the morning and one in the late afternoon. In the interval we would live on bottled goods and water kept in the electric refrigerator in Judge Furber's room. This did very well except for bathing, but the ocean and lagoon were close enough for that.

By the time I unpacked the few things I had brought and had a refreshing shower, it was time for dinner. Our cottage was only fifty yards from the hotel dining room, run by a Mrs. Ward whose husband was attached to the administrative staff as a carpenter-foreman. Food was American style and not too bad, but when Mrs. Ward later gave up personal supervision over the cooking and left it to the tender mercies of Micronesians, it grew considerably worse. The natives thought that food should be served cold, unseasoned and preferably well fried in deep fat.

That afternoon we put on Bermuda shorts and walked through the streets of the American colony, probably twenty households of administrative personnel. A half-mile walk brought us to a native restaurant and recreation center in what was a warehouse and office building housing the largest trade goods importer and copra exporter in the Marshalls. There was also a movie house with wide screen and room for at least five hundred persons to sit comfortably on mats on the concrete floor. Americans were provided with straight-backed collapsible chairs and sat uncomfortably on them in the rear of the auditorium. The show consisted of one feature of respectable age, plus several shorts and serials. I was told that action pictures were favorites on the bill, with wild westerns getting top preference. A snack bar in one corner of the theatre did a thriving business.

A pleasant walk back to our quarters in the cool moonlight was broken just long enough for a cold drink at the attractive Coconut Club, situated on the beach and conveniently located a few yards from the barracks housing unmarried male personnel and transients. As the work day starts at 7:30 A.M., and ends at 4:30 P.M., when the club opens for business, 10:30 is closing time on work nights. The club's well-equipped bar had native attendants and some native patronage, permitted to drink nothing stronger than beer. Several card tables, a billiard table, and some comfortable chairs made up the furnishings.

Sleep that night was something of an adventure. Our quarters were shaded by giant coconut palms and breadfruit trees ranging between us and the ocean. The island, running in a semi-circle along the fringing reef for possibly five miles, was at no point more than 500 yards wide. On one side was the ocean with shallow water from the beach at least 400 feet to the reef, and a sharp drop to very deep water. On the other side was the lagoon, almost enclosed by the islands along the circumference of the reef, but here and there separated by passes leading into the ocean. During the night the waves on the ocean side reached high water mark and kept pounding on the rocky shore just below our cottage. High winds whistled through the palms and the wild swishing of the palm leaves gave one the illusion of angry nature striving to uproot the trees.

By morning the waves had subsided almost to the reef, the swishing of the palms had become a gentle murmur, the air was fresh and clear, and fleecy clouds moved slowly in the sky. It was cool enough for brisk exercise so after a good breakfast the Judge and I walked the few blocks to the court house, where I learned for the first time why he had arranged for both of us to visit this one district and hold court together, a quite unprecedented procedure.

This was to be no ordinary sitting: failure to compose differences between nobles and commoners involved in the score of cases awaiting trial, might lead to violence, perhaps to bloodshed. These cases had all arisen on the Arno Atoll about fifteen miles east of Majuro. It was necessary to determine the right of certain nobles to share the food produced from given tracts of land. By the traditional system the chiefs received a substantial share of food and copra produced on land they controlled, and feeling had been running high against it for years. Many commoners had come to feel that they were being impoverished in order to feed the nobility who performed no useful function.

The land tenure system of the Marshallese resembles Middle Age feudalism. At the top is the *iroij lapalap*, the paramount chief, theoretically supposed to own all the land in his domain. Below him is the *iroij erik*, the subordinate chief supposed to act as overseer on behalf of the paramount chief and see that due honor is paid him by gifts— fish, fruit, a portion of the prize taro and yams, and an agreed percentage of the cocoanut production. The *iroij erik* is also supposed to help the producers clear the land and plan the planting of trees and crops. For his services and the share due the *iroij lapalap*, he usually receives between 25% and 35% of the production.

The producers consist of the *alab* or clan head who directs the actual working of the land and allocates the resulting fruits between himself and the *dri jerbal*, or workers, usually members of the *alab's* clan, who would succeed in turn to that responsibility and dignity.

Once an *iroij* has been installed and recognized by the

alab on his own behalf and on behalf of the workers under
him, it is not in accordance with native custom to deprive
him of his share. The option is available to the commoners
not to bind themselves to a successor *iroij* if they have any
doubt about the validity of his succession; and until his
recognition becomes well nigh universal, he has no claim
to the share of crops which had gone to his predecessor.

Much difficulty had now arisen. The new *iroij* had not
at first been accepted by a substantial body of the people.
In order to add strength to persuasion, he had come upon
certain land and seized "his share" of crops. When a complaint had been made in the district court at Majuro
against his violent action the district judge had enjoined
the *iroij* from proceeding until the case could be tried before the High Court. The *iroij* had nevertheless gone upon
the land once more, whereupon, at the direction of the
High Court, the sheriff and constabulary had gone to
Arno, arrested the *iroij* and imprisoned him for some fifteen
days in the jail at Majuro for contempt of court. The *iroij*
was now back on Arno with his henchmen, supposedly
wroth at this indignity, and awaiting trial.

We had to go to Arno with the clerk of courts and a few
constabulary-men to try these cases and decide them according to native customary law. We expected to hold court
for three weeks, during which we would be isolated from
the outside world except for communication by walkie-
talkie.

We would need food and bedding. There would be no
stores on Arno stocking American provisions, and there was
no hotel or other adequate dwelling. We would find shelter
in the infirmary and we could bring along a native cook who
had experience in preparing food for Americans. We must
remember to bring plenty of cigarettes, coffee and rice to
use as *presentos,* as the natives are notoriously short of the

necessary foreign exchange. I would find this contact with
the primitive culture in its natural surroundings unusually
interesting and rewarding and exciting.

Later that day Miss Griffin and I prepared our list of
household supplies and food, and drove about the island
shopping. We bought 150 pounds of rice, ten cartons of cigarettes, ten pounds of coffee, twenty pounds of sugar, and
many kinds of canned meats, vegetables, fish, fruits and
fruit juices, some crackers and cookies, tea and preserves.
We stopped by the radio station long enough to pick up our
walkie-talkie and learn to operate it. Everything was delivered to the court house, and after we had borrowed towels and bedding from the hospital stores, we were ready.
Judge Furber had already chartered our boat which was to
transport the three of us, Raymond and Judge Saloman,
who was to serve as expert on custom, Jetmar, the district
sheriff and one of his constables, Tion, a representative of
the district administrator, and Raymond's wife who would
serve as cook. We were getting a fifty foot power launch
and it seemed to me that we would have room to spare.
But I failed to take into account the sharp business sense
of a Marshallese sea captain who had reserved the right to
transport at bargain rates some natives who might wish to
make the trip.

CHAPTER 5

THE SETTING AT ARNO

The launch *Evangeline* lay along the pier that juts out from a brace of warehouses and makes Uliga a world port. Ships of over 15,000 tons are able to navigate the passes into Majuro lagoon and unload at the pier which is at least fifty feed wide and more than a city block long. Copra is brought there from all the major island groups in the Marshalls and warehoused until a Trust Territory freighter transports it to Japan.

At last the day of our departure came. We went to the pier shortly after breakfast to check our departure time. Everything was orderly, yet the air was alive with the noisy excitement that surrounds a ship about to get under way. The day before, the hold had been full of copra, and the work of unloading had gone on from late afternoon so that our checkup early the evening before had satisfied us the boat would be ready the next morning as scheduled. Besides the copra in the hold, there was the deck cargo: it was littered with chickens, clucking piteously at the unfeeling brutes who had brought them so far from home.

The next morning at eight, the crew were busy swabbing the decks. The chickens and copra were gone, and the little boat began to justify her name by her freshness but the youth of this *Evangeline* lay far back in an old man's memory.

The skipper finally said she was ready to load; we could bring our gear on board; we would leave presently. This the Judge interpreted to mean two or three hours. Fortunately we did get away by ten, and the time so saved was to become very useful before the day was over.

Back we went to the court house where we had stored our food and supplies, our court records, typewriters and miscellaneous equipment, including the walkie-talkie. All were transported to the boat and stowed in the hold.

Meanwhile the passengers had been gathering. Though the boat was under charter to Trust Territory Government for the purpose of transporting the judicial party to Arno, it was strictly un-Micronesian to sail with an extra foot of space into which some poor native could be crammed. So we found that in addition to the crew of five and our party of eight and a respectable amount of freight, some two dozen bargain excursioners a third of them children, would be crowded into the little fifty-foot launch.

The natives, knowing they were dues-paying members, showed a fine disregard for us and proceeded with their belongings and children to preempt all the decent space on the little craft. Before we steamed out, the only one of our party who was stowed away with any comfort was Miss Griffin. She had taken the precaution of boarding with a rubber mattress and pillow and had staked out enough space for her comfort under the tarpaulin which served as a roof for the after-section. I, on the other hand, was seated near her on the upper deck next to a water cask, with my feet dangling over the heads of the natives lolling comfortably in the cabin below.

For Judge Furber it was even worse. Most of the time he was forced to stand on his feet just outside the wheelhouse. Later he was able to join us in the after-section, but only after people changed positions when the fishing started.

In much longer time than it takes to tell, we finally backed out of our berth. The trip, I was told, was not expected to take over six hours (actually it was eight) and the lagoon had only a faintly provocative ripple. This I was to discover was the old come-on of the sea, that brazen Jezebel, soon to be revealed in all her perfidy.

In any event there I was, perched in my uncomfortable seat. The rail lining the deck was my sole means of holding on, but there was as yet no need of support. We rode buoyantly along the chain of islands in the lagoon, always in sight of land and rarely more than a mile from the closest. Every few hundred yards, beautiful islands appeared all with sandy beaches on which the surf road gently, all with lofty palms and dense shrubbery lining the shores. These islands were very different from Uliga and Rita, along the shores of which the familiar homely corrugated-roofed cottages were sprinkled profusely. The islands we were now passing tended to reaffirm my faith in the tropical isle of the South Seas literature, no ramshackle dwellings visible from a distance, no *benjos* (Japanese for latrine) built over the water, and no rocky beach to mock the enthusiastic bather.

If ever I had hated the sea before, I was soon to develop an unreasoning, vindictive, psychopathic mania. I am still subject to that uncontrollable hatred. You see, it happens that though the Arno atoll is only fifteen miles or so from Majuro, one cannot board ship except on the lagoon side of Majuro. This means that you must first steam to the nearest passage from the lagoon to the ocean and then all the way back on the oceanside of Majuro Atoll. This not only triples the distance to be covered, but in going through the pass you find the ocean massively pouring in and pushing with all its diabolical power to keep the hapless wayfarer from getting out.

Now we had arrived at the pass and here our little bark and its passengers started to take a beating, up and down, again and again, into the trough and up out of the trough, with a resounding crash each time the stern came back into the water. It did not seem possible to me that a craft which looked so frail could long withstand the battering of that vicious, hammering, relentless sea.

And now the passengers began to be affected by the boat's lurching motion. First the youngsters and then a few of the native women, who had been pleasantly lunching an hour before, were led to the rail and supported there by sturdier members. I fully expected to join them momentarily but it was not to be; I had neither eaten nor drunk anything for three hours. I was, however, a victim of my over-active imagination, stimulated by the recollection of my stupid failure to carry my seasickness pills, guaranteed to bring sure relief.

To intensify my misery the water cask on my right kept spilling over in my lap as the boat keeled over from starboard to port and port to starboard and back again. My soaked shoes and trousers in contrast to my relatively fresh appearance above the waist caused me to look weirdly distorted.

When matters became at last no longer bearable, I leaned over to the imperturbable Raymond, and managed to ask whether this was the usual sea one encountered on the crossing to Arno. Oh, no, he answered, sometimes it storms!

So the widly heaving seas, to my overwrought imagination an immediate peril was but an incident in the lives of these seafaring people. Raymond would doubtless have been as terrified by the swiftly moving cars on Chicago's Outer Drive.

The Marshallese are remarkable navigators, accustomed to ranging in outrigger canoes all over their domain which extends some 800 miles north to south and east to west. They claim the ability to appraise the distance from land by close examination of the wave currents. Their knack of finding their way from one island group to another hundreds of miles away without using a compass is considered uncanny. Their sacred burial grounds, to which their chiefs have been brought for centuries, lie on an island far to the northeast.

A story is told of the predicament of one of our navy ships which had rescued some friendly Marshallese on Jaluit Atoll from the clutches of the Japanese, and was transporting them to Majuro. The skipper and his navigation officers set their course but as night fell grave doubts arose about the ship's direction. Everyone was aware that to be off course a few miles might bring them ultimately to San Francisco. They puzzled over the charts and tried to get a bearing from the stars, and then a bright junior reminded them of the Marshallese below deck. They were brought up on the bridge and the captain asked if they could point out the direction to Majuro.

The Marshallese pondered a while, conferred briefly, and finally pointed in a direction somewhat off their present course. They seemed so certain that the skipper, in his uncertainty, decided to follow their advice. They assured him he would enter Majuro harbor in the early morning. He altered his course accordingly, running all through the night in strange waters. And just at the break of day there it was, the atoll looming up before them and they steamed through the pass for the pier at Uliga.

How to fathom the mystery? At the urging of his officers, the captain had the Marshallese brought to the officers' mess, and over cups of steaming coffee, expressed his appreciation. And then he asked the question in the forefront of everybody's mind. How did they know the proper direction to Majuro?

The Marshallese put down their cups, conferred briefly, then straightened up and with a completely straight face their leader said: "It was there all the time."

As we finally made way through the pass, others on our boat seemed not only unconcerned but ready to make sport of the situation. Somebody produced a tangle of fishing lines, a collection of stout cords with a hook on the end. They were untangled and fastened to a stanchion at the stern and one of the crew paid out the lines until they streamed freely in the wake of the boat.

It was explained to me that this was a particularly good time to troll, as we sailed through the pass and into the ocean the turbulent waters usually attracted the gamest fish. That day it proved not to be the case. The face at the stern changed three times, yet nothing happened. Two hours passed. The ocean currents and the wind became somewhat calmer and we could now discern the Arno Atoll far off in the remote distance, first a long solid line of gray, and finally, scattered breaks in the solid line revealed the contours of individual islands.

At this point, Juanita Griffin who had been watching the prospective anglers with thinly concealed superiority, allowed that she would try her hand. The lines were yielded to her and she took her seat along the stern rail. The fish may have been affected by the change in sex; perhaps we came into better fishing waters; in any case, within fifteen minutes there was a strong tug at the line. It was hauled in and there at the end of it was a barracuda, an indignant and bellicose monster at least three feet long, surely well over thirty pounds, and not disposed to submit tamely. He waged a furious battle. It was found that nature had given him stout weapons for the perils he was required to face, but a neck which could resist the headsman's axe was not among them. He died gallantly with a fierce beating of his tail.

Before he had stopped quivering, Raymond's wife was measuring him for the pot. Within a half hour all who wished boiled fish had an ample supply from the little cookstove in the after-compartment; I and a few others waited for the fried filets which came out of the pan later. A fair quantity of these filets, nicely browned, with several cups of hot tea, made an elegant meal just before we made ready to land.

We dropped anchor in a little cove about two hundred yards from shore. Down came the ship's dinghy to which a brand new outboard motor was attached. The necessary screws having been adjusted and all gadgets checked, one of the crew pulled the cord. Nothing happened. He pulled it again, and again. He pulled it twenty times, but alas, there was no reaction. After some twenty minutes and what seemed hours of good-natured joshing, the cantankerous appendage gave a first gasp of activation, then another, and from then on, purred contentedly.

By 6:00 P.M. our belongings were all ashore, and the next load consisted of the Judge, Juanita and myself. The trip to the beach was fast and accurate; we stepped ashore into six inches of water and onto the sandy beach.

Crowds of people had gathered. As we shook the water from our shoes, men and women came forward to grasp our hands and give us the familiar friendly salutation in Marshallese, "*Yokwe*" (pronounced Yokwāy) meaning, "I love you." We responded in the same fashion, which seemed to make everybody happy. Later when I became proficient in Marshallese I would answer, "*Yokwe cum wich.*" "I love all of you."

Raymond and the rest of our party came ashore and then our little cavalcade started for the dispensary where we were to bed down for the weeks of the court sitting. We did not have far to go. The island is not over a quarter-mile wide, and we had disembarked at a point within 100 yards of our destination.

We came to the dispensary as dusk filtered down upon us. What we saw was the usual corrugated-roof structure with siding of salvage lumber, very dilapidated inside and out. There were three rooms, one with three mattresses laid side by side on cots mounted on a platform a few feet above the concrete floor. Apparently it was intended that all three Americans would sleep in close proximity in the same room. I asked Raymond why, if three rooms were available for our use, it happened that all three beds were in one room. He answered that he had advised the Arno authorities by mail that three beds would be needed, two male and one female. The Arno people had therefore prepared the bedroom for sleeping in Micronesian style, with the woman in between the two men.

As tactfully as possible, we adjured Raymond to explain that our sleeping habits were too disorderly to permit sleeping in such close proximity, and that each of us preferred the separate room to which we were accustomed. Our hosts received this explanation with expressions of surprise but nevertheless proceeded to carry out our wishes.

Lamps were lit. We were able to examine our quarters with greater detail. There were of course no electric lights, but only several old-fashioned kerosene lamps which flickered feebly, as if to veil with shadows the unpainted walls and subdue the creaking doors. There was no place to store clothes or toilet articles; there was no running water. After all, the ocean on one side and the lagoon on the other offered ample bathing opportunities, and water for our other needs could be brought from the cistern a few feet away.

I was taken aback by the primitive accommodations, particularly the inadequate lighting. Judge Furber expressed surprise that I had expected anything else and pointed out that this was the best available on the atoll. He argued that lack of the standards to which Americans are accustomed ought not to deprive Micronesians of the justice which America had undertaken to provide and, having assured me that conditions would be made more tolerable the next day, he suggested that we go to bed meanwhile. We put our hospital-loaned pillows and sheets on the beds and shortly after we had dined I retired to my far from comfortable couch. We agreed to get our court call under way the following day, a Saturday, and push the hearing to completion as soon as possible.

I was able the next day to get a clearer picture of the atoll and the life going on about us. The atoll is crescent shaped, the islands closely following each other around the circumference of the reef. Here there was no land-locked lagoon but only a bay along the inside of the crescent, with the land from ocean to bay several hundred yards wide at most. The infirmary in which we were housed looked no fresher in the light of day, but the brilliant sunshine transmuted the salvage lumber siding and weather-beaten frame into something of beauty.

We faced the main street along which were numerous thatched roof dwellings, each fronting on a deep courtyard separated by a hedgerow from its neighbors. Each group of dwellings used a common cistern, a concrete enclosure about three feet above ground and five or six feet below, with an easily raised metal cover. Rain water, the only water suitable for drinking, was carried into the cistern by gutters along the eaves of the dwellings. This was the dry season; the supply was rather low in the cistern serving the infirmary, but it was replenished by a soaking rain the day after our arrival.

Each homesite had a flock of chickens and several pigs, with a brace of dogs to keep peace in the barnyard and incidentally to warn strangers against approaching too near. All the animals had to scrounge for food, without great success. The dogs were gaunt and the chickens given us for the pot by the generous natives inordinately lean.

Behind our dwelling and between it and the beach along the bay, there were several thatched houses inhabited by families related to Raymond's wife. These houses were open several feet above ground, on all sides but one, and seemed to consist of one large room with mat-covered floor. Cooking was done on a grate outside the house, or in a small adjoining cook-house. Near the beach a Japanese-style benjo had been recently constructed; the natives pointed it out to Raymond as intended for use by the judicial party.

We had almost no privacy. Crowds of children gathered to watch us exercise our peculiar customs, among them my colleague's habit of shaving in his shorts outside our dwelling, leaving his face well lathered and walking a few hundred feet to the ocean or bay to wash the soap off with salt water. That he was able to do this each day without skin irritation served to arouse my unreasoning jealousy.

It was my custom to use a safety razor with removable blade, whereas those of the natives who shaved invariably used an open razor blade over and over again. Most Marshallese have little facial hair and shave infrequently, if at all, and when they do the service is performed by some close friend or relative. Moveover they seldom use soap. Some day American shaving habits will overcome Micronesian frugality, but many more important needs vie presently for the Micronesian dollar.

My custom was to have a quantity of water heated for my shave, and with a small mirror attached to the exterior wall of our dwelling, I would stand in my Bermuda shorts and scrape off the beard. Within a few minutes hordes of children would appear, and sitting on their haunches, regard my strange actions with the utmost gravity. Apparently soap and heated water and shaving lotion were phenomena so bewildering as to demand rapt attention in complete silence. After I was pretty well along I would turn to the eager faces and bark like a dog or yell Boo!—enough to send them into peals of laughter but not enough to cause them to leave. The children were uniformly well-behaved, healthy and happy, and probably cleaner than kids of similar age and economic background in the States. The little girls tended to wear their dresses down to their ankles, probably the result of missionary influence which has imposed western dress on the islanders and given them a false sense of modesty.

Meanwhile, on a little stove set up in the hallway beside the dining room, breakfast was being prepared; canned fruit juices, powdered milk and dry cereal, with either bananas, papaya, or pineapple, toast and marmalade, tea or coffee and eggs—when the chickens attended to duty. The friendly natives gave us fruit in embarrassing quantities; and we never knew which of them had favored us. We tried to reciprocate with gifts of cigarettes, coffee and rice, but they had to be parceled out by the imperturbable Raymond, whose sense of propriety was alway dependable.

After breakfast, we settled to an examination of the files we had brought from Majuro. I was able to read the translated copies of court pleadings and the record of each case. Where the contentions of the parties were obscure, as happened frequently, Raymond or Judge Furber could usually answer my questions. When the cases were called at the first call of the trial calendar the day after we arrived, I was sufficiently familiar with the issues to follow the interrogations.

The calendar had been made up by the court reporter and translated into Marshallese; the numerous copies typed by Raymond had been posted in public places where they were examined with quiet solemnity by the litigants and residents. The call was to be made in the courtroom improvised in the school house, which consisted of a one-room wooden structure whose brand new corrugated roof rose to a center gable, with the ends of the roofing slats meeting, almost but not quite, at the height of the gable. This made it possible for rain to fall with some accuracy through the aperture directly onto the table at which the two judges were seated.

We marched from our quarters in a quasi-procession, with the judges leading, carrying briefcases and robes. The court reporter followed with her notebooks and supplies, and the clerk of courts with the files. Then came the sheriff and constabularyman and the local judge, carrying chairs for the judges, the court reporter and themselves, as there were none in the school house. The procession was completed by a fair number of bystanders and children to whom this occasion was a fascinating experience.

As we marched down the main street many people gave us the traditional greeting, *Yokwe,* to which we responded similarly, and many came to shake our hands. Numerous dogs came to sniff our garments, and though obviously puzzled at the strange odors, apparently decided to withhold judgment pending our subsequent behavior. The dogs were among our most interested spectators, save occasionally when they snarled at each other and had to be hustled out of our court room.

We arrived at the schoolhouse and retired to an adjoining

shed to put on our robes. The files were placed on the table which would serve as a joint desk for the judges, and the court reporter and interpreter sat nearby, the people took their seats on the wooden floor, and the sheriff announced the opening of court. We entered and everybody rose. Then, on direction from the sheriff, everybody sat down and the proceedings started.

Judge Furber made a friendly statement about the need for clearing up the old cases and announced that some of them would be set each day in the hope that the calendar could be completed in two weeks. He introduced me as the new Associate Justice who would hear a number of the pre-trial conferences at times conveniently set. I then spoke a few words about what we hoped to accomplish and expressed my pleasure at the quiet and respectful attention from the audience, which augured well for the administration of justice.

This interest on the part of the Marshallese in the judicial process is one of the encouraging facets of the trust relationship assumed by the American government. They all know that the reason for our being there is that only the High Court has legal jurisdiction over cases involving rights in land. In the past, when controversy developed over such cases, they were usually so acrimonious and frequently so bitter that they led to bloodshed—a normal pattern because the loss of a few yards of width across the island, depriving him of a few hundred coconut palms, pandanus or breadfruit, could mean starvation for the loser.

The restriction of such cases to the two American judges as against the 100 miscellaneous judges of various courts throughout the Trust Territory had inspired confidence in the natives, for they knew that where the American judges were familiar with local customary law, they could be depended on to deal objectively with the problems.

The only chairs in the little schoolroom were those for the two judges, the court reporter, and the clerk. Everyone else squatted on the floor, with a goodly number of small children in arms, and an occasional stray dog wandering in to listen gravely. Despite the presence of eighty or more people in this room designed for half that number of school children, the gathering was decorous and attentive to the very end.

As he called each case, Judge Furber asked the litigants and their counsel to advise if they were ready for trial. Almost all announced their readiness; the cases were more than a year old, and our coming had been well advertised, even to distant islands. Where the cases had not yet been set for pre-trial conference, Judge Furber assigned them to me, retaining for himself the first trials and the completion of some which he had already heard partially. He was to officiate in the schoolhouse and I was to have the use of the large Protestant Church across the road. I would also have Raymond as my interpreter, while Judge Furber would use Tion, the young member of the administrative staff on Majuro, and would have advice on custom from Judge Salomon, appointed assessor for this court session.

I was finally in business for myself. That afternoon I convened court in the big church, and called the first case. A table and desk had been placed for me on the platform; below on my left was a small table and chair for Raymond; directly ahead were two benches a few feet apart, on which the opposing parties and their counsel were seated. Behind them on the stone floor were the general public, possibly 100 or more men, women and children. Among the public were members of the *bwij* or clan of the litigants, to lend their moral support (this was not to be a trial but merely a defining of issues).

This was the case against the *iroij* in which he had been

confined in the jail at Majuro for contempt of court. The suit had been brought by one Liwinrak, a plump young woman, on behalf of her mother, the *alab* of the clan, and the workers under her. It alleged that Jiwirak, the *iroij*, had entered on their land under the wrongful claim that he was entitled to his share of production and, when it was refused him, had trespassed and forcibly seized and carried off a quantity of coconuts on account. The suit asked that he account for the nuts he had taken and be restrained from future trespasses.

The *iroij* admitted he had come upon the land after the refusal to pay for his traditional share of the crop, but alleged that he had harvested only enough of the nuts to make the account whole. The right to do so, he claimed, inhered in him as a prerogative of his office under native custom.

From my seat on the rostrum, I studied the faces of Liwinrak and her mother, the *alab* Klene. The latter was of slight build and wore a long white gown, its bodice dotted with flowers. The impassive gaze she leveled at me betrayed no uneasiness. She was obviously accustomed to having the authority and receiving respect as the leading elder of the clan. Her daughter appeared to be of a different breed. She was in her early 30's, with a moon-shaped face the color of cocoa, and long dark hair which fell in two thick braids behind her. She wore a white cotton gown, somewhat skimpy for her broad frame. Apparently ill at ease in the role of leading actor in the drama now about to unfold, she avoided glancing at the bench to her left where sat Jiwirak and his counsel.

Liwinrak was represented as counsel by an articulate, handsome young chap named Jetnil, the brother of the sheriff, and himself a high school graduate employed by the administration at Majuro. He had achieved the status of

trial assistant, evidently as a former assistant prosecutor or
public defender, and was somewhat familiar with American
trial tactics. Though he spoke English acceptably, his remarks were made in Marshallese for the benefit of the
litigants and the public.

I questioned him about the basis of his client's claim. He
admitted that the *iroij* had come upon the land only after
there had been a refusal to pay him. His client had never
recognized Jiwirak as *iroij* after the death of the former
iroij, his adoptive grandmother, and under native custom
he had no right to any share until the *alab* and workers had
given him the traditional gifts of food and fruits and placed
themselves under his protection. It was, therefore, wrong of
him to force his way on to the land and seize coconuts; they
belonged to the workers. Moreover, he said that Jiwirak
was not the rightful successor to the recently deceased
iroij, but did not say who was.

The *iroij* had as counsel a grayhaired, dignified old
gentleman named Levy. He looked a good deal more like a
native king than his client, who was badly in need of a
shave.

A thin sallow face, flecked with scraggly gray whiskers,
a slight figure attired in flowery *aloha* shirt, khaki trousers
and Japanese sandals. Nothing about this man betokened
leadership or dignity. It was easy to believe that Jiwirak
had spent most of his adult life in the shadow of his domi-
nant grandmother, waiting for her to die. The long waiting
and the keen disappointment when she failed to designate
him as her successor had left their impress on his coun-
tenance; and his short imprisonment in the jail at Majuro
had not sweetened his disposition. Despite her failure to
chose him as her heir, Jiwirak's counsel claimed that he
was the only rightful successor and had earlier been confirmed as such in the High Court; he had been recognized

as *iroij* by a majority of the people of Arno, including Liwinrak's mother, the *alab* Klene. He promised to produce evidence that Klene had given the *iroij* food and fruit more than once and had stated before witnesses her intention to recognize him as *iroij* and claim his protection and counsel. He admitted that the *iroij* had removed a quantity of coconuts worth twenty-five dollars but only after it appeared Liwinrak would not honor her mother's commitment.

It took about an hour's questioning to get the facts, careful notes were taken of the answers and admissions, and I advised the parties the proof each would have to supply and who would have the laboring oar to produce evidence on which issues. The case was set for trial several days later and I took up the next pre-trial conference. That night I prepared a draft of the pretrial order after getting more background from Judge Furber and Raymond. The order was dictated to the court reporter, translated by Raymond into Marshallese, and copies of it were distributed to both counsel.

When the trial began I told the plaintiff I had learned of other cases tried within the year in which the court had considered Jiriwak's genealogy and found that he was one of the class of persons entitled to succeed to the privileges of the late *iroij*, providing only that he be recognized by the people in the traditional manner. I said I would follow this rule and not waste time retrying an established issue. There was no dissent.

The trial produced no surprises. There was no evidence of acceptance of the *iroij*'s protection, only a polite hope that it might be done in the future. Since the control of the plaintiff's property was in the hands of two feeble women, it appeared that the aggressive *iroij* had jumped the gun, hoping to accomplish by action what he lacked in claim. I therefore held with the plaintiff that there was a wrongful trespass, that the *iroij* be enjoined from doing it again and that he was to repay to Liwinrak the value of the coconuts.

In other times this decision might have provoked violent action by the *iroij*, accustomed to arbitrary rule and deference to his wishes. But he had already savored the bitter taste of impartial American justice and could only submit with a good grace, hoping for a change in the situation in the years to come.

So the poor widow and her industrious daughter triumphed over the mighty *iroij*, paramount lord over many manors. This was a good lesson in American law which aims to treat everyone with the same consideration, and while giving effect to native custom, as provided in the Code of Laws of Trust Territory, refuses to yield to the arbitrarily exercised power of the king.

The *iroij* did not have to wait long to benefit from the law he had flouted. In the next case he was also the defendant, but under completely different circumstances. This action was brought by one Abijai, an *iroij erik*, or lesser lord, over certain lands in which Jiwirak claimed to be the *iroij lapalap*. What Abijai wanted was a judgment that he had to approve Jiriwak's claim before it could become valid. He had never approved it. From the pleadings and the evidence later, it appeared to me that the *alab* and workers had recognized Jiwirak as their paramount lord against the opposition and hostility of the plaintiff, and had made the traditional gifts of food and fruit to signify their homage. The lesser lord, not wanting his authority diluted by the accession of a lord of higher rank, contended that well-recognized custom permitted all who had interests in the land to collaborate in the choice. This the other parties disputed. So I had to receive evidence on custom.

To discover the kind of service rendered by the two *iroij*, I called in the court's expert who had accompanied us on the trip from Majuro. It appeared that the *iroij erik* was the traditional consultant on planting and marketing problems. He was the one called for advice on the best methods of planting coconut trees and putting in crops. He was able to get the best price by bargaining for the yield of many farms at one time. It was also his duty to collect and deliver the share due the paramount lord as well as to insure that proper respect was shown by delivery of food and fruit.

The *iroij lapalap,* on the other hand, like the feudal lord of old, was umpire over disputes between commoners about their use rights in land, their inheritance of land, the fishing rights on the reefs, and the proper division of work between clans working lands in common. He also passed on the reciprocal obligations and privileges involved in the hierarchical structure of a feudal society. And he had the vital responsibility of safeguarding his people from disease by furnishing them with medical and hospital care—probably the modern equivalent of the witch doctor's activity of long ago. Today it is honored in the Marshalls by bringing the ailing to the government hospital on Majuro, and paying the modest expenses of those under protection of the *iroij.*

Each of the parties offered supporting testimony of some respected elder. The court's expert gave it as his opinion that the wiser and better established rule was that which permits the workers to choose their own paramount lord; otherwise the latter's jealousy or ill-will might deprive the workers of an important advantage. A precautionary note was added that sometimes a paramount lord, who had been opposed by a lesser lord, had a long memory; unless restrained by the court he might attempt to turn the tables on his opponent by giving him unreasonable duties and ultimately ousting him from office.

My decision was for Jiriwak. I upheld the right of choice

by the people, with the right of the *iroij erik's* dissent, and
its free exercise, without subjecting him to reprisals by the
victorious chief, so long as he rendered the service both to
the workers and the land demanded of him by native custom.

The trials were well attended, the people orderly and
attentive. These trials were unique. They recognized a feudal lord's power of accession but required proof of compliance with native custom in a court of justice as against
seizure by brute force; and considering their unique nature
were carried out in good spirit. It was enough for many of
the commoners to establish their contentions that they had
the choice of accepting or rejecting each new *iroij*. The lesson could not fail to sink into the minds of the rulers: they
owed their authority to democratic choice rather than di-
vine right. It is but natural for a spirit of cooperation to
develop where the rights of each group cannot be transgressed without unpleasant consequences.

And so it proved. Before we had left Arno, after the three
weeks of our sitting, the disputes before us had been com-
promised, and the authority of the *iroij* was accepted vol-
untarily by those denying his right to rule by force.

This trend of the commoners to question what they consider usurpation of power by the nobles, is encouraged by
education and by the greater role of the natives in self-
government. Besides the local governments in more than a
score of municipalities, a Marshall Islands Congress, subject
to supervision by the High Commissioner, has existed since
1950. It is composed of two houses, one the House of Nobles
with some twenty-eight representative of the chiefly lines,
and the other the House of Assembly with some forty-two
commoners from the municipalities. This Congress enjoys
increasing self-government with a tendency in the commoners to initiate and control legislation. This is leading the

House of Nobles into an increasing similarity to the English House of Lords, but the process is not accepted tamely by the nobles. Our government policy of encouraging democratic self-government, without taking sides in the power struggle between the two great classes, seems to be paying off in the gradualism which characterizes the development of this society.

Our lives had been following a set pattern, six days of each week, of labor beginning after breakfast and continuing until the flickering beams from our power lamp had become too feeble to read by comfortably. We prepared orders and opinions, dictated them, discussed with the court expert on custom any controversial questions, presided at trials and reconciled native customary law with Anglo-American principles of jurisprudence. Judge Furber and I spent hours discussing the impact of our concept of equity and justice upon the contentions in the cases, and we reached a common understanding of the theories of our decisions. In this way each judge remained free to determine just what the evidence tended to prove, without adopting inconsistent legal theories or differing in applying law to the established facts.

Each afternoon at five, we carried our walkie-talkie down to the beach so as to avoid reception interference from the tall trees surrounding our dwelling. The hour had been pre-arranged with the radio station at Majuro and a wave length kept open for our sole use. First the judge, then I, would open the key and give our call signal. It usually took some time to rouse the operator; our message had to compete with the broadcast of popular music by the Navy Band on Kwajalein. We found it difficult to persuade the radio operator to turn down the music he liked, merely for the sake of helping us get through. That this was our one contact with civilization did not overly impress him, so oc-

casionally he did not answer our call until the Navy broadcast ended. We did, however get through often enough to
reduce the sense of isolation on those narrow sand dunes so
far from American civilization.

The natives were fascinated by the voices which came so
strangely to us out of the queer box topped by a five foot
antenna. They listened to the static with rapt attention. The
children crowded around us, as close as possible to the machine, until their elders reprimanded them sharply. One of
the important pieces of news we were trying to get was the
condition of Raymond's daughter who had just undergone a
serious emergency operation at the hospital. When the news
came that she was out of danger, the crowd reacted like an
audience at an American movie when the cavalry has just
rounded the bend to rescue the settlers from the Indians.

After the broadcast we would take a quick dip in the
ocean, hurrying out to dry in the last rays of the sun before
the chill of twilight. In the tropics there is little dusk, and
surprisingly, for such close proximity to the equator, it gets
too cool for bathing after dusk—at least for people with thin
blood. We would hustle back for a hot meal, canned soup,
meat, fish and rice, followed by hot tea and native fruits.
The judge and I, occasionally with Juanita, would walk to
the village limits about a half mile off, and exchange greetings with fully half the islanders on the way. It must have
been a study in contrasts for the natives to see us in our flowery aloha shirts and Bermuda shorts after our judicial habit
of ankle-length black robe over long-sleeved white shirt and
tie.

Knowing that we were not accustomed to primitive conditions, the natives were most anxious to make our stay as
comfortable as possible. Raymond had heard me grouse
about how difficult it was to take a good cleansing bath in
the ocean. Before the first Sunday was over, a veritable

Trojan horse was seen coming down the village main street, pulled along by a score of men to delighted shouts from a multitude of small rascals at their heels. The monster proved to be a bath-house of homely design but useful: an open cabinet on wheels, with walls made of thatched pandanus leaves, and an entrance door into a dressing compartment. The bathroom was stocked with several pails which, when filled at the cistern, could be doused on your front or back by somebody just below eye level, or by yourself if you wished. Needless to say, I expressed my surprise and pleasure at such a useful gift, and all of us made use of it daily. At bath time the children would gather nearby and chatter ceaselessly about the strange doings of the people from across the sea.

The inhabitants of Arno seemed to live a pleasant lazy life with sufficient food for everyone, and no necessity for working very hard to obtain it. The money crop was copra, the dried fruit of the coconut, which the townswomen gathered out in the forests near the village and carried in fifty pound sacks on their backs to the dwellings in town.

At least three nights a week until about 9 o'clock there was choir practice at the Protestant Church. Our dwelling was only a block from the church so we could sit on our porch and enjoy excellent *a capella* singing. On Sunday we were honored guests at the services which went on intermittently for hours though we attended only for the usual hour appropriate to visitors. Hundreds of voices joined bravely in the hymns, many of them familiar in melody despite the strange language. The correct pitch was given, and the first stanza sung by a young native who had this natural gift of perfect pitch. Everybody seemed to enjoy the singing, and though the many small children caused considerable movement the crowd was on the whole quiet and well-mannered. The Marshallese, though they ap-

peared grave and thoughtful most often, had a lively sense
of humor and a delightful habit of speaking in parables.
When some of them were translated in court, I could appreciate the laughter following a particularly sly dig by
counsel or witness and occasionally let myself unbend
enough to participate.

I remember one such incident, when an expert witness on
custom, one Pigenta, was explaining the difference between
one of noble birth and a commoner. He developed a series
of picturesque, rhetorical questions. He asked whether it
was possible for two pigs to produce a chicken or a tapioca
bush to produce a coconut. It was well known, he insisted,
that only coconut palms could produce coconuts. Therefore
like could only come from like by the rules of nature, and
clearly this applied to man also so that only those of noble
birth could produce offspring with similar qualities.

I could not help saying that in the United States parents
of great beauty occasionally had an ugly child, and parents
of character a child of low behavior. What should be said, I
asked when a child of intelligent parents is born an idiot,
which sometimes happens with us?

His answer was that maybe such things could happen in
the United States, where there was a mixture of peoples,
but with the racially pure Marshallese it was unlikely. If, in
fact, such a thing did happen, the supposedly intelligent
parents would immediately be suspected of being no better
than the child. At this, there was much laughter.

Despite their quarrels with the chiefs, the Marshallese
scrupulously accord the nobles the respect they consider
due the well-born. They are particularly careful not to
stand higher than persons of more exalted rank. Frequently
in coming into the court room where the judges were
seated, the natives would bend until their heads were below the seated dignitaries, then walk to their seats on the

floor. On one occasion at Majuro where I was to try a civil case with Judge Kabua as my expert on native custom, it happened that two chairs had been placed on the platform, one with a high cushion to give its user a little additional height. Entering the courtroom first, I happened to choose the chair without the cushion, thinking it would be somewhat cooler. From the faces of the court officers, I could tell when Kabua sat down that I had committed a grave breach of decorum, because in his higher chair in order to keep his head below mine he was forced to slump down. After the intermission I changed seats, to the relief of Kabua and everybody else.

By Micronesian standards, Marshallese are fairly prosperous. In the district center there are quite a few stores where rice and provisions can be bought, and a brisk business is carried on. Moreover, an excellent job has been done by Grace Neas, the wife of the district administrator, who besides being a fine artist and wonderful hostess, found time to organize the Marshallese women into a guild producing attractive shell handiwork, all of which commands a good price among the Navy and Air Force personnel on nearby Kwajalein.

The Marshallese system of land tenure is organized to provide security for everyone. There are no poorhouses or old people's homes. Everyone is born into land rights which guarantee adequate food with a moderate amount of effort. Although there is still some disagreement on the part of the nobles, the concept of joint ownership of land rights is widely prevalent, with chiefs and commoners possessing well-defined rights and being subject to well-understood obligations.

The day of departure finally dawned. Arrangements had been made for a supply ship to pick us up on its return from the western islands. It proved to be the *Roque,* a beautiful triple-decked steamship of several hundred tons capacity, capable of making ten knots per hour. She dropped anchor one morning as we awaited her on the beach, then lowered an outboard motorboat which sped to shore and took us and our belongings back to the ship, whose captain, a gruff Brooklynite named Cale, greeted us silently, went to his cabin, and returned with a can of cold beer for each of us, making me his friend for life. You can imagine nothing more delicious after weeks of lukewarm liquids.

The ship was loaded with islanders lying on their mats on the main deck under a huge tarpaulin. The few cabins were occupied by ship's officers, and a medical-biological team from Washington returning from an investigation of fish poisoning in the northern islands. Some Marshallese suspected there was some connection between the poisoned fish and the atomic tests conducted from Eniwetok and Bikini in 1954. Examination had failed to show any connection but it was doubtful that the Marshallese would accept the conclusion.

In a few hours we were back at Majuro where my old quarters were waiting. After a full report to the Distad, and a discussion of the appropriate policy in the light of events of the past weeks, I prepared to depart for Ponape to hold my first sitting for criminal trials. Many were on the call, and as Judge Furber was to return to Truk to take up the civil call there I would be alone. A few days later the plane arrived and I left for Ponape and my first island contact with murders and other serious crimes.

CHAPTER 6

HIGH CRIMES ON PONAPE

Ponape Island is the main island of Ponape District in the Eastern Carolines, which includes also Mokil, Pingelap, Kusaie, Nukuoro, Ngatik and Kapingamorangi. Its total land area in some 216 square miles of which 130 square miles form the area of the principal island, high and mountainous. Ponape Island is protected by a fringing reef all around its circumference, pierced by a half-dozen passes into harbor areas. It lies in the same latitude as Majuro, and about 800 miles due west. The district has approximately 14,000 men, women and children, of which about sixty per cent live on Ponape Island. The principal crops are coconuts, breadfruit, yams, kava, taro and bananas.

From the lowlands along the sea, there is a quick rise to high plateau land in the island's center which is dotted with peaks over 2500 feet in height. Much of this central area is made inaccessible by the thick tropical forests where rainfall of more than 300 inches annually is recorded. The difficulty of access results in the waste of magnificent trees which are left by the natives to rot in lieu of transport to a sawmill. Most natives live close enough to the sea to avail themselves of water transport, as the roads outside the district center, Kolonia, are impassable for any but foot passengers.

My trip was to run the duration of the criminal call, at

least two weeks. Before it was over, I would have a fair acquaintance with some native customs and would be able to see something of the island. I was also to dispose of several cases of serious crime, with the soul-searching doubt implicit in any conscientious attempt to judge by American standards the misdeeds of people emergent from a primitive civilization.

Again awaiting me as I disembarked from the picket boat at the pier were Ekener, the Clerk of Courts, and his assistant, Francisco. After the brief formalities of port clearance I asked to be conducted to the court house so that I might examine the files of the cases I would hear. I also wanted to observe how the clerk's office operated in handling public business, and most of all, how criminal trials were conducted in the absence of a professionally trained bar.

There were in general no trained lawyers in the islands, but the domain of criminal jurisprudence was another matter. The government of Trust Territory included two officials, one the district attorney, and the other the public defender, both of them trained American lawyers admitted to the bar in their home states. They had preceded me to Ponape by a week to interrogate witnesses and prepare their cases. Each of them headed an independent department which included assistants from the islands, usually graduates of the Truk high school. Part of the duties of the officers was to train assistants in American jurisprudence, in trial tactics and criminal procedures. Classes were conducted each year in one of the districts, to which the assistants would travel for schooling, usually for up to ten days but sometimes longer. They were also given practical court exposure by participating or at least being present during trials. They were young, from twenty to thirty, intelligent and ambitious and highly regarded by the natives for their facility in English as well as their native tongues, and for their understanding of the American legal system. After months of contact with these men, I came to feel they were the island leaders and administrators of the future.

It was only minutes by well-worn jeep to the court house, a few hundred feet from the main road along the waterfront. It stood on an eminence overlooking the harbor, with access through a circular drive on a roadway composed of rough coral stone and mud. Driving up the hundred or so feet to the crest of the hill in this ancient vehicle after a heavy rain is not conducive to pleasant digestion; but I arrived without more damage than a succession of bounces can inflict.

The building was much larger than the court house at Majuro, perhaps 125 feet long and 25 feet wide. Construction was of the corrugated-metal siding and roof type which I had by now come to associate with Navy production and Trust Territory architectural patterns. When fairly new, their battleship gray color stood out sharply from the surrounding foliage. After ten years without re-painting the building was dilapidated, the metal rotting. Such structures, originally designed for about three years' use, had long since passed their projected span of life.

At one end of the building, a section had been set aside for the land and claims department, where claims were processed against the government for the return of lands taken by the Japanese. The administrators in this office were all natives with an infectious sense of humor. They laughed widely at the most trivial remarks and talked with a fervid endurance equal to that of any filibustering senator. I was to suffer greatly from the happy talk of these natives. The cubicle which, to satisfy tradition, was called the judge's chambers, was not only tiny but exposed to sound, separated only by a thin wooden partition from the land office.

In the storage closets which separated the chambers from
the clerk's office were kept the court files, a safe for money,
valuable papers and supplies. There was just enough room
left for the fifty or so volumes of law, many of them falling
apart from the mildew created by an annual beating of
hundreds of inches of rain.

The rest of the building was court room; near the judges'
bench were the flags of the United States and of the United
Nations.

Native functionaries greeted me and I had a word with
each of them through Ekener or Francisco. Everybody was
pleasant but I could sense their curiosity about me and my
authority as a Justice of the High Court in the criminal trials. Two district judges were there to serve with me; the
code of laws required a three-judge panel on each charge of
first degree murder.

The two judges differed greatly from one another in every way. Andreas Weilbacher was a descendant of a German settler who had intermarried with island nobility. His
six-foot height, blue eyes and fair skin proclaimed his unusual ancestry. Quick of movement and speech, his affabil-
ity and poise defined him as a man of the world accustomed to getting along with people—a born politician. In
addition to the German and Ponapean he had learned as a
boy, he had received schooling in Japanese, and later, in
English. He could speak and write in the four languages.
Though without formal legal education, he was possessed
of good common sense and a wide acquaintance with native law and traditions.

His companion, Iacopus Olmus, the Presiding Judge of
the District Court of Ponape, was a leading noble, respected as the best informed and most capable jurist among
the Ponapeans. Of short, broad figure, with dark brown col-
oration, grave in manner and slow in speech, he understood

English adequately, but out of fear that his lack of facility might subject him to ridicule he was too proud to speak it. I was forced to converse with him through interpreters, though all the time aware that he understood my words as I spoke them. He or Judge Andreas sat with me as assessors during the ensuing trials until the time we sat *en banc* at the trial of Damian and Serapan on a charge of first degree murder.

Before that trial there were a number of less serious cases. One involved the charge of assault with a deadly weapon, brought against a tiny mouse of a woman who sat impassive and indifferent, at the Counsel's table. When she was asked the nature of her plea, the public defender stated that she was pleading guilty and throwing herself upon the mercy of the court. I immediately asked her for personal confirmation and made sure no one had promised her leniency for pleading guilty. I warned her of the maximum punishment of five years in prison, provided for this offense by the Code.

I accepted the plea of guilty and asked the district attorney to advise me of the circumstances of the crime, whether the accused had a record, and what punishment the government recommended. He told the story of the crime in matter of fact tones, pausing after several sentences to let the interpreter translate into Ponapean for the benefit of the large crowd which filled the courtroom.

The story he told seemed utterly uncharacteristic of the mild, unobtrusive little woman who faced me. Apparently she had been widowed some years back and had lately developed an interest in an attractive, somewhat younger man living in the same town. Unfortunately, he had a wife with whom he was on good terms, a plump woman not at all inclined to share her prize with the prisoner. The prisoner had accordingly declared a one-woman war against the

stubborn wife. On one occasion she had thrown a large
stone which landed on a fleshy spot, without serious damage. No charge was made about this incident. However, the
prisoner had come upon her rival while seated one Sunday
in church participating in religious services, and had
promptly plunged a knife in her back. Luckily for both
women, the knife had been deflected, the wound was not
critical, and in a matter of weeks the victim was as good as
new. The prisoner had no previous record of crime, and
had apparently been a good mother and citizen prior to the
incident. In view of the unprovoked assault and serious nature of the crime, the prosecution recommended a two-year
prison term.

I called upon the public defender for a statement of any
facts about the background of the accused which should be
considered in mitigation of guilt, and for his recommenda-
tion of appropriate punishment. The wily public defender
invariably took advantage of each such opportunity, insert-
ing in his narrative a recitation of the circumstances surrounding the crime which was utterly at variance with the
story told by the prosecution; and casting doubt on whether
the accused had in fact committed the crime to which she
had pleaded guilty.

This was a sad case, he said. Too great a burden had
been placed on a frail creature and provocation beyond her
capacity to withstand imposed on her. Actually, there had
been bad blood between the two women for years, occa-
sioned by the victim's insulting remarks and threats. The
victim was much larger and stronger and somewhat younger
—attributes which had made the prisoner apprehensive.
Accordingly, whatever she did was in the nature of self-
defense. This explained the rock which had struck the victim, who was also but somewhat less successfully engaged
in rock-throwing. It also explained the church incident

which occurred when the accused was trying to find a seat in the row behind the victim, who refused to move forward to let her by.

I wanted to know why the accused was carrying a knife into a church of all places, if she were not intending to leave it in the victim's back. The public defender whispered to the accused and after some discussion blandly advised me that the accused was carrying the knife on her way to church, as is customary with Ponapean women, in the hope she might find a ripe fruit to eat. The laughter which went up from the attentive audience revealed appreciation, if not acceptance, of the ingenious explanation.

The counsel then requested a suspended sentence for his client on the ground that she had learned her lesson and was unlikely to stray from grace again. In announcing the sentence I had determined upon, of one year in prison, I reviewed the facts which had impressed me most force-fully. I explained the interest of society in law and order and how essential it was for everybody's security that each citizen abide by the law. I pointed out that it had taken ages to develop to the point where the weak and timid could no longer be victimized with impunity by the strong and ruthless; that in fact the accused was one of a class now enjoying a position of special favor and protection, making it all the more improper to commit acts of violence against another similarly favored.

I also described how the marital relationship is protected by law, and pointed out that there would be little stability in family life if any man or woman were free to try to dis-rupt an harmonious marital partnership. As I had a captive audience which felt compelled to listen with grave atten-tion to the judge's discourse, I said more in the same vein. In the months to come I was to increase the practice be-cause it seemed effective in developing a sense of public morals, as well as making clear to the natives some basic concepts of United States law.

After each few sentences I paused to allow Ekener to translate. Occasionally I had to define my terms more simply; a high school graduate in the islands does not yet have a very large vocabulary. This necessarily slowed up the proceedings even more than is inevitable in the process of translation, but it seemed to me unavoidable and important.

After several other cases of assault with a deadly weapon were similarly disposed of, the call finally narrowed down to the murder trial. There had been some doubt, created mainly by the public defender, as to whether the district attorney would ultimately file an information covering the charge of first degree murder, which would be sternly resisted, as against murder in the second degree, or manslaughter, to which there would be a guilty plea. All doubts were dissipated when the district attorney, on the first day of the trial call, asked leave to file an information, charging murder in the first degree, and announced his readiness for trial. As the two defendants had been kept in jail for some months since their arrest they also wanted a speedy disposition, so the public defender, too, announced readiness for trial.

It opened the next morning in a crowded courtroom; there was a multitude of curious faces, each aperture in the courtroom walls was filled. The clan to which the defendants belonged was represented by many of its members and those of its elders who were able to walk the mile or two from their village to the courthouse. Many mothers nursing their infants were seated on benches along a veranda which ran the length of the courtroom just outside its windows. Whole families had left their modest cottages shortly after daybreak, moving as slowly as the youngest or most feeble required. They had to carry food in their baskets made of braided banana leaves because no one was certain about what could be bought in the native market. Running water was available from a tap just close enough to the judges' chambers to enable even the smallest child to peer in through the open window and watch me at work behind my desk. But no child or adult was impolite enough to tarry longer than needful, or ever guilty of disturbing my meditations by unseemly noise. This was my experience generally with youngsters in these islands—they were usually well-behaved and controllable by their elders, even in boisterous play. In no case can I recall a child going into a tantrum in rebellion against some admonition by a parent. My observations convinced me that "spoiled brats" are not found in a state of nature; they develop that way only as a result of what we are pleased to call the enlightenment of modern civilization.

Court opening had been set for 9 A.M.—a concession to native custom, for the islanders started each day at a leisurely pace and slowed down as the day wore on. Frequently witnesses from distant areas had to come by water: the Constabulary would have to leave the district center by launch, probably at the crack of dawn, and round up the witnesses frequently a mile or two from the nearest landing place. Any witnesses not called to testify on the day of arrival, had to stay overnight in the district center, usually at the home of clan members. In such cases, food had to be provided by the Government, ordinarily in the shape of C-Rations, of which there always seemed to be enough.

There was the problem of allowing adequate time to the counsel for interrogation of witnesses, because most often those coming from distant points would not have told their stories to either prosecutor or defender until arrival in town just before trial. Such delays were customarily part of the trial pattern, recognized as essential in arriving at justice.

The crowd had gathered on the day of this trial somewhat earlier than usual because of the widespread interest in the crime. When I arrived at 7:30 A.M. many people were squatting in front of the courthouse, or seated on the veranda benches. The clerk of courts soon appeared and started to prepare the courtroom for the hearing, straightening the benches, putting chairs around the tables reserved for counsel and clients, and for the court clerk and reporter, and placing two chairs behind the judge's bench for the additional members of the court. In the meantime the judges appeared and joined me in my chambers for discussion about the plan of conduct of this trial.

When it appeared that these native judges had never participated in a murder trial nor sat on a three-judge panel before, I opened the volume containing the Code of Laws of Trust Territory and read the statutory language regarding such trials and explained the meaning whenever it was doubtful. The major provision was to the effect that the judges were to determine by majority vote the guilt or innocence of the accused and fix the punishment, if any, but that rulings on the admission of evidence, or legal questions presented during the trial were within the province of the High Court Justice only. I promised my co-judges to explain in chambers any ruling of mine that might not be clear to them during the trial.

The clerk of courts came in to advise that everything was in readiness. Both counsel and their witnesses awaited the opening of court. I put on my flowing black robe and, followed by Judges Iacopus and Andreas, strode into the courtroom to the bailiff's warning for all to rise. Everybody rose, including those who had been sitting on benches outside the court room. The bailiff advised of the opening of

court and admonished those having business with the court
to attend and present it.

I called the case of Trust Territory Government vs.
Damian and Serapan, and requested the prosecutor to
make his opening statement. He described the Christmas
celebration a few months ago at the home of Thomas, the
uncle of Damian, and told how Damian had slain his uncle
with the aid of his companion Serapan. There had been much
drinking and at the height of the celebration Thomas had
wielded his machete too close to the nose of his nephew
and accidentally nicked the tip, whereupon Damian had
gone back to his own quarters in a neighboring village,
gotten his own machete and returning to the home of
Thomas had almost decapitated him with one blow.

The first witness for the prosecution was one Aluis, a man
of high birth and a kinsman of the deceased and of the defendant Damian. Aluis took the oath gravely. He sat down
in the witness chair facing the counsel table with the left
side of his face toward the bench. He was a strikingly
handsome man in his forties, of better than average height,
his costume an aloha shirt and khaki shorts revealing a
solid physique and powerful arms. He told his story sorrow-
fully, with the restraint of a parent forced to take note of the
serious misdeeds of his offspring.

He told of the family party planning by Thomas, one of
the elders of the clan, and his wife. They lived in a large
house with a number of smaller cottages nearby and a separate cookhouse adjoining. In the main house there was
room for the sleeping mats of many people, and they were
to be used that night by families from distant parts. Customarily each family brought something for the pot, a
chicken or two, a good-sized fish, a substantial taro root, or
breadfruit. Nobody needed to bring coconut or bananas;
they were available in profusion in the neighboring forests.

The party started auspiciously shortly after noontime, with the arrival of guests from the farthest villages. There was ample space for children's play between the cottages so the parents were able to let them run free. There was much glee among the youngsters and they scampered off to play like young savages. As more people kept coming the store of food increased and soon it was time to prepare the supper which would be served before sundown. Many hands were available and before long the diners were squatting on mats before a festive board laden with native delicacies. Nor was food the only interest of host and guests. The men had arranged for what turned out to be excessive quantities of native liquor composed of yeast and coconut juice. I gathered that it must have had an impact equal to a respectable number of Missouri mules.

It is customary at such feasts for food to be served quite cold, or at least as cool as cooked food will get after standing an hour or two in a cool place. There is no artificial refrigeration available to the natives, their food spoils comparatively quickly, and so the tendency is to consume all prepared food even if it means stoking up the human furnace with considerably more fuel than it needs at one time. At any rate, much food was consumed, and so was the fiery liquor—by most of the men and some of the women.

The effects of too rapid consumption of the native drink led to increased activity on the part of the host and some of the guests, each according to his kind. With Thomas, the effect was to release a latent brutality normally restrained by the amenities of tribal life and the strict rules of behavior towards family and guest implicit in island culture. So when his wife did not move fast enough in bringing food to their guests, Thomas became very angry and began to beat her. Nobody raised a voice in protest, nobody tried to stop him. He belabored the poor woman until he tired of the sport.

The unwonted effort and excitement apparently stirred in Thomas recollection of daring deeds by his forbears in warring on other tribes, and the letting of blood and carrying off of women, for he strode to the wall and removed his machete. He brandished it overhead as he staggered around the room conjuring up his ancestors and recounting how they had made their way to these islands and conquered the inhabitants, putting the men to the sword and appropriating their women. Aroused by his own boasting, he whirled the machete around his head and thrust it at an imaginary enemy. He seemed to imagine the enemy in the shape of his kinsmen, and stumbled around the room pretending to lop off heads and arms.

Thomas, by this time, was very drunk. Those who were not quite so drunk managed with a little footwork to dodge his clumsy blows. But there were a few who could not move. Seated on the mats in drunken stupor, they looked out upon the scene through glazed eyes. Among them was Damian, a youth of twenty, a favorite of his uncle Thomas. He had come to the party with his young wife and their baby and her kinsman Serapan, a man in his early forties. When it appeared that her lord and master wanted to stay on and was getting drunk, his wife went home with her infant.

Thomas approached the youth seated on his mat. His wild expression and whirling machete aroused no fear in the nephew; this was, after all, his beloved uncle, the brother of his mother, and therefore, according to native custom, of higher dignity even than the boy's own father. In fact, both one's natural father and the brothers of one's parents are all equally called father, and the mother's eldest

brother is usually the clan leader, with more authority over
the young than their parents.

Damian sat perfectly still. Thomas drew the blade high
over his head, held it aloft for a silent moment in a trace of
remote, imagined fury and slashed down over the head of
his favorite. The boy did not move. The blade flashed
across his eyes and sliced off the tip of his nose. The sudden
pain and rush of blood thrust a sense of clarity into his
mind. The awareness of pain brought him through the maze.
Thomas too must have realized that something unpleasant
had happened. He allowed himself to be disarmed and led
to his mat where he sat quietly, struggling dimly to understand what he had done and why people seemed to be excited about it.

Meanwhile, several guests rushed to attend to Damian.
They tried to stanch the flow of blood, all the while utter-
ing words of consolation. They said he would soon be as
good as new and that the mark of injury would soon be un-
noticeable. Besides, they said, Thomas would undoubtedly
pay substantial reparation for the wound both to his person
and dignity. Nobody thought of taking him to the hospital;
it would only be necessary to answer embarrassing questions there, and on top of all with a visit from the constabulary. Better to avoid it. The bleeding finally stopped anyway and Damian started for home on the arm of his friend
and kinsman Serapan. They were careful to take along with
them a jug of the precious liquor which had helped to bring
about Damian's injury. And so they started for home.

But home was far off, and on such a long trip it was necessary to rest every now and then and to take an invigorat-
ing drink also. The liquor began to work. The pain of the
wound was still there but it seemed less sharp. Damian
began to experience feelings of humiliation; and of anger
at being mutilated.

He drank and brooded. He could become free, he thought, if he could stop worrying about tribal discipline. If he became his own man, he could come and go as he pleased. He could be free to sleep or to rise, to fish or do nothing if he wished, he could be free of obligation to wife and family, to tribe and relative. He had to defy that authoritative uncle. Thomas had no right to treat him that way. He must have revenge for the humiliating wound, inflicted while everybody was looking on. So Damian's rebellion against social pressure coalesced with his resentment at public pain, and at last in some unforgivingly humiliated recess of his mind, the shattering notion came to him that Thomas must die. The awesomeness of the verdict only strengthened his wild resolve.

Both he and Serapan had been drinking steadily. They came to share the resolve, and the kinsmen were now conspirators. They secured their weapons and retraced their steps. They stormed through the jungle, making no effort to conceal their coming. In fact, when they were within the last few hundred yards, they shouted, "Thomas, you are going to die. Sitin, (his native title) you must die!"

But at the house of Thomas things had quieted down. Most of the guests had left and Thomas was sitting on his mat inside the house, still dazed by drink. A little knot of kinsmen were standing in the clearing talking about the day's events, when suddenly two men burst in upon them. Aluis immediately sized up the mischief afoot and moved forward to meet it. He had no weapons but sensed that he must move fast to avert tragedy. He selected Serapan as the larger threat and closed with him, grasping him around the middle. He pinioned him so securely that it was impossible for Serapan to use the machete effectively. Aluis said that when he saw how dangerous Damian looked, he warned his companions to grab him and take away his weapon. They tried but his reaction was too swift. He held them off with fierce swings of the knife, and strode up to Thomas' cottage, calling him to come out.

It is likely that Thomas knew he was in deadly peril, but he did not hesitate. He emerged from his house and in the utter silence and in the dim light staggered to where his beloved nephew was standing. If there was fear on his part he did not reveal it. No word was spoken. Damian raised his arm and brought the heavy knife down on Thomas' neck, almost decapitating him with one blow.

Thomas fell dead. His kinsmen pressed forward. Damian seemed to reach greater heights of passion. He now attacked the wooden poles which supported the roof, but found they were too stout to collapse despite his repeated blows. He ran to the cultivated ground nearby and cut down the growing plants and shrubs. The tender stalks of the banana bushes yielded to his onslaught, and after them, the young palms and papaya trees. When he had done sufficient damage to perform the symbolical act of destroying the fruits of Thomas' life, along with his body, Damian sat down; and meekly surrendered his weapon to Aluis and the others. Many hours later the constabulary came and took him to the jail.

This is the story of the killing of Thomas as narrated by four prosecution witnesses. Through it all the accused sat, indifferent, as if the business did not concern them. They had feared that they in turn would be executed at the hands of their fathers, the elders of the clan. Their fear had been dissipated. Now that the law of Trust Territory was being permitted to take its place over native custom, and the maximum punishment could only be a term of years, however long, there did not seem to be too great concern by the prisoners over the outcome.

The public defender, however, was not inclined to concede any greater liability than was implicit in those facts that could not be denied. When the prosecutor rested his case, the public defender requested the court to reduce the charge from first degree murder to manslaughter. He contended that the killing was the result of great provocation, aggravated by the liquor, and did not constitute premeditated and deliberate murder. He cited cases from courts in the States, holding that first degree murder requires proof of specific intent to commit a felony; and intoxication, if sufficiently established, negates crimes in which a specific intent must be proved, so this case was at most one of manslaughter.

The spirited argument by counsel ended with my recessing court for some hours and studying the authoritative cases cited. This was to be a ruling on a legal question and I alone had jurisdiction, so I studied the question in chambers and read all the cases in the limited library available to me. I concluded that the public defender was right; what was involved here was a case of voluntary manslaughter. My reasoning led me from the admitted fact of intoxication to the unprovoked assault and the defendant's violent reaction to it. Fuel added to the fire incited Damian to a murder with passion. His cutting down the trees was symbolical of the insanity under which he labored. I felt it had been in him from the time he was wounded.

I announced a reduction of the grade of crime to manslaughter—to which the defendants promptly pleaded guilty. It then became necessary for the three judges to deliberate on the length of sentence. We retired to chambers. Through the interpreter I presented the issue to my cojudges and read the applicable sections of the code. The maximum sentence was ten years' imprisonment. A vote was necessary to fix the sentence and any part of it which might be suspended pending good behavior. In addition, the relative responsibility for the crime might require different treatment of the two prisoners: Serapan had not struck any blows and might not have intended to do so.

The native judges pointed out that long prison sentences were self-defeating; they were of no aid in converting prisoners into solid citizens. They reasoned that a prisoner could be sooner reclaimed by daily contact with his family and leaders of the clan. I questioned whether light sentences did not fail the needs of society in deterring crime. They claimed, in answer, that such crimes occurred infrequently, and then only as the result of deep intoxication, whereas when the effect wore off most natives relapsed into their usual peaceful, equable conduct.

The code contained language requiring judges administering the law to consider native custom, and so I felt I must give fullest attention to suggestions by native judges. We finally agreed to fix the punishment of Damian at six years' imprisonment, with the last two to be suspended upon good conduct, and that of Serapan at four years with the last third to be suspended upon good conduct. So ended the first and last murder trial held before me.

Actually there was another murder case on the call; a man had met violent death some six weeks ago. The constabulary had investigated the crime which occurred in a remote village, but had not been able effectively to pin down the assailant. Of course there was much gossip and the police had brought some of the gossipers a long distance by water to be interviewed by the district attorney. But the prosecutor announced he had insufficient evidence to base an adequate case and was forced to dismiss the pending charge. Quite often, I was told, the clan influence is so strong that it is impossible to develop effective evidence of serious crime, which is dealt with in the end by sanctions rooted in clan tradition.

That weekend there was a delightful experience awaiting me, a trip to the ruins of Nan Madol. The district administrator offsets the scarce recreational facilities by making available a number of government-owned small craft for trips to neighboring islands and parts of Ponape reachable only by water. Roads traversable by vehicles extend only a few miles from the district center and lead to paths through thick jungle passable only on foot, so the use of boats by government employees on weekends is greatly prized.

I was pleased to conclude arrangements with Bob Hawley, the weatherbeaten transportation boss, for the loan of a small boat complete with outboard motor and an operator on the coming Saturday for a trip to the world-famous island with the mysterious ruins. On that morning I walked down to the dock and found, to my pleasure, that Hawley had arranged to use his own much faster and more spacious power boat and that we would have two others in our party, Ray Cadwell, the manager of a local trading company, and a new employee of the land and claims office, who had a college background in anthropology. Neither of them had ever visited Nan Madol, and in addition to their lively curiosity, they had thoughtfully provided a portable ice cooler complete with a case of beer.

With Hawley at the helm we speedily got under way and chugged out into the bay. As the navigation rules decreed, we crept along at a snail's pace until close to Langer Island to which the sea-strip was attached. The bay is better than a half-mile wide but the channel for the use of shipping is not over a hundred feet, and shallow water abounds on both sides. Fields of coral are found in many areas in the bay but because the water is clear are not perilous to small craft. At one point the path through the coral beds was of the width of a narrow lane. We slowed down as we passed through the beds of coral, marveling at the wide expanse of water on both sides of the lane between the fields of coral. Soon we could increase speed as we made the turn toward Metalanim, one of the five divisions of Ponape, marked by mangrove swamps along the coast and thick foliage covering almost all the land. Coconut and nipa palms abounded, also breadfruit and mango, and houses of thatch all but invisible amongst them. In the distance we could see the Catholic Mission buildings, with the tall spire on the church, and the cultivated ground adjoining. This was an area well known to Hawley, who was married to the daughter of the ruling king, and had a prosperous plantation of several thousand acres. Both wife and land were productive, with five little Hawleys already here and another on the way.

As we swung away from the land to keep clear of fish traps built by the natives, we came within a few hundred yards of the fringing reef. There, standing upright and seeming poised to enter the bay, was a shining white vessel of at least several hundred tons, stuck fast on the reef since 1951. We were told of the numerous efforts to salvage the vessel, none of them successful beyond the removal of freight and equipment. Only boats of shallow draft could approach over the reef without getting stuck, so although we were quite safe we gave the vicinity a wide berth.

After an hour or so we turned toward land and followed a long stone pier apparently built for loading of copra. In the shallow water on both sides of the pier I pictured small boats being loaded with this important money crop and making runs over the reef to where the freighter rode at anchor out in the ocean. At the landward end of the pier were gathered several natives who greeted Hawley cordially in native tongue. One caught the line he tossed onto the pier and pulled our boat in just long enough for a dark-skinned youth to jump in and we were off. The purpose of the stop was to take on an expert in the tricky waters we were about to reach. Sometimes the passes between the islands were so shallow, we were told, that boats had to be hauled by hand. This time of day the water was not at low tide so we were able to ride into mangrove swamps and pick our way tortuously through slimy water around numerous small islands until we reached our objective. It was a landing platform of heavy flat stone surmounted by several stone steps leading to a structure which looked like a stone fort, but without a roof.

We fastened our line to a tree and clambered off, pausing occasionally to take snapshots of the island and of each other. The structure we reached was actually hollowed out of the ground and had walls of stone planks, many a dozen feet long and about a foot and a half thick, with smooth sides suggestive of logs square cut by modern machinery. There were hundreds of logs placed one on the other with supports of stone piers, to a height of possibly twenty feet. Below the ground floor, built of huge flat stones, was a basement on the bare earth. Here were the living quarters and warehouses for storage of food. Reaching to the walls were stone steps from which a nimble person could climb onto and over the outer walls. One had to be extremely cautious on these stone masses; they were slippery and a slight fall would cause a painful wound. I pondered over what these ruins must have looked like five hundred years ago when they were populated with the Saudeleurs, a tribe which had come from afar, conquered the Ponapean chiefs, and then built these fortresses along the seashore where they lived, controlling the surrounding countryside.

The incredible industry of those people, mining enormous slabs of basaltic rock, transporting great quantities at least five miles over land and then in canoes across the bay, defies imagination. No one had explained the ability of those master craftsmen to cut the rock to uniform thickness and smooth surface without metal tools. No metal is found there. The tools could only have been of wood, stone, bone or shell.

The fortresses extended over a number of islands connected by causeways. As we strayed outside the walls, we encountered a herd of goats grazing in the luxuriant undergrowth; they looked at us in surprise and finally indignation. As we snapped pictures they scampered off, jumping furiously over treacherous stones at a pace which would have broken a human neck. Time and nature had modified man's creative effort, with the unchecked growth of rank underbrush and creepers and a myriad of papaya trees heavy with fruit. The stone outer framework was nearly covered.

Never explored by competent archeologists, the ruins have not been accurately dated. Study by a team of anthropologists, archeologists and historians might discover that restoration to their original condition is justified. It is a fertile field but the prospect of such study are indeed dim; Trust Territory operates on a niggardly budget; it is hard to imagine their finding the money for scientific exploration when economic needs are so pressing.

Our return trip was uneventful, save that we landed minus the case of beer. The humidity is so high, especially at Ponape, that one never seems to get quite enough liquid. From the dock we traveled in Hawley's jeep to the transportation office, and from there I decided to walk the several blocks to my hotel through the native trading center.

The main street is unusually wide with paving of crushed coral rock. There are a score of stores, several barber shops, a pool hall complete with billiard table and hangers-on, a movie theatre, and three or four shops displaying goods brought in from Japan and the United States. The Japanese

imports are much cheaper than the American and of somewhat lower quality. One noticeable feature is the absence
of packaging materials—whatever you buy you take along
just as it is, whether dusty, damaged, or shopworn. There
are no sidewalks, everybody uses the street and a large
number of dogs use it for a continuous siesta right in the
middle of the roadway—a constant threat to sporadic government jeeps and trucks. Most of the natives live in their
own villages out in the countryside so the native dwellings,
either behind or attached to the stores, are few in this area.
There are no shops selling native food, except for the daily
catch of fish, sold at the pier as unloaded by the enterprising fisherman, there is little excess food to sell. Whatever
surplus vegetables and fruits are produced are sold in one
market store near the courthouse, and are not available in
quantity, nor are they in general appetizing to Americans.
There is one restaurant catering to Americans, operated by
a Ponapean of mixed blood named George Higgins. The
food is served in native style—that is, stone cold—pork,
fish or chicken, boiled or fried taro, breadfruit, yams and
coconut. And one's natural interest in novel food is quickly
discouraged by the absence of seasoning.

That evening I dined at the home of Bill Finale, the
acting district administrator who prided himself on his art
as a cook. He and the district attorney had prepared the
main dish, spaghetti and meat balls. More thought and effort was devoted to mixing the sauce than to mixing with
their guests, most of whom were residents of the colony, either government personnel or native-born Ponapeans of
European descent. Everybody was quite gay, however, and
the evening passed pleasantly and quickly. Among the
guests was a priest of the Society of Jesus, Father Costigan,
head of the Catholic Mission on Ponape. With his knowledge of native lore acquired during a ten years' stay in the

district, he was an interesting talker and told me of the variety of problems he had to face during the course of a day, some requiring solutions you could not find in any manual.

One recent case was that of a woman in his parish, just about to bear her thirteenth child, whom he had advised to seek a divorce. Because of her husband's considerable financial standing and the solid support he enjoyed from the ruling king besides, it had become necessary for the priest himself, in order to ensure the wife's receiving justice, to represent the wife in divorce proceedings brought by her husband. The judge of the district court had, however, awarded the divorce to the husband, given him possession of all the children and allowed the wife inadequate alimony; so she appealed and was to be heard before the High Court the following week. I changed the subject at once but promised the good father that if I were going to be the trial judge the mother would have my most careful consideration.

Early Monday morning I was at the courthouse examining the call of cases awaiting trial. Among them was the appeal called to my attention by Father Costigan. The divorce had been granted by Judge Andreas. When court convened and all the undisposed of cases were called, few were ready on both sides; among these was the divorce appeal. Both sides were satisfied to rely on the testimony and the facts admitted before the trial judge. It would therefore be possible for me to hear arguments, read the testimony and probably decide the case before Wednesday, the day that the weekly plane would stop on its trip from Majuro to Guam. Both sides were anxious to finish the case; the wife was restless under the alimony decree and the husband had a new bride waiting, so it did not take long to get into action.

At Father Costigan's side sat his client, a comely lady

who belied her twelve offspring, but was obviously within a matter of days (I feared minutes) of delivering another.

In his opening statement as her attorney, he said how happy the marriage had been until about a year back when the husband, a lusty chap with a roving eye, had developed a strong attachment for a local nurse, who had borne him a child and, with an advantage of fifteen years under the wife, gave promise of matching, if not surpassing her, in productivity.

The birth of the child caused no serious problems. There were plenty of relatives to adopt a child born to the beautiful nurse and the well-to-do theatre operator. In a matriarchy, all children are legitimate, the mother is always known; and there is no disadvantage in being born as the result of a romantic interlude. The nurse continued to perform her duties at the hospital while she enjoyed her dalliance with the plaintiff in an open association known to everybody. An affair of this kind usually ends with the first wife going back to her clan after the elders of both clans meet and agree on a property settlement and the placement of children. In this case, however, the husband had taken the untraditional step of bringing his paramour to live in his home and exercise authority over the children. To this the wife took strong exception. She defied him. Whereupon the husband beat her soundly and cast her from their home.

Being a daughter from a chiefly line, the wife did not submit tamely to this indignity. She went to the clerk of courts and swore out a warrant charging assault and battery under the Trust Territory Code of Laws; the next day the husband was taken into custody. The native judge could do no less than sentence him to fifteen days' imprisonment which, despite all maneuvering, he was forced to serve. This convinced him that his wife no longer loved him, so he

brought suit for an American divorce, asking custody of
the children and freedom to marry the nurse who was now
again with child.

When they came before the district judge, he learned
that they were agreed on the divorce, but not on anything
else. The husband claimed that his incarceration had
caused him to lose face among his friends and in the community; this hurt both his pride and his business (his was
the only movie theatre in town). The case seemed appropriate to the trial judge, so he granted the divorce, throwing
in the custody of the children including a babe in arms and
a few small toddlers, and sending the wife back to her people with alimony of forty dollars a month. The wife asked
that the divorce granted the husband be set aside and
granted to her instead, that she have custody of the children
and alimony befitting the husband's station in life.

I turned to the husband's counsel, who was a trial assistant and a brother of the *Nanmarki* (native king) and
asked him to point out any errors or misstatements by
Father Costigan. He made a voluble statement castigating
the wife. She was sworn to esteem her husband, but had
made him a low creature in the eyes of the community and
of his children. He pointed out further that the husband
was entitled to bring his guests into the home he had provided, and that it befitted native custom to chastise a wife
who so far forgot herself as to question the propriety of her
spouse's offer of hospitality. For a wife to complain to the
authorities about such well-deserved punishment indicated
she no longer wished to enjoy her dignities, and gave the
husband the right to a divorce. Fortunately Inosuke the
husband was a well-to-do man who could afford to be generous and this was the basis of the alimony order, not
ordinarily available in cases of divorce under native custom.

When I read to him the portion of the code on divorce

and asked him to point out where it authorized a divorce under analogous circumstances, he was forced to admit that his case did not come within the grounds enumerated in the statute. When I asked whether the wife had done anything reflecting on her propriety as custodian of the children, he admitted there was no such evidence.

The questioning turned to the alimony. I was interested to know on what scale the family had lived, and the extent of the husband's resources. On these matters no evidence had been taken by the trial judge. Since the children would be no expense he had conceived it to be equitable to allow the wife, while a guest in the home of her clan to which she had perforce retired, only enough for her own maintenance. Her lawyer pointed out that she had been forced to leave her home without taking her clothes or even the pots and pans given by her clan at the time of her marriage.

After inquiring into the prospect of reconciliation and learning that they wished to terminate the marriage, I set the case for decision the following day, in order to spend the afternoon reading the testimony. It was not lengthy. I also discussed his decision with the trial judge and I had no difficulty in determining that the husband had no basis whatsoever for his suit, while the wife, under American law, undoubtedly did; that she was entitled to custody of the children, and substantially more alimony, as well as a possible interest in any property of the husband acquired with their joint funds.

The next day I announced my decision and explained my reasoning. The divorce to the husband was based only on hurt feelings, which the law did not recognize as grounds for divorce. If it did, few married couples would stay long together. The wife was entitled to divorce under Trust Territory Code, but probably not under native custom, which although it considers adultery a deviation from per-

missible conduct, also regards it compensable by payment
to the aggrieved party. But I had decided to leave the
divorce question in the hands of the trial judge, as he would
have to hear evidence on financial and property rights during the new trial which I directed. Meanwhile the wife was
to be reinstated in her home with custody of the children
and adequate funds for temporary support until the final
decree.

An interesting situation developed that day, worth recounting for the picture it gives of the hierarchical structure
of Ponapean society. I had a telephone call from the *Distad*
asking if I would listen to the problem confronting the
Nanmarki of Sokehs in handling some difficulty of tribal
custom. I said yes, of course, and the *Nanmarki* came to my
chambers escorted by Frank Mahony, the district anthropologist, who was to act as interpreter.

The *Nanmarki*, Kalio, was a burly man above average
height, wearing a sport shirt and slacks and a wide-
brimmed straw hat which he kept on throughout the inter-
view. Mahony was a fascinating chap who had lived several
years on Ponape and had mastered the language there, as
he had before that on Truk. He was immensely popular
in both the Ponapean and Trukese villages and knew their
history and traditions as few white men did. Chief Petrus
of the Trukese held Frank in such esteem that a year before
when a food shortage was reported in the wake of a typhoon on Ponape, he sent Frank a fifty pound bag of rice
for his sole use.

After the customary social amenities, Frank explained
the purpose of the visit. The *Nanmarki*, by native custom,
had the privilege of bestowing honorary titles on deserving
nobles. In Sokehs, the principal titles are, in successive order, *Wasai, Naniken, Nalaim* and *Lepen Palikir*. There were
a large number of lesser titles besides, the intent being that

every clan elder carry some honorable distinction to betoken his position in the hierachy. As senior dignitaries died off, their titles were awarded by the *Nanmarki* to others of lower grade, usually the ones just below. While such awards were regulated by custom, it was nevertheless recognized that the *Nanmarki* had discretion in the matter, a prerogative of royalty; he could pass one he considered undeserving and reward another he believed deserving.

Precisely that is what had just occurred. In order to indicate displeasure with certain conduct of the noble next in rank, the *Nanmarki* had passed over him and chosen his junior instead. After an unsuccessful attempt to persuade the *Nanmarki* to reverse his action, the noble had hit on a new idea. He had filed suit in the district court, asking the court to declare that he was rightfully entitled to the honor, and to require the *Nanmarki* to appoint him. Of course the *Nanmarki* was made the defendant and would now have to appear in a court of law to justify his action. At least this is what the noble intended. It did not seem at all incongruous to ask an American court in this modern age to take jurisdiction of this attribute of feudalism. The purpose of the *Nanmarki* in coming to me was to request that the High Court exercise the prerogative it enjoys under the Code, of ousting the district court from its primary jurisdiction and directing it to send up the file for hearing and decision by the High Court.

For a moment as I discussed the matter with Mahony, I felt as a judge must have felt in England during the time of King John, passing upon a plea by one of his barons that the king was violating his own law. My questioning the *Nanmarki* revealed that no financial return but only social prestige was involved in the position demanded by the disappointed noble—though the pain must doubtless be grave indeed.

It did not seem to me that our courts could have jurisdiction over controversies of this kind, and if jurisdiction was doubtful, it would be unwise to encourage natives to bring before us cases involving nothing more serious than frustrated social ambition. I suggested to Frank, however, that the case should proceed in its regular course, with hearing and decision by the native judge, and appeal to the High Court. It would be proper for the *Nanmarki* to stand on his privileges under tribal custom and refuse to submit the charge to decision by the court. If this were denied, the appeal would follow as a matter of right. This satisfied them both, for they would then not have to submit the matter for ultimate decision by the native judge who in this case was not a member of the Nobles' House, but of the People's House. I sensed that the democratic tide encouraged by our teaching of self-government was running high even in the feudal social order of Ponape.

Actually there are five incorporated municipalities on the huge island of Ponape, and one on each of the other large islands of its district. Each municipality sends five nobles headed by the *Nanmarki* to the Nobles' House in the Ponape Congress. The People's House is composed of representatives of the people, one for each three hundred persons in the municipality. The Congress has only advisory status at present, with authority over local taxes, schools, and public improvements. Doubtless it will be a slow process before democratic self-government displaces this formalistic society built up over the centuries.

The system of social organization on Ponape Island is highly stratified. In each district the head is the *Nanmarki*, who as recently as German times, was considered to be the owner of all land in his district. Customarily he married his father's sister's daughter, so that his son would be in the right clan to inherit his dignities in this matrilineal society. The son (or grandson) assumed the title of *Naniken.*

A district consisted of some fifteen to thirty-seven sections, each with an indefinite number of farmsteads, every farmstead inhabited by a biological family. The commoners were required to provide both section and district chief with gifts of food, and to work the lands of the chief a number of days each year, without compensation. In addition they competed in the growing of yams in order to be able to present the chief with the prize specimen. Customarily the chief would reward the winner of the contest with a step-up in title.

Inheritance of land is thought to have followed a matrilineal pattern originally, but the Germans seem to have changed it to patrilineal, and in addition to have solidified ownership of land by individuals instead of by clans as was the aboriginal custom. This they did by requiring all land to be registered in the name of some male, usually the head or a leading member of the clan or family in whose individual name a certificate was issued, describing the land and its size and setting forth the pattern of inheritance. Title was to pass successively to the eldest son. Sale, gift, or rental was permitted but only upon consent of the *Nanmarki* and the German governor.

Women could not hold title to land so it became the practice for some designated male to hold title for his sister, wife, mother or other female relative. With the passing generations, differences arose as to the conditions of such arrangements and considerable litigation inevitably developed within the clan. But these problems have been moving towards settlement with the adoption of the 1957 law of inheritance by the Ponape Island Congress: titles now pass successively to the eldest son or daughter or issue, and unmarried children have the right to live on the ancestral lands and share in the food.

Before leaving the islands, I asked Fred Dupont, the genial public works boss, to drive me out to the new territorial high school, designed to replace the one at Truk, on the banks of a stream close to the center of the island. The campus pattern was similar to that in the states, with separate dormitory buildings for boys and girls, and faculty members; and there was a good-sized manual arts and science building. Construction was of concrete with wooden doors and trim. A huge area had been cleared for a farm to be operated by the high school youngsters under the neighboring agricultural station head, and it was expected that they would grow enough food to be self-sufficient. Besides there was also a neighboring stream for swimming and laundry.

The common sense evidenced in the planning was most impressive. I saw the school in its raw state with many attractive features still to be completed but I could easily see how popular it was bound to be. I am sure it would be worth traveling far to visit.

I left Ponape carrying two dozen eggs I had been able to purchase from the housekeeper for the Catholic Mission, a pleasant lady named Mrs. Finn. I knew these eggs from the pious hens of the mission would be a welcome relief to my wife after months of cold storage eggs. And so it proved.

When I deplaned on Truk, this precious cargo in my brief case was received with an enthusiasm far exceeding my most sanguine expectation. What other possible reason could there have been for the warmth of feeling which greeted me after an absence of only a month? We now settled down to a long stay on Truk and soon came to be as familiar with the life and the people as if we had been there for years. The old-timers are eager to discover what particular sin each newcomer is expiating to justify exile to those distant shores, and the avid desire for confidences works both ways. It did not take long to know all about the American Colony. There was little recreation besides pure gossip, not always the most kindly, a major activity among the women on Truk. As gossip is hardly supposed to be judicial in nature, I had best turn my story over to the lady related to me by marriage.

CHAPTER 7

LIFE IN AN ISLAND PARADISE

We had been on Truk less than two weeks and had just moved into our new home when it became necessary for my husband to leave on his swing through the Marshall and Ponape Districts. I had by then met most of the people in the American colony. A few became my good friends, and we have kept in touch to this day.

My best friend was Ruth Furber, wife of the chief justice. Originally from Wellesley, Massachusetts, Ruth had been on Truk a dozen years with her husband, a dedicated public servant if there ever was one. Actually she was the first lady in all of the districts, having been out longest, and though possibly the oldest in years, was the youngest in heart. She was my most constant companion, and but for her I would have had many more lonely and anxious moments when our husbands were away.

Another favorite of mine was Cy Pickerall, the most outstanding of all women and men, and one of the most sincere, brave and loving persons I've ever met. She had been on Truk as long as Ruth Furber, leading an active life beyond the taste of many men. During my stay Cy was a teacher-trainer, speaking and writing Trukese better than the natives, and before that had been head of the intermediate school. In her current post she would take off for the distant islands, where she would live for weeks with the natives under conditions no woman could find comfortable, to inspect the work of her pupils, who were supposed to be competent teachers in their own communities. Cy was easily recognized in her wide-brimmed disreputable straw hat, driving about in her battered jeep and accompanied by her faithful terrier, named Winipwot after one of the peaks on Moen. An attractive woman in her sixties, Cy was a charming hostess and wonderful company.

The first lady on Truk was the wife of the Distad, Virginia Gallemore, a woman of high principles and great energy, who spent much of her time bettering the lot of the native women. It was she who encouraged them to copy simple handicraft from other islands in materials native to Truk, and find a market for them. The Gallemore home was larger and better furnished than other staff homes, as it was much used for entertaining visiting dignitaries, both native and foreign. Trukese officials were frequent guests, but their wives never. It will take much education to raise the position of women on Truk to equality with the men.

A number of American wives, particularly those without small youngsters, were full-time staff employees and lived very busy lives. This meant getting to work at 7:30 and home at 4:30. You could be sure to see these women at the commissary right after quitting-time, stocking up for the evening and morning meals. Many clerical jobs were staffed by Micronesians with whom these women worked in close contact; and they were usually on very good terms.

A considerable number of wives with small children taught in the school for children of staff members, which was conducted by the organized parents. There was something to do for practically everybody in the group.

I became a full fledged member of the colony very quickly and the routine typical of the lives of all of them was soon mine, too. I had to weather a number of surprises too but by the time my husband returned a month later, things had fallen into a pattern which continued until our first trip together.

The first great shock I experienced was the impact of the drouth Truk was suffering from when we arrived. There had not been a single word of warning from anyone about this possibility. All the literature available to us before leaving the states had warned only of the excessive rains and moisture. I was thoroughly prepared for this peril and was armed with several kinds of mildew-resistant material —so it was with great alarm that I found just the opposite; water was so scarce it was rationed.

This meant an early rising for all housewives, because the water was turned on at 6:30 A.M. and off at 8:30. During this interval we had to do the laundry, draw enough water for mopping, washing luncheon dishes, flushing the toilets, and of course for drinking. At 5 P.M., it was turned on again for dinner and at 8 P.M. off it went. This made a mad scramble for me because I would not, under any circumstances, leave dirty dishes or pots in the sink, else we would have been overcome by ants and by the giant roaches that looked to me more like race horses as they scampered across the floor. It never pained me to see them weaken and expire under a strong spray of "Raid," but I could not bear to see one squashed. Instead we used the broom to stun them, and swept them outdoors for the other insects to finish the job.

In defense of the administration I must say they were constantly trying to improve the water supply, and each year think they have it conquered. The water itself is good, being rain water caught in huge catchments, and even when it sometimes had a rusty appearance we were never afraid of contamination. However, the "water hours" were a great blow to me. I just hadn't imagined not being able to

bathe whenever I wanted to—and in the tropics yet! It was
not too long, thank goodness, before the rains started. And
then life became beautiful.

9:30 A.M. was the time for the coffee hour for which people met each week-day in the club rooms at the hotel. This
was one of the functions which the club sponsored. Doughnuts, orange juice, tomato juice and coffee were available
for a slight fee. This coffee hour really fascinated me. I
never did enjoy it, but I rarely missed going, and in order
to get a ride down to the commissary with Ruth Furber, I
had to go. I liked everyone who attended the coffee klatsch,
but it seemed to me that at this hour, for some reason, they
all showed up somehow differently than when we otherwise
met socially. There was an undercurrent, something un-
spoken. Some had to sit in the same seat next to the same
person, others would have a grouch and fail to say good
morning, or were hurt if someone else failed to. Here is
where one picked up all the gossip and where yesterday's
rumor became today's fact.

After the hour was over (no one but housewives took
that much time) the men and girls who worked in the
District Center took turns in coming over. Ruth Furber and
I would go to the commissary for a daily look and shopping.
This store was a great joy to everyone. It was said to be the
finest in any district and was far superior to those I saw on
Yap or Koror. For this we were grateful to Hank Chatroop,
the manager of the Truk Trading Company, an ex-Chica-
goan and a connoisseur of good things to eat. Considering
the great distance that things had to be shipped we had a
fantastic assortment, all kinds of canned and prepared
foods, things I'd never seen back home—English biscuits
and chocolates, Danish cheeses, Dutch candies, all the
frozen vegetables and fruits, and "T.V. dinners," including
cornish hens, chicken livers, turkeys and tenderloins. Natu-

rally, all meats were frozen too, and though the variety was great, the quality was never first rate. Sometimes the quantities were low, but at no time was there a possibility of anyone going hungry. One dreamed of fresh mushrooms, lettuce and tomatoes, but a little ingenuity could produce some fine substitutes. It was indeed a challenge to give a party, but I attended some very fine ones.

It was hard to get accustomed to powdered milk and cold storage eggs, but after my electric blender came, the milk was quite palatable and with a pinch of curry the eggs seemed very exotic. Before we left, the chickens were producing and eggs could be had in small quantities at a dollar a dozen.

For those of our readers who will be specially interested, prices of some items at the commissary ran like this: Coffee was $1.43 a lb., 3 lbs. of potatoes with sprouts cost 76¢, 3 lbs. of dry onions, sometimes with the same were 69¢, soda crackers 89¢ a tin, Canadian bacon $1.53 a lb. Good Scotch whiskey was $2.39 a fifth, and Beefeaters' Gin $1.23! Unfortunately the last two could not be used three times a day. One absolutely never, at least to my knowledge, started the cocktail hour until after the 4:30 whistle blew.

There were many times during the day when time hung heavy. After a long day of sitting at my new typewriter picking out letters to those at home, I would be enervated to the point of just lying on my back aimlessly staring at a gecko (a small tropical lizard) running up and down the sides of the wall and screens. They were harmless and never bothered to get near a human, but they were helpful in getting rid of flies and other insects. The record player from the native school down the hill would blare loudly up to our house and I could hear "rock 'n' roll" which now seemed to be more native than anything else. The Trukese have no music of their own. They simply adopt the music of those who have been there. I would often hear my maid singing a familiar hymn, in Trukese, of course, or a German-sounding folk song. The big high school, Pacific Islands Central School, where the best students from all the districts came, had an extensive library, and received *Time* and the *New York Times* weekly.

Once a year the students from the school would put on a variety show, and boys and girls from other islands would perform an indigenous dance or song. In Truk, a war dance with huge war clubs was an exciting event, a thing of precision and timing, with the men whirling about, making an intricate pattern and bringing their weapons down on the head of their neighbor unless he turned around fast enough to parry the blow. Another was a polka, a vestige of German days, I assumed. The dancers from Yap and Ponape were the most colorful and the most primitive. My husband keenly enjoyed the Palauan girls in their rather suggestive hip-swaying dance which they performed with backs turned to the audience. On the whole, however, the young people had taken quickly to American ways. The usual attire for the young men, who ranged in age from sixteen to twenty-five (these were high school students) was khaki pants and *aloha* shirt. Most of the girls wore blouses and skirts and all looked very neat and attractive.

It is hard for an American housewife, so unlimited in her movement, to picture the sort of restricted existence day in and day out with the same faces and the same routine, and nowhere at all to go. Surprisingly enough, however, the days passed rather quickly. Lots of time is wasted but there is such an ample supply of it.

Perpetual sunshine can be just as devastating as its opposite. The rainy season can be a welcome relief. My experience was totally different from stories I had read about monsoons and such. Perhaps in other places the reaction would be different, but the rain on Truk was so very beautiful to see! One could see it off across the lagoon, moving slowly and gracefully—and then almost like water turned on in the shower stall it would come down straight and hard, passing so quickly one would be unaware that the sun must have stopped shining for at least a few seconds. This was how it rained usually, but at other times it varied. A high wind could add such fury to it that in just seconds it would sweep in under the eaves of the house, and before one could lower the canvas over the screened windows, the whole room would be flooded. On many days a low hanging cloud would rest atop of the mountain behind the base and hardly a drop would fall on our little community.

No road could be worse than the one that led up to Nob Hill. No matter how often the road equipment did a scraping job, the surface immediately following a hard rain, would be ruined again. The porous coral allowed the water to run off so fast that even after a whole night's soaking, the passing of a truck would raise a cloud of dust.

I think everyone must have been happy to see a little rain every day, and after a particularly hard one it was nice to look up at our only waterfall cascading down, wishing fervently that somehow some of it could be saved for the days when "water hours" would go into effect. But one of the great frustrations of a housewife was to have the laundry done early in the day and, before it could dry, to see several showers drench it over and over. Usually the wind and the sun dried things so quickly, it was a joy; but on those few rainy days nothing was more unpleasant than the odor of dank linens—with nowhere to hang them.

There are so many small, everyday things we Americans take so much for granted that we aren't even aware of, that become important indeed when we have to do without them. I for example missed the morning newspaper in a way that I would never have imagined—it is an institution most of us rely on to start the day off—and I missed as much so seemingly trivial a thing as paper for wrapping garbage. Occasionally, the "Fly Boys" would bring down a few of the Guam dailies, which consisted of perhaps four pages about the size of the *Saturday Evening Post*. And the few people who took the weekly *New York Times* let it go the rounds for those eager to read last week's news. And when paper bags would become scarce, the bones would go to our neighbor's dog Blackie, the coffee grounds I was told were good for the flower beds, and of course, my maid's mother, Araline, would take home whatever had any value. The Public Health Department did as good a job as they could in picking up the trash daily, but many of the cans were rusty and with holes. The only animals who looked well-fed and sassy were the rats—fortunately I never had any in my house but people with dogs and cats would often boast of a goodly catch.

The native marketplace was near the water and close to the pier which was called Baker Dock, named after some sea captain, though some thought it was named after the inter-island supply ship, the *S.S. Baker*, which was an old tub, held together by scotch tape and adhesive. But she always came back to her berth until finally put to rest on Guam. Her skipper was a likeable and engaging fellow named Harry Jennings. Harry was very well read, had good recordings on his hi-fi, and was of a generous nature. Whenever he would come back from a trip, if there was a good catch of fish, he would bring some of it by, or perhaps a tomato or two and some green onions or celery, for which I was always grateful. The market was run under the auspices of the Agriculture Department and showed signs of great improvement during my short stay. On market days, Tuesdays and Fridays, the little screened store opened at 1 o'clock. Boats full of taro, yams and other roots were items to barter, and for sale to the Americans; also melons of all kinds, cucumbers which were coveted and could practically cause a contretemps between females, eggplant, some breadfruit, papaya, pineapple and limes in great profusion. Sometimes there were oranges, a tart green kind but welcome nevertheless, and live crabs done up in a strong pandamus leaf. One invariably asked of Cristie (the young lad from the island of Nama who had charge of the store and collected the money and paid it to the natives): "Does the crab have two legs?"—whereupon a lengthy discussion would take place between him and the person who had brought it in. Always the answer was the same: "Yes, Missus." And more often than not; upon opening the bound up creature, lo and behold, you would find one claw. Regardless of size, a crab retailed for 50¢. For me it was a real delicacy.

Many women would be squatting about the ground near the shelter, some nursing small children, others giggling and munching on mangoes. Others off to the side were playing bingo, the then current craze of the Trukese. Some would come up offering shells for sale, most of them dead and worthless, as the better ones were bought by the Trading Company and shipped to a shell outlet on Guam. It was seldom that anyone brought shells to my door. Sometimes on Sundays a man and child would appear and I would buy a few, not because they were good ones, but because they had usually come so far. The man would always be happy to get a few cigarettes, and if I had any candy, I'd give it to the child.

My friend Ruth was most generous in taking me about in her little Volkswagen. On Tuesday and Fridays she would blow the horn at my back door a minute or two after the work siren called everyone back to work. In my pidgin English I would call to Araline: "She come. Now I go." Most times we would be first to arrive at the marketplace and of course first come first served. I could see signs of resentment among some of the other women who came after us and for a short while I felt a little guilty. In fact twice I decided to take the manhaul down, the large truck with seating space in the rear which carried the dependents' children to school. My intentions were of the noblest until I rode this contraption twice. No bucking bronco was ever wilder, my insides were so badly shaken I soon lost all feelings of guilt. The sales would be spirited, especially if there were cucumbers or chinese cabbage available—anything for a green salad.

After our purchases at the market, we would usually go over to the Truk Trading Company, the Marshall Field of Trust Territory. This was a huge quonset building, with the largest stock in our part of the Pacific: numerous household items, food staples, dress materials, shoes, linens, toys, hardware, shells, flashlights, writing paper, artist supplies, handicraft and a fabulous collection of Japanese cosmetics and hair pomades. This was the most popular luxury the Trukese succumbed to. For Americans, there was a choice of Chanel and other well known brands of perfume or cologne. Only a few natives wore shoes; with more of them the Japanese *zoris*, or sandals, were popular but most of the people from outlying islands and villages were barefoot.

In connection with the Trading Company which, besides its huge building had several storage warehouses, there was a barber shop, a pool hall, a bakery which supplied natives and Americans alike, a restaurant for natives, and a movie house which drew large crowds, especially for Westerns and other action pictures. I was told the most popular, the one which was shown almost monthly and which they particularly loved, was a documentary film of the bombing of Truk!

Along the road down to the dock and Trading Company we would pass "Nama House," a ramshackle building made of old lumber, corrugated tin and whatnot. It looked like the sort of shack one sees in the deep South but larger. Many rooms had been added to it and it was said to house about one hundred people. These people were very poor. They had migrated from the island of Nama which had been severely damaged by one of the typhoons. The women cooked outside or in a lean-to, and the wash was lying about on the grass while numerous little children played about. The little boys would be completely nude and most of the girls wore shirts, often their father's T-shirts. It was said that each time a child was born on this island an adult had to leave, so they naturally came to the district center looking for work. The road was usually crowded with men and women going down to the trading companies, of which there were two besides the big Truk Trading Company. They would all wave gaily, it obviously tickled them to see Mrs. Furber's little Volkswagen. The young men often held hands or had arms about each other. It was a natural thing for friends to do and not in any way to be misconstrued. Most usually had on shorts or khaki pants and *aloha* shirts. Even during the day, all of the department heads wore shorts—all, that is, but the two judges and the public defender, who invariably wore long-sleeved shirts with tie, and of course long tropical trousers, the dignity of the court coming before comfort.

When people read about the living conditions of Americans on duty in foreign lands they frequently note, with some surprise and possibly envy, the native servants obtainable even by comparatively ill-paid staff members. What they do not realize, of course, is the difference in standards which brings the slight pay of these servants within the budget of the modest American family overseas. Moreover, the authorities encourage the employment of native domestic help, as there is too little work available to them, especially the women. In Micronesia, however, it is not always easy to get a maid with a fair background of experience and some knowledge of English. Many of them are frequently plagued with intestinal parasites. I was indeed happy when a lucky chance brought Chieko to my door.

She was part Saipanese and part Trukese, and had a lovely face. She was a large woman of twenty-five, with a sweet smile, slant eyes that bespoke Japanese ancestry, and long thick black hair which she wore either braided, hanging loose with a flower above the ear, or caught up in a knot held up only by its own weight. She was a great joy to me when my husband left for a long court session, for it was then she became less servant and more friend and protector. It was from her that I learned most about the customs of the Trukese people. She in turn was most interested in my life back home and my children, and showed great delight in the nice things we had brought along to make our home here look like our own. She spoke fair English and tried, when we were alone at night, to tell me about many things that had happened during the war, though at that time she was only a small girl. She did, however, remember the "Navy Days" and that was when she had learned (from the pioneer Navy wives) to clean, launder and keep house. There was nothing she would allow me to do in the nature of work except to cook. None of the Trukese women showed any aptitude or desire to cook for Americans. She was also my interpreter for the yard boy.

She would rattle off to him in Trukese, they would together sound much like monkeys chattering, then she would turn to me and say: "He fix, Missus."

So it was with growing alarm that I noticed Chieko was getting larger each week. She already had five children, but when I asked her if she was expecting another, she was not at all sure, answering: "I no sure, no have woman-sickness since last baby." This young woman walked to work each day from the neighboring village of Mechitiu, a distance of about two miles, and uphill half of the way. Because of her increasing weight, she developed varicose veins, and soon I could see a noticeable decline in her work and a lessening of her warm smile. Finally it was obvious, and I asked: "Chieko, who will help me when you have baby?" She brightly responded with, "I work till baby comes, then my mother who work also for Navy wives, come help you for one month. She very good."

One day not long after this conversation, she told me she felt very ill and thought she should go home, to which of course I agreed. The next day, no Chieko, but Mama, who took her place—and began to enjoy it so much, I never got my darling Chieko back.

Her name was Adeline, one probably given to her by a missionary long ago, but as she could not pronounce the "d," she called herself "Araline" and so did I. She vacillated between Protestant and Catholic churches, but at the moment adhered to the latter for she enjoyed American cigarettes and smoking was frowned upon by the Protestants. At first, because she was so slight of stature and very youthful looking, I did not believe she was Chieko's mother. I judged her to be not over forty and she could even have been less, since Trukese girls frequently have children when they are quite young.

I heard her loud knock on the kitchen door and when I opened it, she gave me a cheery, "Good Morning." In very bad English, she happily said, "Chieko have many, many, bad leg, she no can walk to work. I come work for you." She always used the word "many" in place of "very," and more than often her statements sent me into peals of laughter. And work! She certainly did, all day, every day, scrubbing, washing and never tiring. However, I soon found, that while I had a work horse, she ate like one, also.

Her pleasure in everything I owned was a delight, but she was so bold that soon it was as if it all belonged to her—especially cigarettes which disappeared by the handful. *Ichibon* (Japanese for Number One) she would cry, if she particularly liked something, and often found herself the owner of a scarf, a bra, or even a dress, though I never saw her wear any of them to work. Most of the time she wore an ill-fitting dress of sheer material made in the usual Trukese fashion. It was a low neck, short, puff-sleeved affair, with a gathered skirt and usually trimmed with rick-rack, or other braid. Under this she sometimes wore a bra, and a *lava-lava*, which is a piece of calico or printed material made like a sarong, tied about the waist. She often pulled off her dress upon coming inside the house, and donned a blouse which she wore with the *lava-lava* for working. One of her first acts each morning was to start the laundry going, into which she often put her own clothes. I had to watch her constantly and remind her that I didn't at all mind her washing her clothes, in fact I encouraged it, but that she must wait until last for hers. Her "Yes, Missus" was always cheerful, but I am sure when I was not watching she did as she liked. In fact in one instance when my husband was away, I came home to see a full clothesline of men's trousers and shirts. When I scolded and asked, "Ara-

line, you think it fair to wash clothes for your whole village?" she seemed shamefaced for the first time and agreed,
"it not nice."

Many times when I would be reading or writing, she
would walk behind me and look over my shoulder, as if to
read also, though of course she couldn't read a word. Other
times she would plop into a chair opposite me, and with
feet planted firmly on the floor and legs apart (social
graces being the most of which she hadn't) she would stare
at me. We tried to have "happy talk," as she reminded me
of Bloody Mary, differing only in her dress and non-addic-
tion to bettlenut. That delicacy was reserved for the ladies
of Yap whom I was to meet later on in my travels.

It is the custom for Trukese household help to get
luncheon along with the going rate of a dollar a day in
wages. When I discovered that none of them ate breakfast
before coming to work, I made a larger pot of coffee and
showed her how to make toast in the electric toaster and
gave her preserves, peanut butter or butter. This was more
than welcome to her and sometimes she would have cereal
and milk. Luncheon, I had been told, consisted of a cup of
uncooked rice per person, and a tin of canned sardines of
the large variety, sometimes packed in tomato sauce. They
never seemed to tire of this fare, and it was Araline's lot to
cook the rice for herself and Senano, the yard boy. They
were both so hungry most of the time that I never com-
mented on the amount of rice she used, but each day she
cooked a pot large enough, by our standards, for a family
of six. There were always left-overs in the refrigerator, and
almost daily I would give her tidbits which back home
would have been a full meal for anyone. Most of the time
she would say, "Missus, I save, I take home to Chieko."
But sometimes a choice bit would look so good to her that

she would put it on top of the usual heaping bowl of rice, regardless of whether it was meat, potatoes or even spaghetti, and although it was still cold from the icebox. One day I gave her what seemed like an array of delicacies, including a large bowl of clam chowder. Seeing what looked like a well-balanced meal to me, I purposely did not give her the usual can of sardines. She, however, wanted her just due, so with hands on hips she looked coldly at me and asked, "What's the matter, where's the fish?"

It was a great disappointment to me to find that, surrounded though we were by so much water, fresh fish was very scarce, unless some Americans went on an outing and brought us some as a gift. The natives did a lot of fishing and Araline was a great fisherwoman, telling me often how she stayed up all night making a net or pulling in the catch, but she never brought me any. Perhaps I wouldn't have wanted it since the natives had no means of refrigeration, and unless the fish were still flapping, I'm sure we would not have eaten it. I had been given some Japanese glass fishing balls, useful in floating nets, and since they were quite hard to come by, I prized them for use in flower and shell arrangements. When I returned from a trip I missed several, and it remained a mystery until I remembered that my fisherwoman probably couldn't imagine for what earthly reason I wanted them, while to her they served a useful purpose.

Many of the old timers among the American ladies knew about Araline and told me of her cunning. They wondered how I could keep her. On one occasion before I arrived, I was told, her then mistress asked her to bring in cocktail glasses for her two guests. This she promptly did, bringing in four glasses. When the woman asked, "Who is the fourth glass for?" Araline pointed to herself and said casually, "I like, too," knowing full well that it was unlawful to serve liquor to Micronesians. I found her amusing, however, and she did a beautiful job of ironing and of course I still expected Chieko to come back.

Remembering the incident of the cocktail glasses, I thought I would try to teach her something simple, such as bringing in a tray of iced tea and cookies. The day before my regular bridge game, I said to her, "Araline, tomorrow Mrs. Gallemore and other ladies come to play cards. You wear your prettiest dress and I show you how to serve. Okay?" "Yes, Missus."

Imagine my chagrin next day to see not only that she had worn her oldest, most faded dress, but that it was not even clean. However, instead of making much of it, I said, "You make many ironing this afternoon, I serve ladies." After the refreshment was served, and I had apologized to my guests for her slovenly appearance, Araline unbelievably drew up a chair behind me as if to kibitz, all the while making gestures from above and behind my head. "Number One" she said, pointing to me, thus paying me her highest compliment. We were all hysterical. It took many pretexts to get her away from the porch and back to her ironing.

One day soon after the bridge game, Araline received numerous telephone calls, and her excited responses in Trukese seemed to indicate an approaching crisis. At the end of the day she asked, "Missus, you do me many, many favor, you loan me ten dollars, yes?"

I asked her why she needed such a large sum, and she responded that she had to give it to her husband who was leaving the next day for Nama, an island about a day's trip from Moen. I asked no further questions for I knew the Namese were very poor. I assumed that her husband was using the money to help needy relatives on Nama so I gave it to her.

Next day was native market day, which brought me to the

dock to purchase native fruits and vegetables. I had given Araline time off to tell her husband goodbye. When I saw her at the dock and asked if her husband had left, she answered that he had missed the boat. I then said, "Araline, what was the money for?" and she answered, "My husband, he bring me present." I turned away, with a stern resolution never again to be so easy with her.

There were times when she looked quite tired, but she never slowed down in her work. I would ask, "Araline, you look tired, you not well today?" She would answer, "Yes, Missy, I many tired, I no sneep. Last night I just go sneep, when one person knock on door, wake me up for bingo game. We play all night." Bingo was the biggest thing on Truk. It was a terrific fad. Whole villages would meet to play and since it kept the families together, father, mother and children as well, it was not restricted by the administration, though these people could ill afford to gamble for money. Some would win from fifteen to thirty dollars, so Chieko told me, a tremendous sum by Trukese standards. Most often, however, they lost.

All Trukese, both men and women, like to wear flowers in their hair. As is the Hawaiian custom, a flower over the right ear means that one has a sweetheart, and worn over the left ear that one is looking for one. Hibiscus and oleander almost always bloom on Truk, but in certain seasons blossoms become very scarce. At this particular time, the gorgeous flame tree was in flower, which is only surpassed in beauty by the orchid tree, but I was not lucky enough to have any of this rare beauty on my so-called property. We were having the High Commissioner for a visit, and I was making elaborate preparations in entertaining for him. The day of the party I sent Araline out for flowers and branches to decorate the house. She was gone quite a long time and when she returned she was simply loaded with beautiful things, so I was sure she had robbed all my neighbors. I only prayed that they didn't know her, or where she was bringing them, though actually the bushes "belonged" to no one. As she watched me arrange them, and deck the halls, she asked if she might make me a *mauri-mauri* (wreath for the head). This she did, and that night it was a conversation piece. When, with a peculiar expression on her face, she handed it to me I said, "Araline, is anything wrong?" She looked very grave and then, touching my arm, a rare thing for a Trukese to do to an American, she said with a big grin, "I love you." I quite melted then, and forgave her all her shortcomings.

CHAPTER 8

AMERICANS AT HOME ON TRUK

The Truk District is located in an ocean area 300 miles wide and 600 long, in the Central Carolines. In the district there are about 100 islands, of which 39, with land area of 70 square miles, are inhabited. The total district population is over 20,000, far below the figures during Japanese times.

In the geographic center of Trust Territory about 1200 miles west of the Marshall, is the Truk Atoll, an enormous fringing reef surrounding a lagoon about 40 miles wide, in the center of which are located some 14 high volcanic islands, one of them Moen, the administrative headquarters of Truk District. It is also the center of the territorial judicial department, and the home of the two American judges.

The hereditary chiefs have great power, but Truk has proceeded farthest from feudal forms, and has none of the privileges of nobility still respected in the Marshalls and Ponape. In the Truk Congress there is only one house, composed of a delegate from each of the fifteen municipalities in the Atoll and from each of the twenty-four islands outside it. It is the responsibility of the delegates, elected annually, to provide for education and the other needs of the district, by adopting a budget and levying taxes to meet it. A head tax is levied on each individual, sufficient with taxes on business and on the import of luxury items, to defray the modest expense of local government, and elementary schools. Other administrative costs are borne by Trust Territory government which also provides medical and hospital and dental care, higher education, police and public safety and a host of other services. Under the supervision of an American staff officer, these services have substantial numbers of Micronesian employees, many of whom are moving into positions of responsibility as they achieve greater competence. In a truly valid sense, then, it may be said of the American administrators that their greatest success consists of training others to take their jobs.

In all of the districts save Truk, I was a guest, tolerating the modest fare and primitive accommodations because they were the best available. On Truk, and particularly the island of Moen, we were on home base. We were free to develop a sense of proprietorship over our sturdy cottage and unkept grounds around it, until we could take a pardonable pride in our attractive home and tropical garden. It took much effort on the part of our yardboy to clear the matted undergrowth and tame the wild grasses; to build stone walls surrounding the tender plants which sprouted almost but not quite fast enough to escape the voracious African snail. Before very long we were harvesting pineapple of incredible sweetness, myriads of bananas, and succulent papaya. Only Senano knew the exact time to bring in the still green papaya—one more day and the birds would have pierced the tender skin, and no human would then find the remains palatable.

The house also, under the resourceful eye of my wife and the assiduous care of Chieko and later her mother Araline, finally became an abode of cool comfort. I always looked forward to it at the end of the hot dusty day for a cool drink on the stone verandah and an hour's siesta before sundown.

Practically every American family had attractively combined their possessions, transported thousands of miles from the homeland, with native mats for the floor, handiwork for the walls, shells and shell ornaments, weapons, and relics from the sea. Many of the housewives had learned how to use native fruits and vegetables and combined them with dishes from the American commissary to produce tasty menus far beyond the native woman's ability. In fact, their systematic housekeeping, their three adequate meals for their families daily, the seeming opulence (by native standards) of their lives apparently caused a sense of inferiority among the natives, strong enough to prevent true social contact between them. This was not to say that the Americans had a high standard of living; at times it took ingenuity to produce food fit to eat. Nevertheless the fact that the poorest American kitchen was far superior to even the best Micronesian would naturally have made the natives resentful were it not for their admiration and affection for our people.

Soon after I returned from Ponape and the Marshalls, I got to know much better the American staff I had met when I arrived but there were too many to achieve real rapport. And as we equipped our home we came to know the administrative people in the American colony, and became familiar with the performance of the government units.

The executive head was the district administrator Roy Gallemore, called "Distad" in official parlance, a retired Navy submarine captain. He and his wife Virginia lived in a modern cement block dwelling at the top of Telegraph Hill. Their children were married and living in the States. Roy put enormously concentrated effort into his job. He was responsible for the work of some fifty American staff members and about 400 natives, and it was he who interpreted United States authority to the native officials and tribal leaders. Usually informally dressed, in a wide-brimmed straw hat, *aloha* shirt and khaki shorts, he was a man of genial friendly temperament, and the natives, who esteemed him deeply, felt free to approach him in his office or home, night or day. He was warm and hospitable to them in his home and Mrs. Gallemore developed ideas and markets for the native handicraft, so their great popularity was readily understandable. Roy spent many anxious hours trying to reconcile the pleas of his staff for the use of new equipment aging in the warehouse, with the strict injunction of higher authority on Guam to live within a reduced budget allowing no room for replacements of that kind.

His right hand was the assistant Distad, Percy ("Red") Steele, a burly man of great charm and assurance, a retired naval officer of about sixty, who had been a football player and looked it. He was in fact famous as a member of the celebrated Harvard football team which won a Rose Bowl victory in the 1920's. Red had also played professional football and done some coaching. At the time of Pearl Harbor he found himself a resident of the Hawaiian Islands and after a hitch in the Navy took a course in Stanford University's School for Naval Administrators which furnished a good many of our island administrators. It was Red's duty to route the teams of medics, teachers, sanitarians, supply officers and others to the islands, either in the regular supply ship or in the smaller boats which operated inside the Truk lagoon. Frequently he would go along on a tour of inspection or for necessary palaver with the outlying chiefs about some phase of administration.

The third member of the executive staff was the administrative officer Larry Anderson, who had come from California and brought to his job both business experience and enthusiasm for outdoor sports. He supervised the movement of supplies and personnel to and from the islands, and saw to it that the Distad's orders on various island projects were carried out. A man of great drive and a tireless worker, he could be seen in his office late at night, working or meeting with native officials or committees. In whatever leisure time he had he developed the all-district baseball league, a project justly popular with everybody—the natives and staff members and their families. Every afternoon after closing hour, Larry went down to the ball field, supervising ground work by the several dozen convicts customarily used on work requiring strong backs. Saturdays and Sundays he was mostly at the field, as organizer, umpire, and coach as well as teacher of American baseball rules.

It was through Larry's urging that I became sponsor for the baseball team of the Mortlockese living on Moen. This meant supplying the team with baseballs, bats, and in some cases, gloves, but fortunately for me it didn't include baseball shoes. The boys actually preferred to play in their bare feet. It meant running the bases on paths of cinders, so you can imagine the toughness of the feet of those youths.

Although my dignity as sponsor entitled me to participate in skull sessions where rules and strategy were discussed I never did get effective recognition when I told the boys about their habitual mistakes. For example, no Trukese would use two hands in trying to catch a fly ball. He would usually try it with one and of course he usually missed it, in which event he just good-naturedly picked it up and heaved it to the wrong base. I could never persuade them that American professionals always use both hands whenever possible.

The major part of the administration building was occupied by the executive staff and their secretarial help, and the rest by the statistical department, the housing administration, the telephone operator—and the sanitarian, John Brandt, much admired by the Micronesians, partly because of his blond hair, flowing mustache, and god-like physique, partly because of his willingness to travel to any distant island in unseaworthy vessels in carrying out his duties. He surveyed the sanitary facilities, water supply, health habits and exposure to food contamination by rats, cockroaches and other pests. It was part of his job to advise the natives concerning the placement and care of *benjos*. In his work, John had the advantage of close touch with the inhabitants and no one was better informed about the differing native customs on the far islands.

Behind the administration building were two rows of quonset huts, occupied by the medical department, the post office, the land claims office, and by the native finance officer and his staff. Here was the closest approach to a bank on the island, for the finance officer, a Trukese, was authorized to collect all monies due the government and to cash pay warrants and personal checks on distant banks. He had a small loans business on the side, with a safe method of collection of debts at the source because the wages due native employees passed through his hands.

Across the road from the post office was a row of ramshackle structures housing the commissary and attached refrigeration shed, and a tiny barber shop. The commissary was completely native-owned and manned by Micronesians, who spoke English passably well. Actually it was a branch of the Truk Trading Company, the department store located in the main village along the seashore. The manager and only non-native in this enterprise was an American from Chicago, named Hank Chatroop. Gross sales of over $1,000,-000 per year were reported with profit sufficient to pay the native stockholders a 25% annual return on their investments. Peculiarly, this is not considered an extraordinary return by the natives and the market value of the stock is not above par.

The barber shop contained one barber's chair and room to seat not more than two customers. The proprietor was a

Trukese named Marcus, and his shop had been named "Marcus of Moen" by some well-traveled American. It was his custom to use the clippers liberally but the shears only modestly. Usually before starting he would apologize for touching your head: the head is considered a very personal object among Trukese. As there were few towels it was necessary to arrive early in the day to have one to oneself. My biggest surprise occurred when I first had a shave. I noticed Marcus sharpening a Gillette razor blade by holding it in his fingers and stropping it by rubbing it on the inside of a bottle. After getting a satisfactory edge, he held it between his two fingers and proceeded to shave my neck. I expected a mortal wound any second but his deft motion and steady hand piloted the weapon around my ears without incident. Natives pay a dime for the operation and the going rate to the American colony is a quarter and when I added to it a ten-cent tip, it was very well received—an unusual sum.

A few hundred feet down the road was the constabulary and jail, another ancient quonset structure. Inside, it was dim and dingy. The cells surrounded a very large ward room which the prisoners normally occupied during the day. I got the impression, in view of the laxity of supervision, that it would be relatively simple to walk out of the jail, but there would be no place to hide, at least not for long, before hunger took over. Actually the Trukese do not regard jail as cause either for shame or great discomfort. They are usually better fed when under detention and they meanwhile avoid the family chores and tribal obligations. I was told that it is not unusual for wives to visit the cell block and remain locked up with their husbands overnight in a common cell.

There are about a dozen policemen commanded by the district sheriff, one Keago. Nearly all have a fair command of English and are pretty intelligent. Two of them, Mitaro and Peter, were sharp enough to be selected as assistant prosecutors, and were often seen in the courthouse library, checking on the defined essentials of statutory crimes. The Constabulary were always natty in their khaki uniforms, complete with sidearms and tropical helmet. In esprit de corps and military bearing and action this body made a pretty fair showing.

Across the road from the administration building were two large structures standing on twin hills, the hotel and the hospital. The hotel, built on concrete, was a solid one-story building about 150 feet square, containing ten rooms each with private shower, and a large dining room and recreation area with a shuffle-board table, pingpong table, juke box, and service bar where members of the Community Club were served drinks, soft and hard, and short orders. There was also a modest library, several thousand books bearing the marks of constant use by the Trukese. Huge window frames on two sides of the dining room were screened, and in time of storm, wooden panels were fitted into the frames to make a solid wall. An occasional easy chair, and some not so easy, were spotted around the capacious lobby and a badly out-of-tune piano stood in one corner. Though far from luxurious, the hotel, with its tennis court adjoining, was the center of social activity on the island.

The hospital left much to be desired. It also was a solid structure of concrete floors and plastered walls, with an X-ray room and several operating rooms, a few large wards and a number of semi-private rooms. The operating rooms and surgical equipment showed signs of an effort to achieve sterility, but the atmosphere was spoiled by the disorderly clothing of hospital personnel. If anyone had tried to teach either patient or attendants habits of cleanliness, they were not much in evidence especially not in the care of bandages and surgical dressings. Some of the screened windows had been broken, with no apparent concern about the need to keep mosquitoes and flies out of corridors and sickrooms. The facilities, though as good as could be found throughout the islands of the Pacific, were of course far below standards in any small hospital in any small American town. Our staff members, therefore, came in to be treated only for superficial ailments; when more serious trouble threatened they were shipped off to the Navy Hospital on Guam. Many natives were also sent to Guam for treatment but only in really serious cases. Actually a Trukese would have to be very sick to relish the trip to Guam, most of them preferring the daily contact with their families nearby.

Further on down the road and below the hospital hill was a modest-sized quonset, housing the public defender and his staff. His Trukese chief assistant was a young man in his late 20's named Andon, a graduate of the high school and of several years in the territorial college on Guam. A fine interpreter with a calm judicious air, something of a preacher as well as trial assistant, he lived an exemplary life, touching no liquor, always well-behaved and dignified. He had come from the Mortlocks, a chain of islands about 150 miles from Truk. The Mortlockese were by and large the most intelligent and handsomest of the Trukese, and had given Truk a number of valuable administration employees.

Adjoining the public defender's office was the courthouse, also a quonset long and low, facing a large grassy plot. One end of the structure contained the clerk's office and vault on one side of the entrance way, and on the other a modest courtroom with some fifty chairs—not the entire seating capacity, for many natives preferred to sit on the concrete floor particularly during the hot season. At one end of the courtroom was the dais on which were placed the judge's bench and three rickety old chairs, too uncomfortable for even a few minutes' slumber during a dull trial.

Beyond the courtroom was the combination law library

and secretarial quarters fitted with desks and typewriters and a large library table. The library was of proportions so modest that no working lawyer would tolerate it in the states. It did have some unusual volumes concerning island customs, and a good deal of the background material developed during the early days of the Navy occupation, and mimeographed copies of the decisions by my predecessors.

From the library a short hallway led to two private offices, mine, and adjoining it, the Chief Justices'. These rooms were not walled above seven feet or below two feet and the dividing walls were of plaster board, so it was possible for us to converse with each other without leaving our chairs. The outer walls were slotted with wooden shutters which could be closed to keep out the sudden squalls. The front entrance hall was at ground level so that a sudden rain frequently inundated the hall, the clerk's office and part of the courtroom. The natives never complained about the discomfort of walking with wet feet into the courtroom and huddling in the straight backed chairs, but I often thought that such conditions could never be tolerated back home.

Across the courthouse lawn, several hundred feet down the road, were the buildings of the intermediate school, a district-wide junior high school attended by graduates from the elementary schools, which handle pupils in the first six grades and are located in the local communities. Some of these students travel to the intermediate school from their home islands in the Truk lagoon, and of necessity have to receive bed and board. The bed was the usual mat which each student carried from home and rolled up when he was not using it. Board consisted of two meals from the community kitchen, with rice always the basic ingredient. The youngsters range in age from 13 to 17, and the graduates can enter the high school—the only one in Trust Territory—whose buildings line the other side of the road.

Students come there from the far ends of the territory and form little enclaves based on common origin. There are nine distinct languages in Trust Territory, eight of them unintelligible to inhabitants from other districts, and so the *lingua franca* has become English, replacing the previously used Japanese. There were perhaps 140 students in all, of whom at least 80% were males, as girls in that age bracket would be subject to family pressures towards matrimony or at least maternity. Frequently the girls would become pregnant and would be returned to their native islands, a punishment which would surprise them no end for it seemed to them that they were only carrying out their laudable destiny. Bed and board is provided for the students at government expense, with housing similar to that provided for the intermediates, and dining room, showers, a recreation building, and a large ball field at the foot of the hill on which stood a number of homes of American personnel, ours included. The first sound every morning was a phonograph blasting into rock 'n' roll and it was the last sound to follow the setting sun. Like their counterparts in America, Micronesian students love to hear popular music by the hour.

On the staff of both the intermediate and high schools the principal and most department heads were American, and almost all the teachers Micronesian. Some of our teacher-trainers who had speedily learned the native languages made regular trips to the outlying islands to supervise the local teachers, and became the most popular members of the colony in native eyes. Occasionally they invited students to their homes for meals and jam sessions, and made protegés of the most gifted.

The hospital and the department of medicine were under the jurisdiction of Dr. Eugene Mac Donald from Maine, whose office was on Ponape. One other American doctor made his headquarters on Truk but spent much of his time riding circuit over the other districts as well. The medical administrators in each district were mostly Micronesian. There was also a dental department headed by Dr. Jaffe, an American dentist from Brooklyn, whose home base was the Marshalls. He had a number of assistants in each district, available to local needs. In fact it was customary for a team of medical and dental aids, an educational supervisor, and representatives of the district administrator to make periodic trips to outlying islands for inspection and treatment. I joined them on one of these trips and will tell about it in due course.

All the government departments I have described were housed in the administration center near the actual center of Moen Island, and the homes of American personnel were strewn along the hills above the center. The native villages were sprawled along the sea shore, at distances of one to three miles from the district center. Another department, the communications center, was housed on Telegraph Hill, several hundred feet past the hotel and hospital, a low lying structure of cement block mounted with a number of antenna, and air-conditioned to conserve the valuable equipment. All of the personnel were Micronesian, some from as far away as Kusaie and the Marshalls. The head of this department was an American, Karl Kunz, a fascinating story-teller, who lived near the station with his wife Virginia and two well-behaved and promising youngsters aged twelve and eight. We became so enamored of the older son Duncan that we tried to have him sent to live with us in far-away Illinois when his time came to enter high school.

The remaining three departments were some distance from the center. The closest was the Public Works in a long building housing the separate divisions of public works, electricity, carpentry, painting, plumbing, roads and general maintenance, each supervised by an American master mechanic called a snapper. Under him were natives being trained in the various trades, some of them quite proficient. In a separate structure there was an auto repair and maintenance department and across the road was the new power plant, capable of supplying power for a city of 10,000.

Public Works was the department which came in for major criticism by the American colony because it had the responsibility for making life livable, despite the budget and shortage of equipment. It was impossible to keep the roads in condition, constructed as they were of coral dust or basaltic rock, but without cement to bind the mass together. After a hard rain the roads frequently disintegrated or developed huge and dangerous craters.

And there was so much demand for mechanics to make service calls to dwellings which had to compete for the labor with public projects, that much resentment arose against the head of Public Works. Bad public relations by that official aggravated the situation, but when George Knight, a native of Mississippi, took over the job things changed. He came pretty close to satisfying critics of his department. Consistent with the needs of the projects, he did everything reasonable to make the American colony as comfortable as the situation permitted.

Further down the road to the sea was the agriculture department, under a young New Hampshire man, George Davis. His job was to improve the native crops and animals while developing such non-indigenous cultures as could be profitably added to the native economy. The government had brought in a dozen or so huge sows and barrows which were penned in cages along the seashore, giving the pigs and their quarters the advantage of a modest housecleaning at high tide. It was customary for this department to distribute the young piglets around the islands to stimulate the raising of pork as a supplement to the inadequate native

diet. This did not always work out, for the temptation to eat
the young pigs before they could multiply proved too strong
during times of scarcity.

The department also distributed chickens, the only other
domestic animals (save a large number of scrawny cats and
dogs) found on the islands. Somehow the natives never
seemed to get any eggs from their chickens, which ran wild
into the deep underbrush in search of a too scanty living.
The chickens kept in the agriculture station were quite productive, and occasionally it was possible to buy some of the
eggs for our table after the needs of families with small children were first satisfied.

An active educational program was constantly carried on
to improve methods for planting coconut, the chief crop of
the islands. Other plantings were under experiment, much
of it in the more elaborate headquarters of the agriculture
department on Ponape, in the hope that they could be
added to the relatively small number of vegetables and
fruits which, next to rice, gave the islanders their chief subsistence. On one visit I marveled at the rows of young trees
and plants designed for distribution to the other island agri-
culturists. Of all our activities in the islands this is most vital,
next to health, as at present the chief native food, rice,
comes from the United States and requires foreign exchange,
mainly from sales of dried coconut (copra). It is obvious
that improvement in the life-span and fertility of the coconut palm is a matter of grave importance to these islands.

George Davis lived up on Nob Hill two doors from us,
with his clever and attractive wife Sue, and their two small
boys. He made regular trips to the distant islands by small
boat, to inspect new plantings and advise the natives on
methods and practices. While at home on Truk, George
found time to coach the baseball team made up of agriculture department employees and even to fill in on the playing

field when the team was shorthanded. A very personable young man not over thirty, George was a true ambassador of good will in bringing the administration's efforts into sharpest perspective.

The department of supply, was situated a quarter mile further along the road to Moen Village, the main village on the island, which clustered around the dock. Supply consisted of a number of huge corrugated metal warehouses within an enclosure of several acres, strewn with numerous drums of oil and automotive equipment. In the warehouses were stored supplies of all kinds, furniture and household replacements, and belongings of staff members either incoming or awaiting shipment back home. In the yard were underground tanks of gasoline and pumps to pipe the black gold into government vehicles. This department, under the direction of an Hawaiian-American named Alex Mladnich, employed at least a dozen natives regularly, and many more when ship cargo was to be loaded or unloaded. All of them went about their work with the utmost good humor, happy to earn the dollars to buy the products of the United States or Japan in the big Truk department store. As their work involved handling heavy containers, it was customary to send them around the island in groups of half-dozen or so, in a government pick-up truck. Their pleasure in receiving the usual gratuity of several cigarettes upon completing a heavy delivery and installation was heartwarming to see.

It took a few weeks to get acquainted with the staff and their families and longer to become familiar with the work of the various departments. Work generally would go on at a relaxed pace but when there was the pressure of plane departure it would be accelerated. There was only one plane each week, and so everything was geared to plane time. It normally arrived on Monday about noon, remained an hour or so to unload mail and freight and some passengers. It would then take off for Ponape with passengers and mail and freight designed for Ponape and the Marshalls. The schedule called for the plane crew to spend the night at Ponape and leave the next morning for the Marshalls. Tuesday night would be spent in the Marshalls and at daybreak Wednesday the return flight would take off from there.

This return flight imposed a strain on the plane crew, as it meant hitting the ball, or rather the air waves, all day long —a strenuous schedule brought about by the necessity for the plane to reach Guam at the end of the day's journey but before 6:00 P.M., after which commercial planes could not land on Guam. So the crew would try to return to Truk from the Marshalls not later than 2:00 P.M. to allow a good four hours for the hop to Guam. The return trip was aided by the favorable change in time from east to west which cut the sun time by two hours. Actual flying time, however, would still measure between eleven and twelve hours. Between Monday and Wednesday everyone would be busy preparing letters or other materials for Wednesday's flight to Guam, many in answer to communications received on the previous Monday's flight. So the pace of life between Mondays and Wednesdays could become quite hectic.

CHAPTER 9

TRIAL WORK ON TRUK

For the first week no court sessions had been scheduled, so I was free to leaf through a mass of material which had been accumulating for months in the office of the associate justice. There were bulletins from Trust Territory Government on Guam with information on projects, requesting action by departments scattered over the islands. Circulated by district headquarters and handed to each department in turn, these bulletins gave me familiarity with many problems connected with other branches of the government. Matters of great urgency often arose—involving basic constitutional rights and leading to grave differences of opinion between the judiciary and other branches—of course within the exclusive province of the Chief Justice. He would, however, usually discuss them with me, and after we had developed a consensus of views, he would issue a statement.

In this class was the unfortunate incident involving a master seaman on an American vessel calling at Majuro. On shore leave, he was arrested on a charge of taking indecent liberties with a native boy of ten. Because the jail at Uliga was entirely inadequate, the Distad in the Marshalls was anxious for one of us to fly there immediately and try the case. To do this meant giving up our plans for trips to the western side of our territory and holding court sessions there long scheduled. A dispatch was therefore sent suggesting the accused be released on bail but not permitted to leave the Marshalls until one of us could travel there.

This was not done. Further dispatches came from the Marshalls urging a change of decision. Meanwhile the seaman was released in the custody of his captain who confined him to his cabin. Strangely enough the cabin also contained the prisoner's loaded revolver which he used quite effectively that night. As the result, we had a suicide instead of a charge for which the punishment would not have been heavy.

On another occasion the matter of releasing on bail one who was attacking the constitutionality of an ordinance caused a near rift with Paluan officials. The ordinance provided for certain work in road improvement and levied a tax on each head of household, payable either in money or in services. The objector failed to pay the money levy, and when he refused to join the labor battalion, upon order of the magistrate, was jailed. When one of the district judges requested instructions, Judge Furber directed that the prisoner be released on bail until the matter could be heard by the High Court. He was released. But when it appeared that his defiance might imperil compliance by others in this necessary work, the Distad at Palau was persuaded to have him jailed again, on the ground that he was committing a continuing offense each day. This brought a further dispatch from the Chief Justice, this time somewhat sharper, saying that the prisoner was entitled to release on bail until the High Court decided whether there was merit in the prisoner's attack on the law as constituting involuntary servitude.

On a third occasion, there was conflict with the administration on Yap about holding incommunicado one accused of murdering his rival for the affections of a Yapese woman. A bloody bit of clothing had been found in the road leading to the prisoner's home. The evidence pointed to him as effectively as if he had left the tell-tale marks on purpose, but the Chief Justice advised the Yapese authorities to bring him before a magistrate and charge him with the crime; and then the court could consider his release on bail. In the plainest language it was explained that the Code required such action, no matter how clear was the evidence of guilt.

The Chief Justice had the duty, which he delegated to me when he was not present, of supervising the clerks of court, the judges of the lower courts and the constabulary. To make certain that they carried out the procedures provided by the Code, constant vigilance was necessary. Some of the constables had held similar office under the Japanese (who did not require that an arrested person be led before a magistrate, and that he be released on bail when charged with crime). Often they would hold the prisoner the full forty-eight hours permitted by the Code, and try their utmost without actual violence to obtain a confession. Upon Judge Furber's suggestion, I made it a practice, as he did, of personally interrogating both officer and prisoner to make sure the confession was voluntary. And we both were vigilant in checking whether the prisoner had been first advised of his constitutional right not to incriminate himself before his statement was taken down.

Information sometimes came to us of some defect in our legal system. Then we initiated executive or legislative action to cure it. We would act within our traditional responsibility to promote laws in the public interest, but we might feel impelled to go much farther in advocating them than is normally considered judicially objective in the States.

Where the validity of an ordinance was involved, questioning some element of native customary law, the inquiry was usually extensive. Changes were not adopted lightly. The feelings that impelled their original enactment ran very

deep. Native law was protected and in such fields, for example, as the inheritance or transfer of real estate, it controlled unless it had been superseded by a law of Trust
Territory. So I was cautious about a native law when it was
attacked and usually made a full investigation of it. What
was its basic theory? Was it reasonable? One investigation is
clear in my memory, although it did not arise in pursuance
of an appeal against an unreasonable native law. This was
the matter of the anti-liquor regulation of Moen Island and
it arose quite accidentally in the course of my review of
criminal sentences imposed several years back by the native
judges of the District court of Moen Island.

The High Court judges have the duty of examining the
record of all criminal trials held in the lower courts, and
righting any injustice they may find even if it had not been
appealed and even if a defendant had served a sentence.
The record of each trial is preserved in the native language
and, when reviewed by the High Court judge, is interpreted by a court clerk. It is either disposed of or the judge
reverses the decision or takes the action which should
have been taken at the trial.

Reviewing these files is onerous but important because it
is the only way that we can determine whether a citizen's
rights have been impaired through error or omission by
the trial judge, the prosecutor or public defender; and
whether the particular law is valid or unconstitutional.

This task usually falls to the associate justice and is carried on when there are no trials to be taken up. In the Truk
district alone, I believe I examined probably a thousand
files, all of them cases of misdemeanor, running over several
years and ranging from assault and battery to infractions of
motor vehicle ordinances. Almost none involved sex offenses or criminal attacks, doubtless because relations between the sexes start at an early age in the islands. Some of

the offenses were indefinite: "behaving disrespectfully in the presence of a municipal official" was the gist of an ordinance on the island of Uman, whose chief judge was never able to explain what it meant to prohibit. Some represented the administration's effort to inculcate wiser methods of husbandry and fishing. Such ordinances prohibited brush fires, usually set by lazy natives to destroy rotting crops which the administration believed should be worked into the soil to increase its fertility. In such cases the usual defense was an act of God, such as a spark from a non-existent volcano, but the native judges were not easy to persuade and usually meted out a light punishment.

An offense more serious to good husbandry was dynamiting fish—a misdemeanor, tried by a native judge, which would only reach the High Court on appeal. I had no contact with the offenders as none of these cases were appealed, and no opportunity to impress them with the seriousness of the offense.

It arose when a native or a group of them, enterprising enough to break into a government shed and steal dynamite but too lazy to catch fish by a slower method, detonated a stick of the explosive among the school of fish. In this way they could scoop up large quantities in a short time and return home for a well-deserved siesta. But occasionally the dynamite exploded before it hit the water sometimes wounding or killing the dynamiters. You would think that the sight of a maimed body would be an automatic lesson to other natives, but it apparently wasn't. I reviewed a number of such cases and had to agree with the trial judge who found it difficult to impose a jail sentence on a youth who appeared minus an arm, a leg, or his sight. However, after my trip to the Palau Islands and a period of indoctrination by Bob Owen, the district entomologist there, I developed a better approach in all subsequent cases.

The major damage, Owen explained, was not in the government's loss of the dynamite, nor in the disrespect for law and government property manifested in breaking-in and stealing, nor even in the maiming of the natives which made them incapable of working in their clan's labor force. The greatest crime lay in the effect of the dynamite on marine life. It not only stunned or killed the fish, it also destroyed all plant life and the microscopic animals within range of the explosion. It left a graveyard in which nothing would live for possibly several generations. Fertile fishing grounds which the islanders desperately needed for subsistence, were being destroyed in this way. The offense must, therefore, be viewed as a crime against posterity, and each native must be induced to regard it with abhorrence as a threat to the future well-being of his children.

Equipped with this background and fortified with the scientific data assembled by Owen, I was impelled to do a job on the Micronesian judges. These men occupy a position doubly important: first, they are by birth and ability the recognized leaders of the island community; and second, the American authorities have confirmed their traditional supremacy by naming them as judges. I therefore, met with these men in concert and through Misauo, the court clerk, explained the problem.

They listened to my story gravely. Few questions were asked. The chiefs readily understood the implications and responded to the seriousness of the issue. When I had presented the story they pointed out how they had been handling such cases. The punishment had been increased from 90 to 100 days imprisonment (as against the allowable maximum of six months). I advised them not to increase it further, but instead to take sufficient time to explain to each violator precisely why his offense was antisocial, so that it would be clear to the least intelligent native. The judges promised to observe this advice in the future.

Of a different stamp was the incident revolving around the anti-liquor ordinance of Moen. In reviewing the hundreds of files I noticed the large number of violations of the liquor laws and assumed they were cases of intoxication so serious as to create a public spectacle. But I found out otherwise. I found that the law was not against drunkenness but against the mere drinking of liquor. Actually drinking liquor was not punishable if it was done at a social gathering for which the municipal authorities had issued a permit. I was told that the idea was to prevent squandering the family resources on foreign liquor which natives could not drink in moderation. Few natives cared to reveal a proposed party to the authorities so the applications for approval and permission were rarely tested.

There were many cases of youths picked up in the boondocks or along the public highway on weekends, and kept in the lockup until court hearing a few days later. The sentences were from ten to thirty days, sometimes with small fines. For a first offense, the sentence was somewhat lighter.

I kept a running tally of the liquor cases. Fully 50% of the criminal charges and convictions on Truk were for drinking. The number of repeaters also established the strong hold of liquor—on the young people, at least. Mentally, I likened the attempt to enforce this ordinance with that of the Volstead Act in the States, which had taught us that when public opposition makes a law unenforceable it is wise to find some other way.

Armed with the facts, I prepared a memorandum for the Distad pointing out the impact of violation of this unpopular law on the whole complex of law enforcement. I urged further study of the problem together with the Moen authorities, hinting that the law might be successfully attacked on constitutional grounds.

Strangely enough, a few months later while the subject was under consideration by the administrative department, one of the local judges took the bit in his teeth and declared the law unconstitutional. Of course this dealt a severe blow to its enforcement, and though the constabulary continued to make arrests, their zeal was diminished when those arrested were in most cases discharged. The authorities became interested in permitting the drinking of beer, legal in the other districts.

Before I left the islands the legalizing of beer had been overwhelmingly approved by the Truk District Congress and a commission named to submit a draft of legislation to the High Commissioner for approval.

My review of cases was temporarily stayed with the opening of a session of the High Court. The Chief Justice had assigned the Criminal List to me with the understanding that when I had disposed of it I would take over some of the cases on the Civil List which he would in the meanwhile call for trial. As we would both be holding court at the same time, one of us would use the courtroom, while the other would be relegated to the nearby chapel which had only half the courtroom's capacity, and was stiflingly hot besides, without fan or cross-ventilation. Judge Furber considerately decided that whoever had the largest attendance would get the larger room. This rule was applied during each trial, so it required changes between sessions in order to accommodate changes in numbers. Most often, however, I presided in the courtroom because the criminal trials were usually better attended.

There were three contested cases which are clear in my memory, in two of which there were pleas of guilty. Of the latter, one had tragic, and the other comic, overtones.

One was based on charges of assault and maiming, the other on aggravated assault. Both developed against a background of intoxication from the powerful native liquor made from yeast and coconut juice. It proved to be the only point of similarity.

When the first of these cases was called for trial the public defender stated that it ought not properly appear in a criminal court, but be submitted instead to the lineage chief, for it involved a struggle between blood brothers resulting in permanent injury. He pointed out that the clan's welfare required pacification of all serious disputes without going outside the clan; it had its own machinery which could be relied on to settle claims between its members. He said I would find, upon investigation, that the complaining witness wished to drop all charges. In fact, I would find that the prosecution was initiated by the constabulary and not by the aggrieved party.

The district attorney took sharp issue: The government could not agree. Procedures had been set up in the Department of Justice for considering requests for dismissal. They would normally be honored in cases involving violent action between members of a clan or lineage, when the lineage chief certified that the aggrieved party had been forgiven by the victim, and that he, the chief, had taken responsibility for an adequate financial settlement. Obviously in this case no such settlement was in the offing, for the chief had not seconded the request.

Moreover, the facts would show such uncontrollable savagery on the defendant's part that it would raise the question whether he was fit to live in a civilized community until he had earned the right to do so after an appropriate tempering by some years of confinement. The defendant and the aggrieved party had spent their lives from childhood in the same small village as members of a common lineage;

they were the children of sisters, cousins in fact, but considered brothers by native custom. Both men were married. Both had children.

On the night in question they had strolled down the road, arm-in-arm as is customary on Truk among intimate friends, until they came to the village. There, conviviality was rampant. The defendant bought some native liquor and before very long became not only drunk but abusive. His cousin, who had imbibed little, attempted to exercise some restraint but the other man rejected it. He refused to go home and finally when he was about to get into a fight with one of the elders, the "victim" pulled him away and tried to lead him homeward. The defendant became violent and they fought. Both men fell to the ground. The victim, on top, trying to restrain the enraged man by pinning him to the ground got his face too close to the other, who seized his ear between his teeth and kept on biting until it hung in shreds. There was nothing the surgeon could do but cut off the jagged edges and send the victim back to his village.

When it appeared the government would not dismiss the charges, the defendant pleaded guilty and threw himself upon the mercy of the court. At the request of the district attorney the victim came up to the bench and removed the colored handkerchief which covered his head and the injured ear. Nothing was left of the lobe and external ear. All that remained was the aperture, without protection. In questioning the man the public defender brought out that he had forgiven his blood brother, whom he dearly loved, and believed the crime would never have occurred but for the excessive drinking. Evidence was offered of the good reputation of the accused, a family man and regular church goer; and then a request for a suspended sentence, which would have released him from custody, subject to serving the sentence only in the event of subsequent misbehavior.

In denying the request to suspend sentence, I told the
people why I could not accept the forgiveness as a settlement. There were more than the two people involved. All
those who wished to live under law had a vital interest in
public order. Moreover, the government was also involved,
through its obligation to minister to the ailing and to maintain the crippled. Consideration must also be given to deterring criminal acts by punishment. Otherwise people
might feel that whatever they might do when drunk could
be condoned as unpremeditated. All in all, when irrepara-
ble injury had been caused one human being by the wan-
ton conduct of another, a jail sentence seemed wisest. Nor
could I accept the brotherly act of the victim in waiving
claim for punishment as valid for the attitude of society.
Therefore I imposed a sentence of one year, part of which
was suspended during good behavior.

The next case is noteworthy because of the unusual celer-
ity of the defendant in reacting to a situation of utter ab-
surdity. The charge of aggravated assault was brought
against one Yosuo, a giant of a man, for savagely beating
his good friend into a condition requiring weeks of hos-
pitalization. The plea was guilty as charged, so after I ascertained that the defendant knew the possible consequences
of his plea, it was accepted, and the prosecutor started to
make his statement.

It appeared that Yosuo was working in his garden one
afternoon when along came the complaining witness, somewhat drunk. He sat down on a friendly log and the two men
chatted amiably for a while. A pack of cigarettes was produced by the guest but he had no matches, whereupon the
host suggested he go into the house where Yosuo's father
was reclining on his mat, and ask him for one. This the
guest started to do as Yosuo walked out into the forest.

The house was the usual one-room affair with only suffi-

cient room for sleeping mats for Yosuo, his wife and their
two children, and the father. The guest, who was having
great difficulty in keeping erect, greeted the old man, got
his box of matches, and offered him a cigarette. To give him
the cigarette, the guest leaned over but too far for a man in
his condition, and fell on the old man. In the fall his head
hit one of the supporting posts and dislodged a machete
which clattered to the floor. The collision with the post
slashed his head and made it bleed. He landed on top of the
old man's body and head, completely covering him except
for the legs. After a few feeble attempts to move the heavy
weight, the old man lay helpless, hoping desperately that
someone would come and get him out. The guest helped by
the blow and the drink, promptly fell asleep.

This then was the general picture when, a few minutes
later, the wife of the defendant entered the dwelling. All
she could hear were the gentle snores of the guest. All she
could see was the body lying on that of her father-in-law;
only one head showed and that one covered with blood. In
a few seconds of terror she recognized the guest. Hearing no
sound from her father-in-law and seeing the machete on the
floor, she instantly concluded that the old man had been
murdered. She rushed out of the house shrieking, ran to her
husband as he emerged from the forest, and gasped out the
terrible news. His good friend had slain his father, in fact cut
off his head, and was now lying on the old man's mat.

Yosuo looked about for a weapon and found a huge
wooden staff fashioned from a tree trunk. He ran into his
dwelling, burst inside and commenced to belabor his sleeping friend, who awoke and managed in his stupor to beg his
friend to tell him what was happening. When Yosuo in blind
anger roared his reason, his guest protested his innocence
and shifted position enough to free the old man's head and
torso. This gave Yosuo's father a chance to speak, saying,

as I understood quite mildly: "Son, I am still living and in possession of my head, as you can see for yourself."

As the district attorney completed his recitation, Yosuo and his wife sat stoically. The weapon was produced. Its gnarled end and weight aroused wonder that any one beaten with such a weapon could recover. Actually it was its great size that prevented Yosuo from doing permanent damage; it was just too difficult to maneuver in close quarters. The complaining witness stepped up to the bench and exhibited his wounds. He had suffered several broken ribs and some severe cuts and bruises on his head and body which by this time were almost healed. He seemed happy, considering the strength of the defendant and the character of the weapon, to have escaped with no worse injuries and obviously bore no ill will. All this was stressed by the public defender, who pointed out that the defendant Yosuo had never been distinguished for acuteness of perception, and was but the victim of utter confidence in his wife's statements. He further pointed out that while the defendant's father had passed away shortly before the trial, the defendant was still the sole support of his two small children on his government salary, about twenty dollars per month. With the lack of criminal intent as well as the good reputation of the accused, both quite obvious, it was not too difficult to follow the public defender's plea for leniency. And the district attorney made his request for punishment in the lightest possible vein.

For a few moments I meditated on the appropriate penalty as the full courtroom waited. I then proceeded to discuss the evidence and the consequences of Yosuo's act. We were here confronted with an individual slow to comprehend yet quick to act under compelling motivation. Obviously such a man might pass through an entire lifetime without running afoul of the laws against violence. Nevertheless his quick and savage reaction to suggestion without investigating, indicated the need of some action to stand as warning against repetition of this almost fatal result.

I told the defendant that it is good for a man to have confidence in his wife. Very likely in their everyday life he would rarely go wrong in giving credence to her recital of daily events. But this feeling of confidence in a wife's powers of observation should never cause acceptance of judgments that might lead to violence, at least not without some investigation. There was such a thing as trusting one's wife too well. He must therefore resolve never to act against another human being without making sure by his own examination that it was required. And in doing so he must not run afoul of the law.

His precipitate attack, I advised him, actually entitled him to a term in jail, but I was reluctant to send him there. His family needed him. In fact it was even likely that he was too stupid to confine in our jail, where the prisoners were divided into labor contingents utilizing tools and equipment for public works projects. So after due warning of severe punishment upon breach of probation, I gave him a suspended sentence of one year, to the relief of the authorities and most, if not all, of the assembled audience.

The next case, more precisely, series of cases, involved a notorious character named Domingko. He was not a Trukese but a native of Palau, a group of islands far to the southwest. The Palauans are probably the most attractive and most westernized of the Micronesians, the men being taller and the women more comely than the other islanders. Domingko was no exception. He was about six feet tall and his shoulders reminded me of a wrestler.

He worked on Truk as straw boss in charge of laborers on the salvage of numerous Japanese craft lying under the waters of the wide ranging lagoon. The Truk island had

never been taken by frontal attack, they had been by-
passed and starved into surrender at the war's end. After
the Solomons were conquered and airstrips established
there and in New Guinea, the Truk Atoll came in for continuous heavy bombing which sent dozens of Japanese ships
to the bottom. At the end of the war the scrap-hungry Japanese initiated steps towards the salvage of these sunken vessels, which had been constructed, in part, from scrap purchased in the United States. The Micro-Metals Company
was formed with authority to fish the waters of the lagoon
for the rotting hulks, and sell the salvaged metal to Japan.

Thus was completed a full cycle in international trade—
America's sale to Japan of steel scrap, fabricated into in-
struments of war, destroyed in turn by us, subsequently reduced once more into scrap, and ultimately winding up yet
again in Japanese mills.

There were two major grounds of complaint against Domingko. One involved his alleged assault with a deadly
weapon upon a Trukese dockworker who had angered him.
The other involved such charges as kidnaping, assault and
battery, and false imprisonment, all leveled at him by a
rather shopworn Trukese woman named Tosiko.

The first case was the charge of assaulting the laborer. In
addition to the public defender, Domingko's counsel included a Palauan trial assistant who was there, it was explained because Domingko was alleged to know no language but the Palauan. The plan, then, was to conduct the
proceedings in Trukese, translate them into English for the
court, the district attorney and the public defender, and
then into Palauan for the defendant. I suspected during the
trial, however, and later became convinced, that the defendant was sufficiently familiar with both Trukese and English to follow the proceedings in both tongues. By asking
for translation into Palauan, he gained time to think and

advise his counsel of points as his agile brain developed them.

The trial began. There was the usual statement by the district attorney of the facts he expected to prove. The public defender waived his statement, witnesses were sworn, and in a few hours the prosecution developed an effective case.

Domingko was the owner of an ocean-going launch on which he lived while in harbor. The boat was tied up at the dock when Domingko and his crew were not using it for their salvage operations. In the cabin below deck dwelt the woman Tosiko, either as mistress or wife, depending on whether Domingko's prior Palauan marriage had been dissolved, as he claimed. When he was sober, which was only occasionally, life with him passed agreeably for Tosiko. But when he drank, he often beat her in sadistic rage. She finally had too much and so one day ran away to her native island Udot located in the Truk lagoon about a dozen miles west of Moen. She was piloted there in a tiny outrigger by a Trukese dockworker, unaware that she was fleeing from the lordly Palauan.

When Domingko returned that night and learned why Tosiko was not there at the dock, his rage was boundless. Blaming everyone but himself, and especially the treacherous Trukese, he finally discovered that Tosiko was living in the household of her brother Sochi on Udot Island and learned that she had been brought there by the friendly longshoreman, towards whom his wrath turned. Dissembling his feelings he persuaded the man to make the trip once more, this time to bring Tosiko a box of chocolates and her lover's entreaties for a speedy return.

The longshoreman made the trip that day, together with one of Domingko's henchmen, to whom he had assigned the duty of assembling Tosiko's gear and carrying it to the boat.

By nightfall both men returned, empty handed. They found Domingko on his boat, impatiently awaiting them and sufficiently drunk to be quite angry. They told him they had met Tosiko and given her the gift, but she had refused to go with them, saying that her brother Sochi would not let her go. Had she sent back word that she would not have returned in any event, it might have deterred Domingko, at least in part, from what he then did.

The men were walking with him along the deck, attempting to calm his angry mood, when Domingko suddenly darted into the cabin and emerged with a rifle which he pointed at the dockworker with threats against his life. The man jumped off onto the dock and kept running as the shots came after him. Nobody was hurt, but the islanders were badly shaken at the prospect of facing Domingko, both drunk and possessing a deadly weapon. The next day the constabulary were alerted and confiscated the gun, which was now produced and labeled as a prosecution exhibit.

A number of witnesses testified to having seen the weapon in the defendant's hand, pointed at the complaining witness, and hearing gunfire but none had seen the flash of the gun. At the close of the government's case, the public defender moved to have the charge reduced to simple assault, on the ground there was no proof the rifle was a deadly weapon. Admittedly it looked deadly enough, but he claimed it only discharged pellets no larger than a tiny pea and utterly incapable of causing a serious wound.

The district attorney took exception. The rifle, he said, was in fact a Remington and capable of frightening anyone it was pointed at. It was not necessary for a possible victim to test whether his skin would withstand the pellets, the weapon was of a class normally considered deadly, it was pointed at the witness and discharged, and must be considered, together with the defendant's threats, as intended to arouse fear of serious injury.

I took advantage of the fact that the argument occurred on a Friday to adjourn early in order to study whether the prosecution had to establish the deadly character of a weapon from a class including weapons of a dangerous nature. I asked both counsel to study the question over the weekend and to return on Monday prepared to help the court find the answer.

On Monday morning Mr. Gergely, the prosecutor, said he had a statement to make. Although the rifle was, by construction and appearance, to be automatically classified as a dangerous weapon, he had decided in the interest of justice on a test to determine its real danger. He had the constabulary load it with pellets and fire at a tin can from a short distance. He felt constrained to state that the pellets merely caused a slight depression but did not pierce the can. After these experiments he was prepared to reduce the charge from assault with a deadly weapon, a felony, to simple assault, a misdemeanor.

Domingko testified mainly to deny firing, but admitted pointing the gun and threatening, but only in jest, he said. After short argument he was found guilty, but sentence was delayed until the trial of Tosiko's charges against him. Without more ado the prosecutor told the story he expected to substantiate through sworn testimony, involving charges of kidnaping, false imprisonment, and assault and battery.

He started where Domingko had frightened the dockworker away. Having thus lost contact with the fair Tosiko, how could he renew his proposals in a more attractive fashion? Whom could he now use as intermediary? He needed someone persuasive enough to convince Tosiko that her best hope for a secure and happy life lay with him, Domingko. After some deep thought, he found the answer. Himself. No one could do the job as effectively. No one else could accomplish by direct action what could not be gained by persuasion. Surely when Tosiko realized the bounds of his affection which after all impelled him to make the journey to her home, fight off her family if need be, and carry her off in his arms, she could only capitulate and once more accept him as her lord and master.

It did not take long to chart his course. He called in his Trukese henchmen, the half-dozen cronies who regularly drank his liquor, and held a conference. He did most of the talking. One of them owned a good-sized canoe equipped with outboard motor. It was commandeered for the journey to Udot. Three of the rest, and Domingko's brother, were figuratively sworn in as the crew. They would each carry a serviceable machete, while Domingko, as captain, would be equipped with his reputedly deadly rifle. The plan was to leave the Moen dock at about midnight, steam to Udot, find their way to the home of Sochi, break in, induce the sleeping Tosiko to leave with her lover, take her off to the boat, and return to Moen.

The first elements of the plan were carried out smoothly. The boat came alongside Domingko's ship, fuel was pumped aboard, the conspirators got under way on the short run to Udot and they reached it in an hour. Slowly they crept into the harbor, showing no lights and expecting to hear some questioning voice momentarily. There was none, and soon they were entering the narrow pass which leads into the inner lagoon and anchoring in a little cove near the village where Sochi dwelt.

Two men stayed with the canoe; the other three, including Domingko and his brother, Mori, started off. They came to Sochi's house which they had visited in times past and found easily. It was more substantial than the usual Trukese dwellings. Of one story, it was built of timbers and siding, with a number of sliding windows at chest level. It stood grim and uninviting in the heavy darkness. Mori went boldly to the front door and banged on it repeatedly, loudly demanding admittance. For a few minutes nothing happened. Then one of the sliding windows was opened and a head appeared palely visible in the dim dark. It was Tosiko. Domingko grabbed the open sill, slung himself up and clambered into the room.

It turned out to be Tosiko's bedroom. In one corner lay her mat with a mosquito net fastened above. Alongside lay another mat, indicating the recent presence of someone else. It was learned later that the other mat had been occupied by Tosiko's former husband, to whom she had become reconciled on returning to Udot. With rare judgment if not valor, upon hearing the pounding, he had surmised the truth and made his escape through the front door.

Domingko meanwhile confronted his erstwhile sweetheart and demanded that she return with him. This she categorically refused, declaring what Domingko could never accept, namely that she no longer loved him. Failing to move her by argument, he cut down the mosquito net with a machete. He then rolled it up, rolled up her sleeping mat too and handed both objects out the window to his two comrades waiting below. He then seized Tosiko and handed her over the sill to Mori; after jumping out he reclaimed her and started for the boat, carrying her in his arms. She did not resist, knowing from past experience that it would only arouse the brutality which had often caused her pain.

While Domingko and his companions were approaching their boat, other events were taking shape to rob him of his prize. The husband who had been so rudely disturbed had dashed for the village and into the Catholic Mission. There he roused the sleeping priest, Father Almus, and speedily told him what was up. As happened, the priest had recently solemnized the union between Tosiko and her new husband, and was well acquainted with Domingko, who was also a Catholic and a member of his flock. Both men got into the Mission's boat at once and chugged along shore until they reached the narrow passage into the inner lagoon. Here they anchored the boat, virtually blocking the passage through which Domingko must come in order to reach the open sea.

Exhilarated with the apparent success of his mission, Domingko took a generous swig from the long bottle stowed in the boat and offered drink to the others. None refused. There was no reason to hurry; the night was clear and cool. So they tarried, for the time fate needed.

Finally, Domingko gave the signal to cast off and his boat got under way. He had first taken the precaution to throw a tarpaulin over Tosiko so that she could not be seen from the shore. He also gave her a precautionary kick as a reminder that silence is golden. Soon the narrow inlet came into view and in the dark he made out a boat anchored across it; the boat seemed to be taking up most of the eighteen feet of navigable clearance. It did not at first disturb Domingko for he conceived the occupants to be mere Trukese, who could never hope to cope with him. But when he saw at last the stern Jesuit priest, the confidence went out of him. Seeing that the priest's only companion was a youth, he put a bold face on the matter and asked Father Almus if he needed help to move his boat out of the passage.

To this the priest responded that he had no intention of moving. He had come to show Domingko the evil of his ways and to keep him from committing a crime against God and law by running off with a woman married to another under the solemn rites of the church—and he pointed to the youth. They were now close up and Domingko could see Tosiko's new husband, but ignoring him, Domingko asked how such a ceremony could be conducted while Tosiko was married to him; he had taken her to wife according to native custom. She had come to him openly and placed her sleeping mat in his chamber; afterwards he had invited her family and the heads of her clan to a feast and they had all attended. It was obvious, therefore, that the requirements of a native marriage had been carried out, and nothing had occurred since to disturb the relation.

So the strange colloquy went on across the space of night between them. In answer the priest reminded Domingko he still had a wife in Palau who had borne him a daughter, and so his union with Tosiko could not be valid under native custom until he had complied with the requirements of custom in terminating the previous marriage. To Domingko's statement that he considered this marriage to have terminated, the priest turned a deaf ear. The most he could do would be to take Tosiko under his protection until her matrimonial complications were straightened out.

Domingko was in a dilemma. It was difficult to stand up to the priest and particularly to use force against him. But his patience was wearing thin. The prospect of leaving without his bride and suffering loss of face among the lowly Trukese proved too strong for Domingko to stomach. He decided to take matters into his own hands and force an exit through the clogged passage; and he jumped into the shallow water and started to push the obstructing boat out of the way.

Meanwhile Tosiko, aroused by the altercation, poked her head out from under the tarpaulin, looked breathlessly about her until things became clearer in the shadowy dark, and after a bit, the rest of her eased slowly out of the canvas covering. When nobody appeared to pay her any attention, and while Domingko was in the water pulling the Mission boat, she saw her chance and seized it. She jumped into the water and in a few moments waded to the mainland where she took to her heels and disappeared into the welcoming darkness. This sudden denouement took everybody by surprise and quite effectively settled the matter. Domingko and his party realized it would be practically impossible to follow Tosiko in the dark and find her in the thick tropical forest. Father Almus, now relieved of further responsibility, hauled in the anchor and returned toward the Mission. With the passage now clear, Domingko hoisted himself into the boat and took off on the return to Moen.

The aftermath of this frustrated plan to carry off Tosiko was her complaint, probably instigated by her brother Sochi, in order to ward off other attempts. There was some evidence that he had threatened his sister: she could never return to the family home and share in the crops from the clan landholdings if she were to consort once more with Domingko. This is an effective deterrent for a native woman, who is required to yield to the authority of her eldest brother in regulating her family life and even in bringing up her children. If he is the clan leader, he has the added authority to determine who is to farm which clan lands, and who is to share in the production. To be cast out of the tribe is a serious matter for a female even if she marries well, because upon the death of her husband, if his clan does not wish to keep her she has no place to go. Trukese women, therefore, are prone to listen to the admonitions of the elder brother and to remain on good terms with the clan if possible.

How did Domingko and his counsel meet the evidence of abduction and forcible restraint of movement? Mainly by concocting a fantastic story of voluntary flight by Tosiko with her lover, attributing it to her anxiety to be rid of supervision by her brother and family. Her flight from the boat they explained by saying that she was then under the eyes of the priest; her subsequent court action they laid to pressure from her brother.

The defense received a critical blow when one of the men who had made the trip with Domingko turned up as a rebuttal witness for the government. A youth of twenty, he was one of the pair left to guard the boat. He had taken some liquor and the tossing of the boat had made him too ill to be of much use. He corroborated the government's evidence on all essential points and on cross-examination freely admitted animus against Domingko. There rankled in his mind a thoughtless breach of friendship, perpetrated when Domingko had failed to include him in his offer to take the other defense witnesses to lunch during the trial, and left him standing alone as the others drove off in a jeep. Of such small accidents are our large destinies often made.

After full argument, examining the Code to see whether a case had been made on all the charges, I came to the conclusion that it had, and entered a finding of guilty. I requested counsel to give me their recommendations for sentence, and then a further surprise occurred. Mr. Gergely, in his usual competent manner, pointed out the seriousness of the offenses and the necessity of making the defendant an example, in order to deter others from such action. He recommended sentences of a term of years for each offense, to run concurrently.

Mr. Edwards, the public defender, voiced Domingko's disappointment because he had had hopes of achieving United States citizenship and ultimately residing on Guam. There was a substantial colony of Palauans there, but no more would be accepted for permanent residence unless as citizens of the United States. And citizenship would not be granted a convicted felon. Actually, he argued, the case boiled down to a lover's quarrel. At most Domingko was guilty of pursuing his light of love a little too aggressively perhaps, but as for his allegedly brutal treatment of Tosiko, Trukese women liked their men to be masterful and express their affection with considerable emphasis. Possibly the defendant had exceeded customary bounds but that did not indicate a felonious intent.

Domingko's employer was in court to vouch for his chararter and good behavior, and to advise on steps already taken toward eventual citizenship. If the charges could be reduced to the class of misdemeanor, Domingko would be content to accept his punishment without demur, though he felt even a misdemeanor had not been established.

After these arguments, I recessed court for several hours and retired to my chambers for study. It seemed to me that legal tomes would not be the most satisfactory basis for a just decision. A study of the history and culture of the Trukese would more likely give the right answer, I felt, so I selected several works from our library prepared by Trust Territory anthropologists. Two of them, Fischer and Tobin, as well as others of international reputation, had written interesting monographs, giving considerable background material in this field.

My reading did support the conception, advanced by the public defender, of a large measure of force characterizing relations between the sexes, surprisingly enough, for the Trukese male seems so benevolent, if not meek—at any rate in the presence of strangers. Apparently, he makes up for this mildness of demeanor, in the nuptial chamber. Seeing the events against this background it seemed to me fair to conclude that Domingko, as a Palauan, was unwilling to lag behind the Trukese, and deemed it essential for his self-esteem to go to greater extremes.

When court convened that afternoon, I delivered a lengthy analysis of the facts and the theory of my decision. I pointed out that although it was doubtless commendable by Trukese custom to pursue a female with great ardor, it was a perilous course if it led into her nuptial chamber at the side of another. It was only man's conceit to believe that no matter what ill treatment he inflicted on his beloved, she could bear it with greater fortitude than the prospect of leaving him. If society usually left the relations of man and woman strictly between themselves, it did so in the expectation that no criminal statute would be transgressed thereby, especially when other people would be injured.

I said, however, that possibly I had been more severe in my initial declaration of guilt than the facts required. To become a citizen of the United States was such a worthy aspiration that the court should not unreasonably hamper it. Nor was I able to say that the actions complained of showed a depraved or lawless character, but rather a wilful and impetuous nature which needed some measure of restraint.

Accordingly, I felt that justice would be served by vacating the finding of guilty on the charges of kidnaping and false imprisonment, and letting it stand on the charges of assault and battery. I then sentenced him to the maximum punishment on these charges, six months in jail, and warned him not to molest Tosiko or her family. I drew up an order of commitment and before that day ended Domingko was taken by the Sheriff to serve his sentence in the district jail.

It did not entirely close the chapter. After the first thirty days, Domingko's employer made a strenuous effort to obtain an executive pardon from the District Administrator. When I was consulted I said I had no feeling about it—my province was only to judge—and if the executive department felt that he merited a relaxation of sentence, the responsibility was theirs. I took this attitude the more readily as I had by then learned that the fair Tosiko had left her latest mate and visited Domingko at the jail, and had in fact spent the night in his cell. When I would pass him by in the group of convicts employed in public works, he would give me a big grin to indicate that he bore no malice. I have the feeling that if we could have kept Domingko off liquor and in jail indefinitely he and Tosiko could have been very happy in their little jail cell.

The last criminal trial which stays with me from that Spring sitting is one involving a handsome young athlete named Koro Paul, who lived outside of Moen Village in a typical mongrel dwelling, partly wooden siding, partly corrugated iron roof. With him lived his young bride and child, with another on the way. He worked part time in one of the village stores, which made him eligible to join the baseball team, one of the sixteen in the league organized by Larry Anderson.

The village merchants took great pride in their team and they were equipped with snappy gray uniforms, and shoes. Naturally this exposed the team to good-natured joshing by their opponents, most of whom were shoeless and wore nondescript costumes. I recalled that each time Koro got up to bat the opposing bench would utter broad remarks about the beauty of his figure and the utter grace with which he fanned the ball.

Now he was in court and beside him his young wife with a child suckling at her breast. The charge was assault with a deadly weapon. The plea was not guilty and the trial opened with the testimony of Asano, the complaining witness.

From his story it appeared that he was a whilom friend

of the defendant, accustomed to stopping at his house after working hours. These visits were partly social, but occasionally other purposes were served, as Koro was the native equivalent of a bootlegger. Apparently the natives admire our western culture even when it is anti-social. The liquor was of course a native brew, a combination of yeast and coconut juice, sold at fifty cents for a bottle about as long as one's arm from the elbow to, say, the end of the middle finger.

On the day in dispute, Asano had been drinking rather freely elsewhere. Perhaps that accounted for the trouble which befell him. In any event he came to Koro's house about dusk, ordered a flask of native brew, and took advantage of old acquaintance to sit down on the stoop just outside the front door and drink his liquor there. As he drank he conversed in friendly fashion with Koro and his wife, but after some time Koro found duties elsewhere and his wife too found it necessary to pass from the house down the front stoop. After she had come in and out several times she said some things to her husband upon his return which caused him to get into a violent argument with Asano. He ordered him to leave and as he was leaving attempted to wrestle him to the ground. Asano was more powerful than the smaller, slighter man, but after a few blows were struck, he staggered off down the highway on the road to town.

Apparently Koro was not satisfied with this mild termination of an affair in which he considered his honor violated. He aroused his brother who lived nearby, and together they took off after Asano. He was not hard to trace, he had caught up with some kindred spirits who were standing alongside the road conversing in loud tones. The tropical night had by then descended but the moonlight made it possible to see with reasonable clarity. Upon reaching Asano and his companions, Koro stated that he had a serious complaint to make about Asano's treatment of his wife. When Asano said he knew nothing of any mistreatment Koro demanded to know whether Asano had not taken personal liberties with her as she passed by up and down the front stoop while he sat there. The inference was that Asano had reached under her short skirt as she walked by. When he continued to deny that he had taken any such liberties, Koro tried again to wrestle him to the ground and again he was unsuccessful. According to Asano's testimony and that of two bystanders, Koro then struck him with something metallic and shiny, and Asano fell to the ground, bleeding profusely from his scalp. He was taken to the hospital where stitches were required to close the wound.

On cross-examination, the witnesses were unable to say whether the object used was sharp, or even a weapon. They did say, however, that it gave off a metallic sound when it struck Asano's head and that he fell down several times. The inference was that Asano's crown had been broken by striking the road and the rough stones which lay on the shoulders. No weapon was found later near the scene but the hospital report indicated that the wound was caused by a sharp metallic object. It seemed to me that the state had made out a *prima facie* case, which could not be gainsaid without some testimony by Koro and possibly his wife. When I denied the public defender's motion for a not guilty finding, it became necessary for Koro to take the stand. He admitted the scuffling, but denied that he had used a weapon. Two prosecution witnesses had placed a shiny metallic object in Koro's hand before he struck Asano whose head then immediately began to bleed and I would have had no difficulty in deciding against Koro. But in cross-examination, the district attorney brought out that Koro and his wife had then been arrested on a charge of selling intoxicating liquor; that both had pleaded guilty and received suspended sentences. This offense was a misdemeanor, assault and battery with a dangerous weapon was a felony. It appeared that the prosecution had split up the transaction between Asano and Koro Paul into a number of offenses; the misdemeanor had been tried first; the felony was reserved for later action. In this way the government could make sure of an additional string to its bow by charging a defendant with several offenses arising out of the one transaction, with the likelihood that the defendant would be found guilty of one or more.

The troublesome question, now presented for the first time, was whether the second trial constituted double jeopardy, which is prohibited by Trust Territory Code, as it is in the bill of rights of our Federal and State Constitutions. In general this doctrine provides that one cannot be tried twice for the same offense. True enough, Koro had been charged with a separate violation of law arising out of the common subject matter, but both offenses seemed entirely distinct. I told both counsel my fear that it would be impossible for me to pronounce judgment without an investigation of the legal authorities, and invited them to make their own studies. The several hours allowed for this purpose turned out to be inadequate for all of us.

As I was unable to resolve my doubts, I had strong reason to discharge the defendant, particularly as he might not have pleaded guilty to the misdemeanor had he known of the possible charge of the felony. After a detailed analysis of the case, however, I did not do so. I believed that Koro Paul was guilty of assault and battery with a dangerous weapon. He had pleaded guilty to the charge of selling intoxicating liquor. Had he received anything but a suspended sentence, I would probably have discharged him on the ground of double jeopardy. But as he had served no time, was it in the public interest for me to do so and thus make it

impossible for the government to establish the limitations of
the double jeopardy rule, since the government had no right
of appeal to a higher court from my ruling? I decided to obtain a final decision from the court of appeal, which could be
had only on appeal by the defendant. So I found him guilty
and gave him a term of imprisonment sufficient to insure an
appeal. This strategy paid off. Koro Paul did file an appeal
and it brought about a full consideration of this question for
the first time in Trust Territory. The decision that his constitutional rights had been infringed by being tried twice for
the same offense resulted in his release.

Comparatively few cases like Koro Paul's with sexual
overtones, are presented to Trust Territory Courts. Out of
more than seventy felonies I tried only one case of rape or
attempted rape. It involved an attack by a youth on his
neighbor, a married woman in late pregnancy whom he had
fancied for a considerable time. It was only because of the
possible consequence of a violent attact on a pregnant
woman that the case even came to trial.

An interesting note at the trial was the impact of taboos
on the relationship between brother and sister, exposed because the complaint had been lodged by the elder brother
of the victim. He testified for the prosecution to establish
the pertinent physical surroundings. When the victim
took the stand and the questions called for her story of
the attack, the prosecutor asked for a short recess in order
to permit her brother to leave the courtroom while she testified to the intimate facts of the attack. Native custom made
it taboo for details of her body and particularly her sexual
organs to be divulged in his presence.

I learned subsequently that the taboos forbid a female
undressing in the presence of father or brother, or letting
them see her nude; and no suggestive stories or jokes can
be told in their common presence. But with other kinds of

relationships it is quite another story. The marital relationship, for example, is broad enough to embrace the unmarried sisters of the wife who are at the service of the husband when his wife is pregnant or unavailable. And relations between young unmarried couples are free and easy, without restraint by their elders. Children born of such unions are readily adoptable or stay with the mother, grandmother, sister or other close relative.

There was one practice which had caused considerable nuisance and often strong resentment. Some of the Trukese youths indulged in what was called "night-crawling". They would crawl into the room of some sleeping couple in the dead of night and share the mat of the woman. It was reported that some women were such sound sleepers that they failed to awaken in the embrace of the interloper. Apparently these daring youths lived a charmed life for no reported capture or punishment seems to have occurred. It is of course barely possible that some of the "sleeping" wives were conscious of what was transpiring even if their husbands were not.

It appears to be consistent with native custom for Trukese maidens to entertain favorite suitors who call on them when the family has retired, and an ingenious method has been developed to insure the girl's recognizing the youth in the darkness. The boy carries, as a calling card, a delicately carved and painted bamboo staff known as a "love stick," whose distinctive designs have with practice become familiar to the maiden. The young man must in turn become familiar with the plan of the house, so that he can discover precisely where along the side of the house, he can find the mat of his loved one. He then thrusts the love stick through the thatched walls, where it can be felt by the maiden. If she recognizes it as belonging to the right caller, she will pull the love stick and its possessor through the wall; otherwise she will push it out. Our maid Chieko, in commenting on a love stick we had purchased as a souvenir, pointed out that the number of ridges on it indicated the number of times its possessor had been disappointed in his quest. This I am inclined to doubt—on the theory that men are somewhat more likely to boast of their conquests than of their failures.

After the criminal list was disposed of, there were many civil cases still requiring attention. Judge Furber divided them with me, and we continued with trials each day until the time came for my journey to Yap and the Palaus for an extensive court sitting. The civil trials on Truk were all of the same general character, each involving disputes over the ownership or use-rights of land. In each the issues had been carefully stated in a pre-trial order adopted after a conference between the judge and both parties and their counsel. The counsel in such cases were not trained lawyers but ex-government prosecutors or defenders, considered to have sufficient ability to represent others.

The civil trials were always well attended, often by most of the adult members of a clan or lineage. Every case involved the vital question of basic subsistence. Which party would enjoy the right to take food from land and trees? It was absolutely essential to follow the evidence with great care and come to a sound decision. In every such case, the court's written opinion included the salient facts and the legal theory, because, with the numerous cases, the decision can take weeks to prepare and much of its effect is diminished by the passage of time, to say nothing of the participants' inability to understand the printed word thoroughly. I therefore would sum up the evidence at the close of each case, announce my judgment, and give the reasons and legal theory upon which I based it. The court clerk told me this was a most effective method in helping the people to understand the judicial process and its specific functions.

Many cases came up years too late; sometimes witnesses were dead, sometimes memories failed. Sometimes rights had been waived because a man had recognized a state of affairs which years later he challenged. I had to explain regretfully that the court could not unsettle rights long established, which should have been challenged years before.

Other cases, between descendants of a chief and the members of his clan, involved such technical questions as whether a gift of title to a piece of land by a chief to his descendants had been approved by the clan and was therefore valid or whether it bestowed merely the use-rights during the lives of designated heirs. Unless the evidence was clearly inconsistent I held that community rights prevailed over individual claims, on the principle that land originally held in common should continue to be held in common unless it had been clearly conveyed away by the chief with the consent of all the clan elders. This accorded with customary law.

Land on Truk can be owned individually but the main pattern is a lineage ownership passing through matrilineal lines. Children obtain land by inheritance through their mothers or her clan or lineage. They cannot inherit from the father. The same holds for the wife. She inherits not from husband or father but from mother and her uncles and aunts. Of course there are exceptions: a gift to a child about to marry, consented to by the opposite clan, gifts of land to pay for nursing of old people, and reparation for adultery and personal injury.

There was one kind of case which always privately amused me: the kind in which there was evidence of a previous trial before the Japanese authorities and in which either the parties or their ancestors had participated. Inevitably it turned out not only that the decision was claimed by both parties but that numerous witnesses on both sides attested to it. They were naturally free to do this because there were then no written records. I was usually able to tell which side was the more truthful simply by asking questions to establish who made use of the land during the intervening years. Some of the native "lawyers" however, were sharp enough to have caught the importance of use and came up with many an ingenious explanation.

For example, when the evidence showed clearly that for years after an "unfavorable" decision, the purported losing party remained in possession of the land and enjoyed the crops, the explanation was that the clan chief had threatened the winner with punishment if the decision were enforced. In another case it was claimed that the party in possession customarily brought a substantial share of the crops to the alleged winner, who graciously permitted the loser to remain on the place. In other cases, the parties disagreed not only about the decision but where the trial had occurred, who had participated in it and what the contentions had been.

Usually these disputes were between close relatives, engaged in desperate contests to determine which relative and lineage would enjoy a property. If a satisfactory crop was gathered all would participate, but in times of scarcity the shares would be disproportionate. Because of the incentive to imagine the facts helpful to their position, it was unsafe to rely on the testimony of any witnesses. More reliable was the evidence given by former officials and the elders and leaders of the clans. Many gave testimony of great importance, even though, because based on hearsay, it was not to be countenanced in an American court.

We now know at least that such problems will not arise again, because the regulations adopted by our courts call for written pleadings and decisions filed permanently in a public office.

At about the time of these trials I was made aware of deep unrest among the most intelligent and best educated Micronesian members of the administration staff, men in their twenties who lived in ramshackle housing. Some came from distant islands and so had no easy access to the native foods possessed by resident clan members. The economic pressure upon them plus the lack of decent living conditions tended to embitter them and cause eruption into protests which came to my ears.

I was first advised by Misauo Petrus, the young clerk of courts, of the petition prepared by a dozen of them requesting running water and electric power. They were all familiar with the facilities American families had, and felt they had reached the level of civilization where they should have such facilities too. The petition also sought to make their dwellings habitable by certain moderate structural repairs which they offered to do with their own hands, in order to avoid the cost of labor.

I felt emboldened to discuss the petition with Roy Gallemore. Though sympathetic to the requests, he pointed out that it was against administration policy to furnish facilities to the natives beyond their means, except where they were required for health, or public use. This explained the free hospital and medical and dental services, the furnishing of school buildings, and the educational facilities without charge, as well as the transportation of natives to and from their native islands in government boats. About the amenities of civilized living, however, it was the feeling of the High Commissioner that to bestow on some of the emancipated young people privileges not available to everyone in general would tend to disrupt the close family relationship of the natives. Moreover, it would hardly build a social structure sound enough to develop into self-government, if we were to subsidize them with facilities not normally part of the native life which they could not afford on their own. A consistent policy for all of Micronesia needed to be approached on a high level; it was coming to the fore in other areas as well as Truk. As for the young Trukese petitioners, the fact was that they were living in a government house without charge, a privilege not available to the American colony. Anything more would have to bear some relation to the cost involved.

This foreshadows the difficulties likely to arise with the democratic development of these islands. With the increase in population and the younger members growing into an educational elite, their emancipation from tribal discipline and economic control will become intensified. Against a background of constant population increase, caused by improved medical services, the pressure is bound to mount for the rewards to the enterprising which are typical of our Western civilization. It is hard to envision economic development in these islands with their meager agricultural base and lack of minerals and natural resources. And the effect on the economy which would be caused by the removal of the American colony with its expenditures for food and services seems to demand a long period of preparation.

The Trukese are not stupid. They have ample capacity for learning the mechanical trades, a constant process in the Public Works Department. The American leaders there take great pride in teaching good mechanics. Trainees still require supervision because they lack confidence, but it is only a matter of time before confidence and initiative develop. What is apparent now, however, is the irresponsibility and waste in their use of the present modest family earnings—small by our standards but adequate when measured by Asiatic or island standards.

The craze for bingo hit the islands several years back and distorted the sense of thrift which they had developed on the government payroll. At first the women encouraged community bingo parties in order to give their families a common recreational activity. Pretty soon the evening bingo games, which started in the native villages, spread to the administration center, where the game is played for money from morning to evening by housewives unable to control their urge to gamble. The wagers of five cents a card are small by our standards, but the loss can be the husband's day's pay. The wages are at most a dollar and a half per day. Some government workers have fallen into the hands of loan sharks—precisely the kind of situation found in many of the great cities of the United States.

The most successful of the moneylenders during my stay on Truk was the finance officer, a native of the Mortlocks. Somewhat less than thirty, this young man had the duty of making up the payroll of all native employees, each of whom was paid in cash placed in an envelope delivered twice monthly to the finance office. The going interest rate was ten per cent each payday. This, of course, made the effective rate at least 240 per cent per year. What made this plan particularly effective was the control exerted by the finance officer on distributing the pay envelopes. All he had to do was to get the worker to sign the book in receipt of payment, and then open the envelope and take out both the amount loaned and the interest. When this practice came to the attention of George Knight, the Public Works boss, he complained to the Distad who issued a strict injunction against anyone except the recipient opening a pay envelope, and against any private business being conducted on government property. This made collections less direct, the moneylender's representatives contacting the borrowers as they left the finance office. But in the absence of laws regulating usury, nothing more could be done. When I left the islands the matter was still unsettled, pending investigation. The blessings brought by civilization have brought with them the curses which apparently go hand in hand. Possibly, it would have been better to have left this island paradise untouched and unspoiled.

CHAPTER 10

YAP—THE GRASS SKIRT PARADISE

Soon after my husband returned from his trip to the Marshalls it was time for him to go away again. Having him gone for five weeks, home for two and then off again for an extended sitting expected to last about three months was more than I had bargained for.

The newness of the islands, the remoteness of it all and the loneliness at night had taken their toll. I had been assured that "nothing" ever happened to an American lady but there were stories about, and actually there had been an incident on Truk just before we arrived. It involved the wife of one of the senior officials, who carried telltale marks around her throat from beating off an ardent suitor while her husband was away on a field trip. The Trukese are most curious about American ways, especially about our national habit of wearing night clothes upon retiring, a practice which the islanders find interesting though strange. Our house was practically open to all lookers—we had no shutters or shades—and I felt as though I were living in a goldfish bowl. I developed a good case of insomnia. I had the feeling there were prying eyes watching me from the heavy jungle growth in front of our house. I must also admit that although my new friends were wonderful to me, and I was included in all social functions, it was not easy to be all alone. So it was that we asked for permission for me to go along with the judicial party on its next tour of duty, which was granted.

It is a rule of Trust Territory that dependents are allowed two free trips a year to any of the districts, but are not eligible to go during the first six months—a restriction that seemed particularly silly to me. Of course, most of the staff members did not travel, so they were home with their wives; others who did, usually had families with whom the wife had to stay at home. But in my case, and there were others, the hardest part was being left alone too soon. It is naturally easier after six months, when one is pretty well acclimated and has made a place in the community.

I had forgotten that before leaving the States, while reading all that we could about the Carolines, I had remarked that Yap was the one district I would not want to visit. It sounded so far "out of this world" that I had absolutely no desire to see it, but rather than miss the whole tour I girded myself for a rough experience, and vowed there would not be the slightest complaint from me.

We started off on May 16th for Guam, where we spent one night before our westward journey. Our party consisted of my husband, the prosecutor, Al Gergely, a young man of twenty-nine, the public defender Roscoe Edwards, a bachelor of undetermined age, Juanita Griffin the court reporter, and a veteran of many years in government service, Joe Driskell, head of Public Safety, and me. I might add, incidentally, that Juanita Griffin had been evacuated from more danger spots in the Orient and North Africa than any soldier I'd ever met, and she took much delight in these trips. She was a wonderful sport, loved fishing and people, and called practically everyone "my love."

Yap is about a three-hour flight from Guam and the approach to the island group was most exciting. As we circled above I could see thatched roofs dotting the shore line. As in

Truk Harbor, a half sunken ship rested upon the reef just at the opening of the pass to guide us into the lagoon where we landed in the water. This was my first water landing and a real thrill. The water was calm and before we were aware of it we were tied to a buoy a few hundred yards from shore. Soon we heard the chug of a barge which secured itself against the plane and several young men started unloading onto it the mail and cargo. They were almost nude, wearing only the native dress of Yap, a *thuu,* a skimpy tight-fitting loin cloth ending in a curlicue behind them. Their strong brown bodies glistened in the noonday heat.

The Distad, Bob Halvorsen, and his assistants were on board the barge to greet us and when we arrived at the dock at Colonia, the district center, we were welcomed, and smothered with beautiful leis of hibiscus and frangi pangi. It was heartwarming and most characteristic of the South Sea Islands. But the contrasts in this faraway little place were also very striking. The one responsible for the beautiful flowers was a stunning creature, a tall handsome Hawaiian girl named Laverne Deas dressed more appropriately for Honolulu or Miami Beach than for this remote place. She was Halvorsen's secretary and looked like the star of a Michener story, but she turned out to be happily married and the mother of several beautiful children.

Our host the Distad took us up the dusty road in his dilapidated jeep to the hotel—a most depressing building. Lunch was depressing too. We entered onto a screened porch which served as a dining room in which there were two tables, each seating six and impressively set with white damask cloths. There were four sleeping rooms, two of them opening onto the dining porch. In the one bathroom the water had been turned off, but there was a small bottle of water on the wash basin for use in washing. We had been informed about the water shortage on Yap, but until one experiences it, it is not to be believed. The color of this water resembled weak tea.

We were taken to our quarters after lunch and my eyes were popping on the way. I was not prepared for the many Yapese women who reject Western clothes. We passed numerous women in long ankle-length grass skirts and nothing else. They were all sizes and shapes, and walked rather proudly and gracefully. I noticed that some women wore a black ribbon about their necks, hanging between their breasts. This, as I learned later, was a token of maturity. The school was close by and many young men and boys were about, clad only in a *thuu*, some in black and red cloth, others in red and white, each in his clan color.

Our guest house, attached to Mr. Halvorsen's home just down the hill from the hotel was a great surprise, a modern apartment which had just been redecorated. We had a commodious living room, a kitchenette complete with electric refrigeration and stove, a bedroom and bath. The walls were of stained wood with a pleasant odor and the floors were all asphalt tile. As accommodations they were in fact the best that either of us had seen anywhere in all the districts. Mr. Halvorsen told me that the water line we were on was separate from the rest of the center and might have a trickle in the pipes most of the day, although the main valves were turned off all but one hour in the morning and one in the evening. He also had a catchment on the roof which added to our supply. To my delight I found we did indeed have a small trickle of water most of the day. Every drop we drank or used for ice was boiled, though I was told it was unnecessary. On the whole, for those two weeks we consumed very little *aqua pura,* existing mainly on canned fruit juices and soups.

Yap had the smallest American colony in the islands, seven families and several bachelors and they usually ate their meals in the hotel. It is impossible adequately to describe the fare we were served. From the beginning, we decided to miss breakfast, so I stocked our pantry from the scanty shelves of the Yap commissary. We had instant coffee, fruit juice, canned fruit, cheese and crackers every morning. Lunch and dinner we had to eat at the hotel. It was then that I began to realize how fortunate we were on Truk. An average meal here consisted of canned soup, a greasy stew or pork roast, a canned vegetable such as green beans served hot and also served cold as a salad with a little vinegar dressing. There was always bread on the table and peanut butter and jelly which was all we could eat most of the time. Usually before meals we would have some snacks in our apartment in order to spoil our appetites. The hotel was run by one of the bachelors who must have left all the planning to the Yapese couple who did the cooking and serving. There were, however, many compensations to offset the virtues of the culinary department.

As in all the districts, the Americans were eager to welcome us. Most of their social activities were centered in the community club which had been built and decorated by its members. They had a good library, card tables and chess, comfortable chairs and the usual juke box, and there was something doing almost nightly.

Mr. Halvorsen graciously offered us his jeep which we used for the half-mile ride to the hotel at least once a day. On the first weekend we were able to explore a bit; we drove some distance outside Colonia. The approach to most of the outlying villages there led through lanes clean-cut and lined with hibiscus bushes which almost hid the houses from view. We passed one homestead with several dwellings around a central court, the women, sitting on the ground with the pigs and chickens, not particularly interested in us even when we asked to take pictures. The pig is a very important animal here. We were told that sometimes when a runt is born to a large litter, it is not rare for a Yapese mother to nurse it until it is able to forage for itself.

One of the interesting landmarks we stopped to visit was a money temple. For centuries Yapese wealth was measured by the stone money called *fei* which belonged to its most important citizens or their clans. They were huge oval stones, four or five feet in diameter, all with a hole in the center, some weighing up to 500 pounds. In ancient days, hundreds of natives would sail in their canoes to the Palau Islands where the stones were quarried, and the fleet of outriggers would then attempt to transport the heavy stone wheels by tying them to poles which in turn were locked to the canoes. In the heavy seas many boats and people were naturally lost, but their fascination for the worthless rocks was so great that the pilgrimage to the Palaus would take place each year, with a tragic cost in lives and treasure. One could see them everywhere, sometimes leaning against a building or lying flat in the dirt. We were told that no one would attempt to steal or remove them. Though given away sometimes or sold to another clan, they were never moved from their original resting place and everyone knew the rightful owners.

They were particularly numerous in the courtyard and approaches to traditional clan headquarters, which were housed in a stone structure called a money temple, the walls of which were built in part of smaller pieces of *fei*.

There were slots here and there to provide air and light, but no windows. In ancient times the clan gathered here to worship their gods and take part in feasts and clan celebrations, but now, with the conversion of most natives to Christianity, the money temples have fallen into disuse and stand as huge abandoned monuments to a bygone age.

There was nobody on the premises as we peered into the gloom behind the wall apertures. One of the openings was shaped like the window of a bank teller's cage, at least that is how it looked to my husband. Pretending that he wanted to convert some American bills into stone money, he put his money down on the window-sill and demanded the exchange. No one appeared out of the dim past to serve him, but it made a striking tableau and I recorded it with my camera.

That same day we also passed a large building with a high-pitched thatch roof, looking a little like a church without a steeple, about seventy-five feet long and half as high. It was the all-men's house (a clubhouse for men only and the one attractive maiden who lived with them). It was said that when her term of service was over, she was much in demand as a consort for a well-born male. I was told there were also all-women's houses where the mature women lived during certain times of the month when they would be *tabu* and secluded from men. This sense of modesty was another of the contradictions and contrasts.

One could always recognize an older man of high caste, whether by the tattoo on his body or the wooden comb that he wore in the long hair piled high on his head. All the young men had their hair cut short and so could not wear these combs. Almost all the men and women chewed betel nut and carried with them a woven bag of pandanus leaves to hold the nuts and ground lime with which they dusted it. Several of the teachers offered me this delicacy which they assured me was quite palatable and produced a stimulating effect, but after seeing so many red and drooling mouths, all looking as though they had come form a mass extractionist, I refrained. I did, however, succumb to a betel nut bag, which I still own and sometimes use as a summer pocketbook. Besides the red juice which discolors the lips, the teeth of the betel nut chewer are always blackened. The head of the dental department told us, however, that the

Yapese have the best tooth structure of all the islanders.

The days were long for me on Yap. I had no duties and the other housewives had many. I was able to read extensively and write long overdue letters describing the beauties of this lovely, lush place. Each day I would walk to the courthouse about lunch time in order to drive up the hill to the "Palace" which we now called the hotel. On this outing I would sometimes stop in the new one-room cottage which served as the courthouse, and quietly watch, and wait until the siren blew for lunch. On one occasion a small group were sitting about the counsel table and I noticed that a tall woman attired in a grass skirt hung low on her hips seemed to be the center of attraction and the main actor. Later my husband told me that this was a pre-trial conference and the lady in the grass skirt was a lawyer—no less—not a tutored lawyer but a very vociferous one. This was his first experience in listening to a Portia with no bra, and I suspect he sort of slowed up the procedure. I later learned she had won the case, which gave me a wonderful opportunity to charge my husband with deciding the case on the basis of bosoms, not law.

One of the books I read with the greatest interest was *His Majesty O'Keefe,* a novel based on the true story of the fabulous character who was a sea captain from Georgia, washed ashore on this little known island in the 90's. His story sounds indeed stranger than fiction, but we met at least one man who remembered him—a native judge named Judge Fanechoor, also a high chieftain and well-known magician in these parts. It was even rumored that the judge is no longer welcome on his home island of Ilithi because he was believed to be responsible for a typhoon which struck that island. We found him intelligent, charming and most generous both with folklore and native craft. He remembered O'Keefe and verified the story of his kingdom.

Our most unforgettable day we spent with the Russell
Curtiss family on their sailboat. Russ was the manager of the
Yap Trading Company and his wife Verna was one of the
most charming and talented women I met in any of the districts. She had not only designed the house in which they
lived, Japanese in style but taught sewing and cooking to
the natives. Those women who did wear Western clothes
were usually dressed in one of Verna's blouses and skirts.
Yap was the only district that sold sweet rolls, coffee cake
and doughnuts in the Trading Company, and it was Verna
who had shown them how.

The sailboat was a twenty-six footer or so with an auxiliary
motor. Neither my husband nor I had ever handled a sailboat before, so you can imagine what I felt when our skipper said, "Judge, take the tiller."

We were off. It was a beautiful Sunday morning and we
got an early start, about 9:30. Along with us were the three
Curtiss children and two extra little stowaways who joined
us as we cast off. It was easy to steer out through the channel as we had the big navy ship on the reef at the opening
of the pass to guide us into the open ocean. As we passed it
Russ showed us the chart and pointed to Maap, the island
about fifteen miles away which was our destination. There
was a gentle swell in the mighty sea but the sailing was
smooth. We were always in sight of land, but between us
lay the dangerous reef barely below the water line. The little boys soon dropped a line from the boat and before long
had pulled in a beautiful bluetail. The day could not have
been more perfect. The ship and the water alone would
have been enough, without the excitement of entering into
a new pass and weaving in and out between the coral rocks
which we could detect by the shadows beneath the green
water. Coming back, retracing our route at low tide, it
would all be a completely different picture.

We dropped anchor close to a sandy beach and alongside a natural stone pier which jutted out from the shore lined with mangrove trees. The beach was not over a dozen feet wide at high water. Behind it was a forest of palms, pandanus and breadfruit with the occasional vivid green of the slender betel nut tree. The beach looked better from afar, with gnarled bits of driftwood dotting the sand. The water looked cool but after wading in up to our hips and finding it very warm we decided against a swim. We had been completely fooled. Our hosts had thoughtfully brought along an ice-box filled with cold juices and beer, and our lunch was an international affair, starting with *Sashimi* (raw fish fillets) and ending with home-made pizza. As we ate our lunch, it was almost as though we were a Swiss Family Robinson, we seemed so alone—until out of the woods came a strange sight, a white man in khaki trousers and shirt, a jaunty straw hat on his head and a large woven basket slung over his shoulder. I would have thought he was carrying a large supply of betel nuts but then I noticed two tiny feet sticking through the opening. The man was Father Bailey, one of the Jesuit priests from the Mission whom we had met at Colonia, and he was followed by a young woman obviously the mother and by the grandmother. We chatted with this dedicated man who had served on Yap a dozen years and was loved by all he served, and my husband kidded him about the necessity of carrying members of his flock in order to get them to attend services. To this Father Bailey rejoined he would gladly carry the mother and, if need be the grandmother, in such a good cause.

Our return was not quite as simple as our arrival. We did not start back until late afternoon when low tide was upon us. Our boat which had been riding comfortably at its berth had now become wedged on the rocks below, and getting her to move was a real headache. The men jumped into the water and pushed, but to no avail. Finally after they had watched our ineffectual attempts for a few minutes, a group of Yapese men nearby came over and offered their aid and in no time we were off the rocks and under way. But the way out of the little bay was treacherous. In the clear water we could see many huge boulders on the bottom and had to pass around them in the shallow water. It became necessary for Russ to stand in the bow, peering intently into the waters below and giving steering signals to my husband at the tiller. It was slow traveling but finally we passed through the channel and reached the open sea.

On the gentle ocean we rode comfortably, keeping a few hundred yards distance from the fringing reef which encloses the entire island. With low tide the coral heads were visible as the waves dashed over them in fine spray. Whenever the distance to the rocks seemed to lessen, I became nervous so I kept my eye on my husband as he strove to keep the boat pointed towards the entrance to Colonia Harbor. On one occasion he became confused when the helm didn't answer the direction in which he had turned away from the rocks, in a matter of seconds it seemed as though we were headed directly for the cruel barrier. I cried out to Russ for help and back he came from his fishing lines to straighten us out. We reached the pass into Colonia Harbor at sunset. It was a day I shall always remember as one spent so close to a state of nature that it was a shock to be guided back to civilization by the great rusting ship which showed us the way home.

Above the hotel, on the highest point of Colonia, stood the Catholic Mission. There were two tall concrete buildings, one occupied by the Maryknoll Sisters and the other by the priests who taught in the Mission School. We strolled about the old courtyard which dated back to the early 1800's, and here was a very old cemetery with tombstones engraved with both Spanish and German names. On the way back, a class in catechism was just ending, and several dozen women and children poured out of the building, the women, naturally, in grass skirts. We left in our jeep and on the way down the wind caught at my scarf and blew it away. We stopped so that I might run back and retrieve it, when I saw that a young Yapese woman had just picked it up. I smiled and thanked her and held out my hand, and she most haughtily and disdainfully returned it to me. I often wondered later whether I should have made her a gift of it, but it did not occur to me until too late. On most occasions, however, the people were friendly and would even pose with me when I asked for a picture.

The most outstanding and sophisticated party we ever attended was on this primitive island. It was a base affair including many of the Yapese who worked in the District Center, and all the Americans. It was a *luau* with all the trimmings, including the building of a high compound surrounding the garden of the clubhouse, which was lighted only with torches. We were served first a rum brew from a huge clam shell, and later sat on freshly woven mats at long low tables laden with pineapples, coconuts and other tropical fruits. The Americans were asked to wear native dress so the array of Dorothy Lamours, beachcombers, and shipwrecked sailors intermingled with brown-skinned bare-chested men and women was a sight to behold. Music came from a juke box with strong support from the guitar of the gifted Sam Deas, the husband of the lovely girl who had greeted us on the dock at our arrival. She demonstrated her versatility in an authentic hula dance, as good as any I had seen anywhere, including Hawaii. But the high spot of the evening was the jitterbug dancing of the young native women in their grass skirts. What poise and self-confidence!

The entire two weeks seemed sheer fantasy. A few days

before our departure, news came of a typhoon heading our way. All indications were that it would surely hit, many did not care, if only it would break the long drought. There were rumors that the plane would not come down for us and the assistant Distad, in charge while Bob Halvorsen was away at Guam, attempted to persuade my husband to radio headquarters to send the plane immediately so we could be evacuated before the typhoon arrived. This the judge refused to do, saying that headquarters knew our position and were better aware of our peril than we were. It would therefore behoove us to await developments with confidence that the government would not neglect us.

The next day, however, it seemed as if we were going to be struck. The first warning came when a terrific siren blew into the midmorning activities. Roofs and windows were lashed down and the center started girding itself for the worst. It looked like D-day. I offered my services to the Distad for whatever might come. But then we heard that a shift in direction had carried the typhoon off to be lost at sea.

On our second Sunday we crossed the island in search of a village we were told was really beautiful. It was just after a small shower (which did nothing to augment the water supply) and the ground was steaming. The road seemed very good to us. We must have traveled six or seven miles from Colonia, when we passed an abandoned Japanese airfield where forty or more Japanese fighter planes littered the ground, just as they had been shot down or destroyed on the ground. The strip was overgrown with tall grasses and trees. We wondered why the administration did not make use of this for a landing field, and when I asked I was told it was too far out and too expensive to put into condition. This seemed too bad because the choppy lagoon waters were sometimes so perilous that the weekly plane had to pass over poor little Yap.

Undoubtedly we missed a turn in the road and all of a sudden we were nowhere. The road just seemed to end—we even had a hard time turning the jeep around. When I saw the hibiscus lanes so neatly swept I sensed that we were near a settlement, and all of a sudden two small naked boys started to cry. They screamed so that I was afraid someone would think they were being beaten, and soon a woman came out. She was dragging a long palm branch behind her. I tried a greeting and pointed to the camera around my neck and made some sign language. Apparently she understood, for she dropped the branch, straightened her skirt, pulled herself up very erect, and gathered the children close to her. The picture was fairly good, but the children in front of her did not help it.

At last we received news that the skies were clear again and Taloa (the name of our small airline) would come for us, a day late, to take us farther westward on to the Palau Island Group.

Our noisy little bird circling the lagoon and descending for us was a welcome sight. The same committee saw us off, again with the friendly blossoms about our necks, but this time I wore one which I valued greatly. It was made entirely from the fragrant white frangi pangi blossoms and had been given to me by Mr. Halvorsen's houseboy. It must have been his own idea, as Mr. Halvorsen had been away on Guam for a week, and to think that he presented it to me without any suggestion from an American was very flattering and touching. Now I never hear the beautiful music of Tschaikowsky's "Swan Lake," which this boy played over and over again next door to our suite, without thinking back fondly to Yap, the island of surprises.

CHAPTER 11

YAP: INTELLIGENCE, VIOLENCE, LAW

An American can be transplanted anywhere in Micronesia without feeling strange and can travel over its roads without observing conditions very different from his native land, except only on Yap. Here one encounters a civilization truly unique, a way of life maintained stubbornly by the natives, despite fifty years of colonization by Western nations and a much longer period of missionary influence.

From Spanish sovereignty in the 19th Century, to control by Germany which purchased the islands in the early days of this century, the Yapese passed under Japanese control at the start of World War I and under American control at the end of World War II. Until the Yapese understood the difference between administration by the former controlling powers and that of the United States they were not inclined to cooperate even in projects designed for their sole benefit. When they realized that our trusteeship imposed duties on us without hope of material gain, the Yapese became willing to be aided in emerging from a primitive culture into the complexities of the 20th Century.

The four main islands, separated by narrow passages, have a total area slightly less than forty square miles, with some 3200 inhabitants. Other Yap islands, strewn over hundreds of miles of ocean, bring the total land area to some eighty-five square miles with a total population of 5250. Until recent years the population had been rapidly decreasing; it appeared to be a program of race suicide, manifested in widely practiced abortion. The natives seemed to have lost incentive to live and reproduce, partly perhaps because they did not believe in the ability of their gods to withstand the competition of Western culture, and partly because so many lives had been lost in foolhardy wars. Whatever the reason, it is clear from the number of households that the Yapese population has dwindled from at least 15,000 on the main islands a hundred years ago. The turn has come with the advent of American trusteeship, and they have now achieved a progressive birth versus death rate.

High Court sessions are held twice yearly. There is no direct flight from Truk, but the plane which services the Marshalls and Ponape terminates on Guam, whence it leaves the next morning for the 450-mile hop to Yap. This was the course we took when my wife and I enplaned with a full load of passengers and freight one Wednesday afternoon in the middle of May.

In our party were the district attorney, the public defender Roscoe Edwards and the court reporter Juanita Griffin. I expected to conclude the criminal cases first, then to dispose of any civil business and appellate cases and in the remaining time to conduct a school. The class would be composed of the local judges, prosecutors and defenders; magistrates, court officials and members of the constabulary; and those on the administration staff who could be spared. Such schools are conducted every other year in each district by one of the high court judges. Similar schools are conducted on a territory-wide basis each year by the District Attorney and the Public Defender; their assistants are brought to the place designated and given intensive training for several weeks in the fundamentals of their profession. In this way the administration hopes to achieve, among the intelligent young Micronesians, a fairly rapid indoctrination in the principles and background of Anglo-Saxon justice, and United States criminal law and court procedure. The lecturer is required to organize his material personally and to conduct a practical workshop. So I prepared an outline of topics and work in my course covering civil and criminal procedure. This I had completed with valuable suggestions from Judge Furber before leaving for Guam.

Our trip was uneventful save for the failure of the landing gear to operate until we had made a few passes over the island. We were over the narrow part of the island, about eight miles wide and in a matter of minutes we passed from one coast to the other, then banked to turn back, all the while through dense low-lying clouds. There were three airfields and a lot of air traffic and it seemed a miracle that nothing was near us as we passed up and back.

We landed at the Navy airfield, then lined up for customs, operated by the government of Guam. A Trust Territory representative was on hand and we were soon registering in the Hotel Tropics, planning our evening's entertainment. After the heat and humidity of Truk and the islands to the east, it was the height of luxury to dine in an air-conditioned restaurant and then enjoy an air-cooled movie.

Up next morning at dawn, we were checked in at the airport and took off before the sleep had left our eyes. By noon we saw before us the fringing reef and in front of it the light blues and greens delineating shallow waters. From the air these islands seemed more lush than the others, with thicker forests and river banks carpeted with heavy grasses. We soon found out that Yap has no problem of subsistence: there are many unoccupied homes and untilled fields, and production of food is plentiful. Despite the abundance of fruits and vegetables, I was unable to find any market in Colonia where native foods were displayed. From this I learned that the Yapese have no interest in commercial farming and no desire to produce more food than they need for the present. They do not sell produce. The only way you can get it is by gift, and Roscoe Edwards one day shared with us some fine pineapples received from a grateful native.

We disembarked on the dock and met a few of the staff and their wives able to find the time and transportation. Among the greeters was a little brown man in khaki shorts and colorful aloha shirt, with an air of dignity and importance. He greeted me in perfect English. This was Judge Fanechoor, chief justice of the District Court, a leading chief in the islands, and with him was the clerk of courts, a burly young man in his middle twenties, named Feichin Faimau. These were the men I sought out in the courthouse that afternoon after we were settled in our quarters.

The judge, considerably older then he looked, was able to recall incidents in the life of David O'Keefe, the Savannah skipper shipwrecked on Yap in the 1880's, who became the ruler of the islands until his death in 1901. But knowing what I did of the story-telling art practiced by the tribal elders from time immemorial, I was inclined to discount the judge's claim to personal acquaintance with O'Keefe.

What was more to the point, and vitally important in disputes awaiting hearing, was the background of land tenure and inheritance on Yap, which the judge proceeded to clarify for me. It turned out that Yap enjoys a feudal system of tenure: the land, or more particularly the estate, called *tabinaw*, controls the individual or the clan, as the case may be. An estate on Yap is not only the family seat with a distinctive name, distinguished further by being built on a

stone platform, but it also includes certain rights in accessory lands and properties. For example, the *tabinaw* Fanifi-
chug includes, besides the house and lands and accessory
buildings surrounding the stone platform, some farm lands,
a taro patch or two, some palm and breadfruit trees, and
fishing rights in a portion of the lagoon enclosed by the
fringing reef. Title to this estate passes to the eldest son or
eldest brother, but only in trust for the members of the clan.
The holder of title can designate which family members
shall reside in what dwelling and enjoy use-rights from a
farm or forest or fishing grounds. Usually the person installed in an estate owes certain duties to the tribal elder,
such as first fruits of crops and fish, and is on call for necessary communal labor. If these duties are disregarded, the
elder has authority to come upon the land and destroy crops
and trees, and in extreme cases, to dispossess the occupants.
With the excess and fertility of workable land, some of these
ancient customs are less stringent now.

Our discussion took place in the tiny office in "downtown"
Colonia, shared by the judge, the clerk of courts and the
public defender. The judge very courteously installed me
in his niche and moved his belongings from the desk which
I then took over. I found Feichin to be an engaging young
man of serious mien, a former schoolteacher. He had even
attended the territorial college on Guam and spoke and
wrote English adequately. He told me he lacked confidence
in his ability as interpreter and hoped I would not need him
for this duty, his feeling being that he could not readily
translate English into Yapese. I suggested it would be wise
for him to try even if it took longer, as he would surely improve with practice. He agreed to try, at least in the legal
arguments without the complication of testimony.

From time to time Feichin would bring a court file to my
desk and question me about some rule or the meaning of

some terminology. I felt that here was the intelligent mind at work, miraculous in people who had practiced witchcraft just a few generations back and were still addicted to an occasional bit of magic. In contrast to this mental acuity was Feichin's betel nut bag on his hip, and his enjoyment of the ancient Yapese custom of chewing betelnut. This he did by wrapping the nut in a sprig of pepperleaf and dipping it in powdered lime. I found the habit to be so ingrained even in Yapese of the highest education and intelligence, that I considered it better to go along with the practice even in my courtroom, rather than provoke resentment by perhaps ill-conceived and misunderstood discipline. But I never did get used to the sight of these intelligent natives chewing the juicy, unwholesome looking red mess and spitting it out in front of the courthouse door.

The courthouse was one room, about fifteen by twenty, with screened windows all around and doors at each end. The front door faced the constabulary headquarters and jail across the road. The jail grounds included a large lawn area stretching down to the banks of the channel between the islands. On the bank was an elaborate *benjo* built on piles over the deep water and obviously catering to western customs with separate facilities for men and women.

The front door into the courthouse was a screen door, but the one at the rear, being solid, permitted me to step out into a little areaway where I could don and doff my robe in private, and stand with staff members or court officials while they enjoyed the customary cigarette during recess. After court sessions I would walk the several hundred feet to the office of the Clerk of Courts, where the jeep assigned to me was parked. If it had not been seized by the constabulary or the administration for other necessary duty, I would get in, and with some coaxing, nurse the ancient and capricious motor up the gentle hill about a half-mile to the

hotel. On the way I would pass the thriving enterprise
known as the Yap Trading Company, where you could buy
anything from a bolt of cloth to a string of Yapese shell
money. You could also get an ice-cream soda there in company with a pack of almost nude brown-skinned youngsters
of both sexes, not unlike the corner drugstore coke addicts
of American cities.

Then came the community clubhouse, where you could
buy alcoholic and soft drinks, then the radio station (the
only air-conditioned structure on Yap), the commissary
lightly stocked with American foods, the Public Works ga-
rage and service facility, the hospital clinic, and finally, the
hotel. By then the road became steeper, as the hotel structure sat on an eminence several hundred feet above sea
level, but still not the highest ground on the island, which
had been preempted many years before by the Catholic
Mission. The mission property, easily the most desirable
building site on the islands, stretched along a fork of the
main road. It contained several large buildings: a home for
nuns, a school, a church, and a home for the resident priests.
Built of concrete or lumber, rather than the favorite tropical
materials of corrugated metal roof and siding, these buildings were austere in design.

I made an extensive survey of the mission property because one of the cases involved the mission's claim to ownership of almost the entire administrative center in Colonia—
a claim apparently based upon colonization and control of
the center by Spanish priests of the Capuchin order who
had traveled to Yap from the Philippines in the last quarter
of the nineteenth century. The mission's attorney, a Mr.
Phelan, had accompanied us from Guam and recommended
that I examine the site and its environs in order to become
familiar with the physical facts. As depositions of two ancient employees of the mission, now residing on Guam, had

still to be taken, the case was not ready when called on the first day of court, so I granted authority to take the testimony, and continued the case to be tried by Judge Furber at the next court sitting.

Another matter disposed of without trial was brought by a lady named Zurun on behalf of her clan, which wanted to have its use rights to certain lands and fish traps confirmed. The contesting party was a neighboring clan, descended from a common ancestor with the first. The question I was to resolve was whether one or the other could stay in possession of the land until a trial could settle it. Both clans were fishing in the disputed waters and should one bring in a larger catch, hostilities were always likely to develop.

The plaintiff turned out to be a tall, slim, dark-skinned woman in her forties. As befitted a Yapese matron, she appeared in court wearing the traditional grass skirt, with nothing above the waist except the black ribbon betokening maturity and rank, which was wound about her neck and hung down between her breasts. I was advised that a woman was rarely entrusted with the headship of a clan, even if limited to presenting a specific controversy. But after she said that she would personally represent her clan without a trial assistant, there was no further cause for surprise. For she represented the clan expertly, and that against an experienced practitioner who ranked as the first assistant public defender, sufficiently educated to understand American law books and the Code of Laws of Trust Territory.

The proceeding might be likened to a motion for an injunction to restrain interference with the status quo. Usually it is not difficult for a court in the states to determine the status of a controversy, so as to enter an order for protection of rights pending full hearing. In this case the problem was difficult: both clans were enjoying the fruits of the land and

sea, though possibly at different times. Each wished to continue, at least until trial date when one or the other would
be dispossessed. It was only after searching questions of
both parties, with Judge Fanechoor's advice, that I determined that the lady and her clan should retain sole possession for the time being. Zurun and her people had been
pressing for a trial for some time and were now ready but
the defendants had not shown such diligence and even now,
because witnesses were absent, could not go to trial. The
diligent party, I ruled, should temporarily enjoy the crops
and fish, subject to subsequent trial. In retrospect, I am not
sure my ruling was based as much on the forceful pleading
of the Yapese Portia as on the fascinating ripple of her
breasts when she extended her arms in driving a telling
point home.

With the civil list disposed of, I called for trial the charge
of aggravated assault against one Bugulru, a descendant of
the chiefs of Gatchapar, one of the populous districts during the time of O'Keefe, but now much reduced in size and
importance. Its falling off had occurred during the time of his
grandfather, also named Bugulru, who had unwisely backed
his magician Inifel against O'Keefe's champion, the dwarf
Fatumak. In the ensuing deadly test of rites, charms and
incantations between the two magicians, the victory was
gained by Fatumak through shrewd use of psychological
weapons. Extending his bony finger towards Inifel, he had
predicted his death that very night. And that night indeed,
Inifel was literally frightened to death, unable at the fatal
test to cope with the superior magic of his enemy.

The use of magic and the aid of sinister forces extant in
the universe were resorted to by the Yapese chiefs from
early times. It is in fact questionable whether Christian
religious practice so widespread on Yap today, has eradi-
cated the influence of devotees of the occult and mystical.

One occasionally comes across an action by a native manifesting at first full confidence in the forces of darkness, and complete bafflement later when they have not operated according to the ancient rules.

The complaint against Bugulru was that he had imbibed freely of *achif* (the native fire-water) one night, and become incensed at his friend, the complainant, who had failed to show proper deference to his tales about his great ancestors and their intimacy with the spirits animating the universe. He had conjured up ancestral spirits to provoke storm clouds and brilliant flashes in the heavens. He had caused a flight of birds to be directed out to sea against their habit of taking refuge from imminent storm in sheltering trees. He had established rapport with the gods of wind and water, calling them solemnly by name and receiving proof of their presence by a noisy rustling of leaves and waving of branches. This evidence made not the slightest impression on the complaining witness who had become overboldened by the fiery native liquor.

When Bugulru found himself unable to inspire proper reverence for his illustrious forebears, unable moreover to dispel his friend's scoffing at the undeniable evidence of familiarity with the invisible gods, he became infuriated. At such lack of understanding, he could do nothing less than draw his machete and cut off a slice of scalp accompanied by a quantity of hair. The victim could ill afford to lose either. Even after the benefit of such repair as the native surgeon could effect, the wound still looked raw some months later; and of course the surface was—and alas would always remain—barren.

Since the facts relating to the charge were thoroughly established by the prosecution, the burden passed to the defense of making an adequate answer under their plea of not guilty. They produced evidence of native custom to

show that disrespect for one's ancestors merited punishment
in certain cases. They argued that the complainant's flagrant
conduct justified the attack, at least under native custom,
which under certain circumstances enumerated in the Trust
Territory Code, have the force of law.

When the argument was prolonged until the time of ad-
journment, court was recessed until the following morning.
When we reconvened, the District Attorney was ready with
his answer: True enough, the Code required that consideration be given to native custom, but only where it was not
inconsistent with written laws adopted by any legislative
branch of government. This particular custom was at odds
with the penalties provided by the code; it could not stand;
it should be disregarded. This was my judgment. After listening to the prisoner's past record and the recommendations of both sides I sentenced Bugulru to a short term in
prison. He was led away by the constabulary, obviously
greatly perplexed and muttering to himself.

Later that day, Roscoe Edwards, the Public Defender, explained the prisoner's peculiar actions. He had taken the
precaution of ensuring a favorable verdict by directing
against me a mild hex, designed to promote enough confusion and uncertainty to make a finding of guilty impossible. The hex was accomplished by strewing bits of leaves
along the road I must traverse from the courthouse to my
quarters. Accompanied with appropriate incantations ad-
dressed to an all-powerful spirit, it had to be done in the
dead of night. He had advised his lawyer of the action he
was taking and the purpose of it, in the expectation that
Edwards would advise me of my peril. Apparently the native magicians were wise enough to use the psychological
approach as insurance against failure, and to work on the
mind of the victim through suggestion and prediction. But
the hex was doomed to failure in my case because under our

system of justice the lips of counsel are sealed in regard to anything smacking of influence on the court. I therefore did not learn of this attempt until it was too late to affect Bugul-ru's fate. I last saw him as he toiled with the road gang clearing underbrush, still mystified at my immunity from the powerful forces discharged in my direction.

Since neither the government nor the defense wished to start the next contested trial that day, I called for legal arguments in the several criminal appeals awaiting hearing by the High Court sitting as a court of appeal. These appeals— from judgments of conviction and fine imposed by the District Court in traffic cases and cases of disorderly conduct —were all made by the Yapese chief public defender, a young man named John, who based them upon his reading of our set of *American Jurisprudence* volumes. John was possessed of a lively imagination and understanding, but had not as yet developed good judgment, and his appeals, which often involved small fines and matters of slight consequence, would be characterized as frivolous in United States courts.

For example, he appealed in one case to reverse the court's fine of $25.00 for violation of the Motor Vehicle Code, upon the ground that other persons were fined only $5.00 the same day for the same offense in a different part of the district center. This, he argued, was discriminatory because it showed a failure to give his client the equal protection of the laws guaranteed by the Constitution. In answer, I pointed out that the maximum fine for speeding within the district center was $100.00; it was the court's discretion in each case to determine how much below that figure the particular circumstances of each offense justified. If one traveled at a high rate of speed down a crowded thoroughfare, it would be quite different from exceeding the limits in a little-traveled zone. The punishments varied within a court's power and could not be criticized unless clearly unreasonable.

In another appeal John complained that one landowner had received a small fine for setting fire to his brush and thus readily clearing his land of decaying vegetation. But this easy way was prohibited by law for two reasons: first, to guard against spreading fire during the dry season, and second, to allow the soil to benefit from the decaying material. It had been shown that the native practice of burning the remnant of their crops and the wild grasses and scrub timber and shrubbery not only tends to deprive the land of needed replenishment, but is also a major cause of the restricted range of crops in the islands. This had been carefully demonstrated over and over by the agricultural staff and most natives had finally become enlightened, but there were still some who were too lazy to break up the soil and spade this natural fertilizer into it. They were invariably caught and fined.

John's appeal was based upon the excessive fine levied upon a repeated offender in contrast to the suspension of penalty where ignorance of the law was successfully pleaded, and a lesser penalty for a first offender. Here I made the same answer, pointing to the maximum penalty and the court's discretion in fixing stricter penalties for repeated violators. Though the appeal did not involve the law's reasonableness or the Government's right to restrict an owner from burning over his matured croplands—which in the States would certainly have been challenged on appeal —I took the opportunity to discuss publicly the purpose behind the law and its essential wisdom. The close attention paid to my remarks as translated, indicated the interest of these intelligent natives in programs designed for their benefit. Also, I refused to accept the District Attorney's characterization of these appeals as frivolous, since it gave me an opportunity to conduct a class in the basic theories of social welfare as the background for appropriate exercise of legislative power.

The next morning both sides announced readiness for trial of charges of aggravated assault and assault with a deadly weapon brought against one Yengis. The charges rose out of an attack with a spear-gun, used by the natives to bring in large fish. The defendant had been confined in jail for the weeks between the attack and the opening of the next term of the High Court. This was unusual. Modest bail is all that is ordinarily required, since it is difficult to get far from the islands except in a large boat, and almost impossible to hide for long, particularly if one is not popular with natives in the distant villages, which was the case here. However, the reason for the prolonged imprisonment before trial was soon made apparent.

The large fish on whom the gun had been used in this case turned out to be an athletic man of average height wearing only the scarlet ceremonial *thuu* (loin-cloth) of his clan. He was a neighbor of the defendant and a fisherman from one of the outlying villages, from which people had come the long distance for the trial, those who had relatives near Colonia staying with them until the trial's end. The little courthouse was literally packed. The story of this attack was known to everyone, interest in the trial was at fever heat, and many young boys and girls crowded into every available nook.

The District Attorney told the story of the attack and sketched the evidence he expected to offer. When his turn came the Public Defender declined to make a statement, at least not until the Government's evidence was in, and so the trial opened with the testimony of Umo, the fisherman.

He told of the never-to-be forgotten day when he came up against the weapons and ill-will of the defendant. It happened that Yengis had a son of twelve, who went around the village pilfering tools and other articles, despite constant reproof by his parents. One day, in deep rage, Yengis vowed he would teach his son a lesson for all time. He pinioned the boy at his side, extended the fingers of his right hand, and with a blow of the machete lopped off the tip of his index finger. Then, releasing the crying lad, he promised to continue cutting off his finger tips as further thefts occurred. The barbaric action came to the attention of his neighbor Umo's wife, who reported it to the constabulary. A warrant was sworn out upon the charge of maiming and Yengis was confined in the jail. But when the case came on for hearing, the boy was too terrified to tell a story implicating his father, so the judge was forced to release him without penalty.

The indignity of the temporary confinement to a man accustomed to a wide berth when people passed him on the road rankled in the heart of Yengis, and he made broad allusions to misfortune about to overtake Umo and his family. He spent much time sharpening his machete and the knives he normally carried in his belt. He was seen by his neighbors discharging his spear-gun repeatedly into the bark of a palm tree. From time to time husks of cocoanut and rotting fruits would be found on Umo's grounds, obviously propelled by his neighbor's arm. Nothing more serious occurred than an occasional exchange of epithets until one day when Umo, combing out one of his nets and stringing it on some poles, chanced to look around and found Yengis behind him, with his spear-gun cocked. The release of the heavy elastic spring would imbed the spear into Umo's back.

The fisherman turned quickly and attempted to grab the muzzle of the gun. As he did so, with one hand holding the spear point extending from the muzzle, Yengis yanked it away with great force, tearing Umo's fingers with the sharp points of the spear. Before the gun could be pointed at him again, Umo was on his assailant, grabbing again at the deadly spear but it was too difficult to hold the small point protruding from the barrel with Yengis trying to wrest it away. This time the spear tore a gash in Umo's thigh. Despite his wounds, he kept up the unequal battle and was cut on his chest and arms, until help finally came from neighboring villagers, who disarmed Yengis and brought Umo to the hospital where his wounds were tended. Weeks later at the trial he exhibited the lacerations which were almost healed, with no apparent lasting effect but the scars.

The gun was also exhibited. It was rather a crude affair. By pulling back an elastic band attached to the stock of the gun you released the spear from a long barrel. It seemed that this action was adequate to project the spear with sufficient force to pierce the body of a good sized fish, so the status of the gun as a deadly weapon appeared conceded.

Corroborating evidence came from Umo's wife and some of the villagers who arrived on the scene in time to disarm Yengis, and the burden of proof then passed to the defense who asked for time for a brief consultation. The Public Defender and his Yapese assistants conferred briefly and then advised the court that they had decided to offer no defense, but intended instead to offer evidence in mitigation of the offense. I therefore made a finding of guilty and set the hearing of penalty for the following day. The prosecution, it developed later, had been diligent in obtaining affidavits to support the contention that this case merited the fullest penalty the law could impose. Since this meant an aggregate sentence of ten years' imprisonment, which in the islands is considered quite severe, the government had gone to great pains to justify it.

The following morning the Public Defender offered testimony of the defendant's previous good behavior—he regularly attended church; he had never been convicted of a penal offense; he was an industrious man of family, living with his wife and their three children—and recommended a combined sentence of one year, with six months suspension of sentence.

The District Attorney then offered to read some ten affidavits by persons who had been viciously assaulted by the defendant, which he contended the court should consider in aggravation of his guilt. Of course the Public Defender vehemently objected to the consideration of statements by people not before the Court; moreover, there was no opportunity for cross-examination. I was inclined to agree with him, but the District Attorney produced legal authorities which established such procedure to be proper, so I directed the affidavits to be read into the record and sat back to listen.

The affidavits had of course been taken and written in Yapese, which is a very descriptive language, with no glossing over of meanings. The members of the constabulary who had obtained the affidavits had been directed to obtain the facts of each occurrence in detail, and therefore they were specific and complete with regard to each offense. Most of them had to do with beatings by Yengis without provocation; with threats and even attempts to use dangerous and deadly weapons; and finally with several cases of rape. The officers who obtained the latter statements did a masterly job of description, one of the stories being in such vivid detail as to make me blush for the court reporter intent on getting every word. Finally, taking note of the young boys and girls who were far less embarrassed than I, I stopped the recital of these events with the statement that they could be read to the reporter and thus made part of the record.

The composite picture was of a dangerous bully, roaming

roads and fields far from the district center, causing injury and terror whenever he became drunk. No man was safe from his predatory impulses, no woman or girl from his lust —in our parlance a mean and ornery cuss. He certainly merited severe punishment and, more important, the community had to be protected from his ravaging nature. When I imposed the maximum penalty and he was led away, everybody in the courtroom breathed a sigh of relief. Later I was informed that he had escaped and caused a reign of terror among those who had testified against him, but he was not at liberty more than a few weeks. He dared not appear near his own village but the necessity to forage for food in a hostile countryside ultimately gave the police a lead to his capture.

I last saw Yengis several days after the trial as I walked along the dusty road from clerk's office to courthouse. He was one of a group of prisoners clearing the heavy underbrush which grew along the road and widened out to make a dense thicket near the courthouse. Each man was equipped with a sharp machete as he worked over the ground, seated on his haunches. There were some seven or eight men in the little group, with one police officer in uniform standing over them. As I approached he saluted me, raising his arm enough for me to notice that his side arm was not in the holster. His sole weapon appeared to be the bamboo wand he carried, somewhat like an officer's swagger stick.

As I walked by, Yengis straightened up. First I looked at his machete and then our eyes met. I realized the police officer had no weapon adequate to protect himself, let alone me, if the prisoner chose to attack. In a few minutes I reached the relative protection of the courthouse and the opportunity had passed.

I spent the remainder of the day organizing my material

for the school I was to conduct in the next four days. After invitations for it had gone out, I had been forced to make special arrangements for a change in interpreters as Feichin did not feel himself equipped to cope with technical translation. Actually we had had a number of near-breakdowns in our criminal trials when lengthy answers were given which required a good memory of what were sometimes involved explanations. Both counsel and I had exercised patience in order to help Feichin over the rough spots. At times as he strove to find the correct English phrase to give the reporter, he had garbled the answers, sweating profusely and turning red. Now he asked to be relieved of classroom duties but promised to be on hand during all sessions for the experience it would give him.

Under the circumstances I turned for aid to the Distad, Bob Halvorsen, who advised that the best translator available was one of his assistants named Gilmar, whom he would assign to me for duty. Gilmar was a graduate of Pics, the territorial high school on Truk, and had had several years of schooling at the University of Hawaii. The next day he reported at court opening, looking like an American collegiate with his khaki shorts and bright *aloha* shirt, a well-built, brown-skinned young man in his late twenties, handsome, poised and possessed of a sense of humor. It was a delight to talk with him, his understanding of English was superb, and his diction and pronunciation excellent. I have since learned that he serves on the contributing staff of the Micronesian Reporter, the territorial monthly magazine.

After the usual Micronesian delay in opening any public meeting, caused in part by distance and in part by indolence, we got under way. About a dozen "pupils" were present, three of them the sitting District Judges, several of them magistrates and community judges, and the rest, prosecutors and a few of the constabulary. I announced that the first session would be a historical review of the basis of the United States legal system, followed by a discussion of the Trust Territory Constitution and Bill of Rights, and a brief examination of the Statutes. The second session would take up in detail the Rules of Criminal Procedure which the High Court had placed in effect several years before, and the following day, the Rules of Civil Procedure. The closing session would be an exposition of the method of preparing pleadings in civil and criminal cases, with the class participating in the drafting process.

Matters proceeded pretty much on schedule. As these were lecture sessions, I had to conduct classes for several hours each morning and afternoon. The pause for necessary translation served a double purpose; it gave those whose inadequate knowledge of English prevented ready understanding of legal phraseology the advantage of translation into their native tongue, and it gave my vocal cords a needed rest in the long sessions. One fact was definitely established: Gilmar had remarkable gifts of lucid and meticulous exposition in making clear the abstract principles and detailed examples which formed the framework of my discourse. Like most of the others, however, he took advantage of the recess I allowed each hour, to chew the ever-present betelnut.

On the fourth day, we tried to put into practice the rules of procedure for drafting pleadings. I asked the class to prepare a suit on behalf of a mythical plaintiff claiming the defendant had trespassed on his land, removed a quantity of crops, and assaulted his daughter when she tried to stop him. The drafts were interesting and were criticized by the entire class. The stars were the young men who had at least a high school education, and there was a surprisingly good performance by Judge Fanechoor, the dean of the District Judges. The classes proved that the Yapese have considerable intelligence and capacity for understanding Western culture and legal background. They are now at the point where political organization is becoming increasingly popular: witness the creation of the Yapese Island Council, composed of representatives from each of the ten municipal districts, who meet regularly and adopt legislation in education, public works, local taxes and community problems. It is possible to envision the assumption, not too many years from now, of all legislative power in the Council, and a democratic government. As soon as the Yapese are prepared to concede that Western ideas of government have sufficient value to be adopted into their political system, this will come about.

School ended the day before our plane was due to arrive for the short hop to the Palaus, and an elaborate party was given for the judicial party at the community club, which numerous Yapese attended, particularly those having some official contact with the Administration. The next day we left Yap, with expressions of good will to the American staff and the natives whom we had come to know and respect in our few weeks' stay.

CHAPTER 12

DON'T STAY AWAY TOO LONG!

The little plane to take my husband and me even farther southwestward to Koror, district center of the Palau Islands, was a welcome sight as it circled Yap. It was a day late. On looking at the map it seemed we would be just as close to the Philippines, so I jestingly suggested to our pilot that it would be nicer to head in that direction—a touch of civilization and a good meal would have been truly enjoyable.

It was only about an hour and a half's ride and we made the trip without incident. I was always reluctant to get into this little doddle bug of a plane, knowing how patched and beaten up such planes were, but God must have been in His Heaven to bring it in always on time. I also knew that the men who handled it were good mechanics and just as anxious as we to arrive at those tiny dots on the map. As we took off, I got a little wet from the spray which percolated through the roof but after the shortage of water on Yap I really didn't mind.

Quite a group were waiting for us on the ramp at Koror. Here we made another water landing but the plane taxied from the harbor to a ramp up which it wobbled on its wheels to a concrete platform far enough out of the water to be moored there for the night. We were told these planes could stay in the water up to seven hours without damage but I was sure it would never last up to seven minutes if forced down in rough waters. Nevertheless here we were, and as we descended, I caught my first glimpse of those unique and interesting islands. They stuck up like huge green mushrooms, dense with vegetation, but solid rock at the base and utterly inaccessible. There were literally hundreds of them surrounding Koror; they could well be named the "Thousand Islands of the Pacific." Koror was one of the few inhabited ones, Babelthuap another, and not too far away were Peleliu and Angaur.

The Distad, Don Heron, and his wife Nan, greeted us cordially, and drove us in a Trust Territory Chevrolet sedan to their home where we had a refreshing drink while we waited for our luggage to be taken to the hotel. This center was very different from Yap and Truk. It was spread out, and the American homes were separated from one another by a large section of native dwellings, Japanese in design and all orderly, most with lovely flower gardens. For the first time in the tropics, I saw gardenias and rose bushes in profusion, and many other familiar blossoms. There were quite a few stores, barber shops and even restaurants, and the whole atmosphere was more Western (with a slight Japanese flavor) than I had noticed in the other islands. The Palauan girls were particularly pretty, neat and well dressed.

When we were finally taken to the Royal Palauan Hotel, I was most agreeably surprised. It didn't reflect any similarity to the Royal Hawaiian, but it did look like a hotel. The lobby was large and attractively furnished in the usual rattan. A large screened picture window walled one end, a long bar was on another wall, and the rear quarter, which served as the dining room, looked towards the back entrance. Corridors on the sides of this big room led to the bedrooms. Much to our delight we were taken to the end of one hall and found that our quarters, by Trust Territory standards, were lavish indeed, consisting of bedroom, sitting room and bath—unrestricted water privileges. The decor had been neglected, but it was clean. There were two large arm chairs and a coffee table in the small sitting room, plus a hot locker. The bedroom had twin beds, a dresser and hot closet, and best of all, in the corridor outside our rooms was a refrigerator and in it we and other guests kept a water bottle, fruit juices and sundries.

The only hotel guests were the judicial party. We had added two new members, one named Feichin Faimau, the clerk of courts from Yap; the other an assistant public defender from Truk whom we already knew. Both were nice shy boys, particularly Andon from Truk who was quite religious and serious. Feichin and I became good friends and he told me of his aspirations which showed him to be quite ambitious. He seemed to enjoy listening to talk about my children and our life back home in the States. One other person ate the evening meal with us, a young bachelor who lived nearby, the manager of the Western Carolines Trading Company. He had lived on Koror for six years and spoke Palauan fluently. Everyone seemed to love Mr. Seid whose first name was Sid, and when pronounced by a native, Sid and Seid sounded the same.

The lobby with its revolving ceiling fans and comfortable chairs was the only cool place in the hotel, and at 4:30 P.M., the end of the work day, it began to buzz. If I was still in my room I soon recognized that the hour had come for if I didn't hear the tinkle of ice, there was always the sound of a record player and a voice plaintively singing *Don't Stay Away Too Long*. It was undoubtedly the favorite of Josh, the bar boy, as he played it over and over again. The melody and the words were constantly in my ears, "I miss your smiling face" ad infinitum. But it did not get on my nerves too much; it just gave a sort of romantic air to the place.

Josh was the son of a high chief from one of the distant islands, and was very westernized in attitude and appearance. He played a good game of chess which he had learned from Sid Seid, who was now in the process of teaching my husband to play. Each night Sid and the Judge would play a round or so after which, if there was no one else around, Josh would ask to play. It was good practice for my husband whose ardent desire was to beat his teacher. The one annoying thing about Josh was his laziness. If he came in early before the bar opened, or stayed after his customers had left, he would lie down on the sofa and make himself comfortable enough for a nap. But no one else seemed to mind.

Kim, part Palauan and part Japanese, and a former Kamakaze pilot, was the cook and maitre d'hotel of this establishment. He was very good on some things and tried to give us a diversified menu, with fresh fish at least once a week. Occasionally we would have a pot of fresh clam chowder and often a plate of *sashimi* was on the bar at the cocktail hour. Flattery went a long way with him and he did his best to please us.

The commissary was within a block of the hotel, and I would daily replenish our supply of juices and tidbits for snacks.

The administration building, within another block, had an unusually well-stocked library which had been started and catalogued by Mrs. Heron, and one became a member by paying fifty cents a month. Many of the books were new and ranged from best-sellers, both fiction and non-fiction, to the latest mysteries. It was a joy to take a variety of books, as many as I could carry, and have the leisure to catch up on my reading. On Truk, one was too busy with household duties, guests and cooking to concentrate seriously. The Palauan sun was deadly, Koror being only six degrees and twenty minutes from the Equator. After my daily walk either to the library or to the agriculture station where I could buy fresh bananas and really fresh eggs which Kim would cook for us to specifications, I would take a cold shower and lie down in front of the fan to read. Some days I would have as many as five showers and enjoy the uninterrupted luxury of reading without disturbance. At home I had often read about far away and exotic places; now, in reverse, I read about metropolitan centers and sophisticated people.

On Koror, one could call a taxi, operated by some native who owned a jeep, and he would take you down to the Western Carolines Trading Company a few miles away. To get there one traveled through the native district with its numerous stores and restaurants. There was in fact one street called Geisha Lane which boasted several saloons or night clubs, but I never had the pleasure of seeing it at night—because there would frequently be a ruckus and often a real fight, which my husband felt he should not witness, as he might have to sit in judgment later if it turned out to be a felony.

I had thought the roads on Truk were bad but that was before I rode on those in the town of Koror. They were so bumpy that you almost had to hold your stomach to keep it in place, and no one could travel more than ten miles an hour. The Trading Company was fun. It stocked jewelry and tableware from Thailand, and *saris* and batik from India.

As manager of the big trading company, Sid Seid had built up a thriving export business in native handicraft and shell articles. The people of Palau seemed to have a more artistic bent and were better craftsmen than those in the other districts. There were several fine woodcarvers whose work brought in princely amounts. I saw coffee tables of dark wood with beautifully carved tops that sold for more than a hundred dollars and some lovely serving bowls copied from ancient ritual bowls. The famous Palauan wooden monkey men were symbolic of the district, as were the long rectangular story boards, most in bright colors and all hand carved, that told a complete story of some incident in Palauan history. Each came with a typewritten explanation. Most of the stories were so salacious, however, that it was hard to find one I thought suitable to bring back home. The Palauans of the olden days were lusty, bloody and downright pornographic. We bought some of the monkey men and wooden serving pieces, and had some bowls carved for us, but it was just my luck for my husband to have to sentence to prison the leading woodcarver available! All about the grounds of the huge quonset buildings of the Trading Company were hundreds of giant clam shells, some weighing up to a hundred pounds, one of which, filled with tropical plants, now graces my fireplace as a constant reminder of this unforgettable place.

One of the show places on this island was the *abai*, the community house for all gatherings, a large open building made with heavy wooden beams and rafters holding up a tremendous thatched roof. Although wherever there was a wooden beam decorated with figures depicting a legend or some notable happening in the lives of this island people, it looked a little like a church without either steeple or walls. Council meetings were held there; at other times people congregated just to gossip; and in one corner a ping pong table for the youths gave a modern touch. One lavish event we attended there was the graduation of the Trust Territory School of Nursing—the fifth such ceremony—carried out with much dignity and pomp, with speeches by various native officials delivered in Palauan and then translated into English; but the major talk, translated from English to

Palauan, was given by a Navy Captain from the U.S. Naval Hospital in Guam. An impressive candle lighting service was conducted by one of the instructors, with the nine graduates participating, after which there was some beautiful singing by the student body. The affair culminated with a surprisingly palatable "feast," consisting of potted pigeons, taro and breadfruit.

Judge Fanechoor from Yap had come to Koror to study the court procedures there and to visit his daughter Tina, now married to Francis Mahoney, former anthropologist and now the assistant distad. They were a charming, attractive couple and entertained us royally—an occasion befitting the grace of this lovely girl, daughter of a chief of high rank.

One day at lunch, my husband told me we were invited by Judge Fanechoor to witness at a nearby village, an unusual ceremony seldom witnessed by outsiders. They came for me late in the afternoon and we drove by jeep to a village I had never seen. Upon approaching, we saw hundreds of people converging on the small settlement. Women were carrying on their heads small short-legged tables piled with fruit or cooked food. The courtyards and porches of all the huts were crowded with children and adults, and in general, people were milling about in the large open squares. Judge Fanechoor had told us that this was the celebration of a young mother's first appearance after the birth of her first child. This was the tenth day, and up until the moment she came out of her hut, no one had seen her except those who had cared for her and the baby since the day of birth. For ten days she had been bathed in hot seaweed and oils.

When she finally appeared she was so weak it was necessary to lead her to the center of the square where she stood for her ovation. She did indeed look like a strange goddess. Her entire body had been anointed with turmeric and her skin was a golden copper color. She wore a ceremonial grass skirt above which she had a narrow belt of shells. Her breasts were painted or stained a deep purple and she wore lipstick. Her long hair was in a high up-swept fashion, with flowers and pearls intertwined. Natives clicked cameras, old women smoked cigarettes. The young mother gave us a tremendous smile and posed graciously for our pictures. We were told later that she was rather well educated and had worked for the Administration as switchboard operator in the district center building.

Picnicking was the favorite way to spend a weekend here as in all the centers. Several Americans had their own power boats, the fastest and most luxurious belonging to our friend Sid, who with his friend Myron Kerner, head of the U.S. Weather Bureau for Micronesia, took us on one of their deep sea fishing outings. We spent an unforgettable day on one of the nearby islands, a day so perfect as to make all the hardships worth the price of coming to these remote parts.

We left civilization early in the morning—laden with a stateside picnic plus wine, beer and pop, all packed in deep ice—bound for a small, remote island not far from the tip of Peleliu which lies outside of the reef fringing the Palau Islands. To get there is was necessary to traverse the narrow passes between the small mushroom-like caps of islands which lay in the bay on which the boat dock fronted, and came close enough to many of the islets to discover why they were uninhabited. At low tide the limestone base was exposed on all sides showing the impassable nature of the rocky inclines. Each islet rose from this expanse of rock to a high central point, with many trees and thick underbrush covering all the land. It seemed next to impossible to gain a foothold from the water's edge, and if one gained it, to keep from falling back into the water.

After passing these "Thousand Islands of the Pacific," we came into the principal bay used for navigation and saw beyond it the open water to the south. As we went through the wide mouth of the pass, we started to smack the waves, and Sid cut down speed to eliminate excessive bounce. Soon we were past the fringing reef, then took a wide turn to starboard and after half an hour of glorious sunshine and surf, we drove up to shallow water in the lee of a small heavily wooded island, its front yard a lovely sandy beach. Here we dropped anchor and all of us waded ashore carrying food and supplies for the day, among them Myron's transistor radio which we promptly tuned in to nearby Australia.

After unloading, the two fishermen took off in the boat into deep water, leaving my husband and me on what now resembled a deserted island. The sand was fine and clear and it was cool in the shade of the heavy foilage. Behind us was a jungle of trees. We made ourselves comfortable with mats, cold drinks and our books and listened to the beautiful music of Rachmaninoff's "Rhapsody on a Theme by Paganini," being transmitted from Melbourne. The calm sea, the fleecy clouds, the entire scene, made me feel as if we were the only people in the world.

All of a sudden, I realized we were not. Three little dark heads peeped out from the bushes and as I gave them a friendly greeting, they crept closer to the place from which the music was coming. As they spoke only Palauan, we talked in sign language for a while and after we became friends, they started gleefully to build holes in the sand in which they made a stick trap, then covered it over. When Sid and Myron returned later, I told them it was obviously meant for them, whereupon they pretended to fall into the trap and sent the little imps into shrieks of laughter. A little later, their father, having just returned from a fishing trip

himself, joined the party. He was called a *rubak,* a respected elder. He partook of our food and beer, making
elaborate apologies for not having a suitable gift for us and
vowing to send one when he next came to Koror. In spite of
his protest, the gift never came, but I do have his picture
and one of myself standing beside his outrigger canoe. He
spoke no English, but conversed volubly in his own tongue
with Sid, whose Palauan was like a native's. On the ride
home we took another route, and could see in the distance
the tip of Peleliu, scene of a bloody battle in not so peaceful
days.

On other Sundays, we refused the hospitable offers of
avid American fishermen and shellers to accompany them
on all-day forays. It was usually a long day, and as neither
of us was good enough to swim as far out as the reef, it
would have meant sitting in wet bathing suits too long for
comfort, while at the same time being beset by the numerous flies and bugs. Kim would fix an assortment of sandwiches, slaw and pickles, and place them on the dining table
in a screen cage to keep out the insects, and we could help
ourselves to lunch whenever and as often as we wished.

As in the other districts, we had been assigned a battered
jeep to be used for recreation. One Sunday, being alone in
the hotel, we decided to explore. Getting our "wheels"
started was an operation which took great patience, and
getting it to stop was doubtful, since its brakes were very
temperamental. We finally made it to the main road and
took off for the distant hills where we had never been before. All went well at first. We passed a number of villages,
and many people who waved happily, and I guess curi-
ously, wondering where we could be going. We chugged
upward and upon reaching the heights, stopped to look
back and down at the beauty of the dense foilage surround-

ing the blue waters with Koror almost hidden from view. Naturally the motor stalled, and despite all our coaxing nothing happened, not even a spark. We were sitting in the middle of a muddy pool of water, of all places to be stopped, so it was of no avail for my husband to try to push and I to steer. At first it seemed quite funny and we laughed at our plight. Soon our merriment turned to real concern. We were not close to any settlement and there would be a problem of caring for the jeep if we walked back. Besides it was much too far to walk, especially in the heat of afternoon.

Naturally, it was I who was elected to walk down hill to the nearest settlement. I was to take it easy and rest when necessary. It proved to be near the bottom of the hill, and as I approached, seeing women and children sitting close to their homes, I called to one family, "Yoohoo, can anyone help the Judge? He is stuck in a water hole." There was much conversation for a few moments and soon six strong looking teen-agers walked off in his direction. No one spoke further to me, but I noticed that some women who had been clad in only bra and skirt went inside their thatched cottages and donned blouses. I did not have long to wait when I heard the loud chug of the ancient motor and I had to run at top speed to catch up with my driver, who was racing down hill, having all he could do to apply the brakes. My husband told me that when the boys reached him, they merely picked up the jeep, turned it around and gave him a push down hill.

I made several shopping trips to the various stores and was interested to see that most of their merchandise was imported from Japan. I found that fancy nylon underwear, lavish with lace, was most popular. At the semi-outdoor movie theatre, which was patronized by both natives and

Americans, one would see young native women in sweaters and skirts, while American women usually wore cool cottons.

The theatre structure was made from metal strips, salvaged from an airfield somewhere, mounted on bars to become the seats which were therefore indescribably uncomfortable. We always took a pillow, which did little to help us enjoy the movie. The sound track was bad and the place was noisy, but it was recreation, after a fashion. Fresh popcorn was sold at the entrance, the picture changed twice a week and the place was crowded most nights. As manager of the chief trading goods company, Sid also ran the theatre, and more than once I saw him fearlessly throw out a bunch of unruly youths. This took nerve, as many carried knives and were not afraid to use them. I doubt, however, that any of them would have dared to harm him, for he was greatly respected for his courage as a diver, his ability to converse with the Palauans in their own tongue, and his close personal and business relationships with them.

I noticed that one of the rooms in the other wing of the hotel housed a barber's chair and when I inquired I was told that one of the native barbers often came to cut the hair of visiting dignitaries. Both the Judge and I were badly in need of a grooming so I arranged an appointment, but when I saw the coiffeur, I was a bit shaken by his unusually youthful appearance. He was a slight boy, with one leg visibly shorter than the other, and he was obviously abashed when I sat down in his chair to find that he was expected to shear my locks. Clearly his clientele must have been exclusively male and to add to his embarrassment the doorway was filling up with spectators as in the hospital at Truk. There was quite a gallery. The barber was growing noticeably nervous, and for a moment I was fearful of losing an ear or sustaining some wound or other, when Marie the assistant hotel manager came to my rescue. Marie was a very stylish native girl who studied the Sears Roebuck catalogue by the hour. After much conversation in Palauan, she took the scissors in hand and did a very creditable job. "Why," I asked, "didn't you tell me in the first place you could do it? Why did we have to get this man to leave his shop and come all the way to the hotel here just for me?" Marie didn't explain.

The crew that flew the inter-island planes came to Koror on Thursdays, and spent the night in the hotel before the turn-around back to Guam and, as they were all young and full of fun, always livened up the place. They always occupied the twin of our suite at the extreme end of the other wing. During our visit all went smoothly, but I was told an amusing story of an event that had occurred some time before we came. On one of their flights down, they had brought with them from one of the other districts an American staff member who was noted for his extreme piety. So far did this man carry his convictions that he would never join in the base parties or even sit in on the convivial drinking at the club bar. The fliers themselves were most careful about drinking and usually drank only a few glasses of beer, which I thought were well deserved after some of the trips I had heard about. On this weekend one of them decided to play a practical joke on the pious American.

It used to be possible for a bold Palauan girl to sneak into the hotel through the doors at the end of each wing and, without passing through the lobby, reach the room of her date for the evening, then leave the same way in the morning. Since the Administration frowned on promiscuous conduct, the hotel management had barred the doors of the wings and made it necessary to come in through the front entrance. But on that night some one had left the rear door open, and at about 1 A.M. had smuggled in one of the attractive native girls, who had eagerly entered into the plot. She knocked on his door and woke him. When he came to the door and asked, "Who's there?" she whispered, "I come for your wash." He said, "That's fine, but come for it in the morning." Whereupon she answered, "I can't, I can only do my washing at night." He protested, but afraid to lose a good chance of having his laundry done, he timidly opened the door. She charged in. She was a voluptuous girl and started to undress, making clear meanwhile her intention of sharing his bed. The poor man was so frightened that he grabbed a sheet from the bed and ran into the lobby, where he stayed, refusing to go back to his room until morning. Needless to say everybody else in the hotel was in a hilarious mood.

One room was marked "gift shop" and on plane days Sid Seid would open it up, as the crew were great shoppers both for themselves and friends on Guam who wanted story boards and monkey men. I had done most of my shopping at the big store because it gave me a place to go, and before we left I had sent to Truk via the inter-island ship the "Gunner's Knot," two tridacnas (giant clam shells), two wooden salad bowls, several handcarved fork and spoon sets, some handwoven place mats and half-a-dozen monkey men. I realized that with the weight they would add to our already bulging suitcases, we would never get aboard the plane. My prize purchase was a set of six bracelets made from the trochus shell, the one from which mother-of-pearl is made. I could have used many more for gifts to take home, but it was as hard to prod the Palauans into the work of making them as it was the Trukese. I had to practically beg for the six I did obtain. I thought them rather expensive for island handicraft, but they were unusual. Now they make both a conversation piece and a clatter on my arms.

In ten weeks, my judge's work was finished, at least for

that sitting, and we were looking forward to our return to home base. I had realized by then how lucky we were to be housed on Truk. It had the best climate, the best assortment of foods, and the largest and gayest group of people, but our visit to Koror was good for me. I enjoyed its hospitality and became better acquainted with tropical living and the native way of life. And I am still haunted by the song played endlessly by Josh, the barboy, *Don't Stay Away Too Long.*

CHAPTER 13

PALAU, THE FUTURE PARADISE

If our trip to Yap may be described as an experience with a primitive civilization, our Palauan visit may be characterized as life in the South Seas, Western style. In sharp contrast to the Yapese, their neighbors to the southwest are anxious to acquire Western culture and to enjoy the material comforts of our life, which are still almost unattainable luxuries to them. Here the Japanese influence and interest was strongest. There was considerable intermarriage and more than merely passive acquiescence in Japan's plan for a South Seas empire. Aggressive and ambitious, the Palauan younger generation is knocking on the door to economic self-sufficiency. Its opening will lead to the breakdown of the old tribal controls, and it is the interplay of these old and new forces that causes the dislocations and tensions evident there today. In ten years, I venture to predict, a substantial change in clan authority will have come about. Some of the fascinating problems thrown up by this simmering volcano came within my jurisdiction and I will describe them in my story.

The Palau islands are the farthest west of Micronesia, some 800 miles southwest of Guam, about 500 miles east of the Philippines and the same distance north of New Guinea. This places them directly north of the center of Australia and directly south of Japan. The islands have an area of some 175 square miles of which about five-sixths are within the large island of Babelthuap (pronounced "Bab-bledop"). It is on this island that the largest number of people live, about fifty per cent of the total of 8500 inhabitants in all of Palau. Separated from it by a shallow inlet, the island of Koror, the next most populous center, is the chief business, educational and administrative center of Palau, though its area is less than three square miles. In the bay, just off a small island connected to Koror by a series of causeways, is the water landing used by the airline, and the ramp on which the planes come to rest.

As we approached Palau on our routine flight we could see the hundreds of small islands within the bounding reef which encloses almost all the major islands. I learned later that there are about 350 islands within the protection of the reef, some only a few acres in area, all thickly wooded and many, with their high limestone shoreline, inaccessible. From the sky they looked invitingly green and cool, and since the limestone base was not visible from above, my impression grew of masses of trees growing out of the ocean. Later we were able to navigate in a power boat around these islands and at low tide to discover in the rocky walls along the sea numerous caves which had been utilized by the indefatigable Japanese to store food and munitions, and even as a base for the placement of cannon pointed toward Koror.

According to custom we were greeted by the Distad and members of his staff and by several judges of the District Court. The acting clerk of courts and the assistant prosecutors and defenders were also present on the sea ramp, all of them able to converse in acceptable English. All wore western style clothes, white or khaki trousers or shorts, and *aloha* shirts. Arrangements had already been made for a call of cases the next morning, but if I wished to confer with any of them that afternoon, they would be ready for me in the new courthouse.

With our bags stowed on one of the ancient jeeps which had met us, we proceeded to the Royal Palauan Hotel along a road which led across causeways through dense thickets, past several small villages, until it came into the main thoroughfare in the outer limits of Koror Municipality and widened into a width comfortable for two vehicles; and for possibly half a mile it was fairly level and in passable repair. However, once you left this main road, even toward and into the main shopping center, the roads became gutted with holes and ridges, and you just had to go slowly.

We passed the territorial agricultural station, with several acres of tall corn and tapioca waving at a respectable height, and you could see the giant ears of taro plants, watermelon vines, banana trees and pineapple clumps. Obviously nature was prodigal in Palau and repaid honest toil.

Across the road were the ample grounds of the Department of Public Works, with open storage for trucks and construction materials in a large front yard, surrounded by a number of low quonset structures housing the various Public Works units. A little further along was the hospital behind a spacious lawn and wide spreading breadfruit trees. Close by was the front yard of the hotel, and in the rear, about a hundred feet from the road the one-story structure bearing the ambitious name of Royal Palauan Hotel. This was to be our home for the ten weeks of our stay. Here we climbed down and were assigned one of the two suites of parlor, bedroom and bath.

After a short rest I decided to walk down to the courthouse. I was particularly intrigued by the stories I had heard of an air-conditioned library. On the way, a distance of about three blocks, I passed and greeted many natives, mostly young, clean looking and friendly. The temperature was in the low nineties, where it had been for weeks during the afternoons. There had been slight rainfall, but Koror is not dependent on rain for its water supply so the only loss was of the coolness which comes with tropical storms. I quickly learned that the best way to walk was to cross the street to the side where overhanging trees afforded some shade.

I found the courthouse. It was a solid structure of stone and cement block, with concrete floors and glass windows— the only ones I saw in Micronesia outside of Guam. There were two courtrooms of good size, the larger one designed for use by the High Court, with adequate judicial chambers and conference room. The chairs, desks and equipment were all new and well designed. The planning had been approved by Judge Furber so the essential needs of the judicial department had been met. Fans were available both for courtrooms and chambers, and three comfortable chairs for the occasional three-judge court had been installed. Because it was a remodeled structure, based on the existing framework, with its steel and high columns, the ceilings were at least a dozen feet high. Actually the buildings had been erected by the Japanese as an administrative center, and had taken a direct bomb hit. As restored and adapted to the use of the judiciary, it was so unlike the normal quonset construction with metal siding and concave roof, that it had come to be called the "Taj Mahal."

True enough, there was an air-conditioned library and vault for court files and, adjoining it, the office of the Clerk of Courts which contained the usual filing cabinets, typewriters, tables and other paraphernalia typical of such offices everywhere. But the most important feature of all was the water cooler just outside the door of the chambers, where sweet water from the heights of Babelthuap was always on tap. The simple pleasure of clear cold water in this dehydrating climate, in copious quantities for drinking and adequate for bathing, was indescribable.

As I sat in the courtroom trying the chairs for size, the presiding district judge, Pablo Ringang, was announced. Through Anthony, the acting clerk of courts, we had a pleasant conversation, mainly about the cases awaiting trial and the number of weeks we would hold court. Judge Ringang wished to set some of his cases for trial, which would require the attendance of both the District Attorney and the Public Defender, and was anxious to select dates compatible with my call, and we resolved this matter easily. He then advised me of the necessity of shutting down the entire judicial department the first two weeks in July, for the annual trochus hunt, which brought me into contact with one of the unique practices of the islands.

It appeared that fishing for trochus was one of the important activities of the male population, since trochus shells were greatly prized. The entire catch was sold to the Japanese who used them in the manufacture of pearl buttons and ornaments, and in order to guard against decimation of the beds which was bound to follow upon unlimited access, the taking of trochus was limited by law to a few weeks of the year. It was one of the important means of obtaining foreign exchange so every Palauan family made sure to have some able-bodied representative at the annual hunt, in which the entire populace participated. The three district judges would therefore not be available to hold court or to assist me as assessor, nor would any of the court clerks appear for duty.

This was a serious blow to the program I was developing to dispose completely of some sixty cases awaiting trial, most of them civil cases which had been pending for a considerable period, and among them forty cases involving appeals from the Land Claims Administration, to the speedy disposition of which I had been alerted in Washington at the time of my induction. Besides, my team of two lawyers and the court reporter might be kept idle for two weeks, with nothing to show for the expense of transporting and maintaining us for that period. However, I promised Judge Ringang to study the matter and see what could be done to excuse him and his associates without stopping the wheels of justice completely.

On the way back to the hotel I turned off the road along the hospital and walked into one of the native villages. It differed markedly from the villages I had seen on Truk and in the Marshalls. Here the homes more closely resembled those of Western style, with considerably more stone or stone trim and heavy timber and much less thatch and corrugated iron salvage. Palauan society had come most heavily under the influence of the Japanese, and their homes and gardens still bear the characteristic imprint of neatness and order; there is also greater interest in sanitation and public health. The houses appeared to have such furniture as tables and chairs and an occasional bed, but sleeping mats still remained predominant. Most of the homes seemed to be equipped with running water, certainly unique for native quarters, and as I learned later, many have electric power and light. There has developed among the Palauans a strong feeling for the advantages of electric refrigeration and stoves, which one can observe in the homes of well-to-do natives.

Returning to the hotel, I passed the American Commissary, conducted as a branch of the Western Carolines Trading Company, a company completely Micronesian owned and controlled, probably the most successful business in the islands. Its success, I learned, was due to the enterprise and skill in management of a young Californian named Sid Seid, who had come to Palau six years earlier as an officer on a freighter, and had been fascinated by the outdoor life and the friendly people. He soon learned to speak and write Palauan, and young and old affectionately called him "Mr. Sid." Mr. Sid and we became good friends, of which more anon.

The store had almost as complete a stock as Truk had of canned goods, frozen foods, fruits and vegetables, as well as liquid refreshment, from every part of the world. Palau permits the sale of beer to natives, but no strong liquor, and Palauans shop for coffee, tea, rice, sugar, flour, cigarettes and beer, and occasionally, some of the frozen meats and fish. They live mainly, however, on what their gardens and trees produce, supplemented by daily resort to the bountiful sea.

The next morning I conducted the call of cases before a very large attendance. The call had been advertised some days before in all the municipalities of Koror and Babelthuap, and almost all the parties to pending litigation were present. The three district judges, Ringang, Rubasch Fritz and Charles Gibbons, the chief magistrates of many of the towns, and the District Attorney and the Public Defender and their native staffs, were also present. Almost all the cases, civil, criminal and appellate, were ready for trial or would be during the time fixed for our stay.

I had examined each file and knew the status of each case. Most of them, with the exception of the Land Appeals, had proceeded to the point of pre-trial conference, hence the legal and factual issues had been agreed upon. These cases I assigned places on the call and advised the parties they would be tried right after the trochus holiday. The criminal cases, entitled to priority, I set for immediate trial. The Land Claims Appeals were held for further study and conference with the two lawyers and ultimately disposed of in the manner I will hereafter narrate.

Later that day we started the first criminal trial. It involved a charge of criminal assault by a native youth against an American foreman. There was a plea of guilty, with a request that I consider extenuating circumstances. The youth had apparently been employed by the administration and assigned to the supply warehouse under the supervision of the prosecuting witness. When certain items of inventory turned up missing (by no means a rare occurrence), the defendant lost his job at the instigation of the supervisor. Shortly afterwards, on a week-end visit to a beer hall on Geisha Lane, the native honky-tonk district, the two men came face to face as the supervisor waited outside the hall. The defendant walked some distance away, stopped and picked up a convenient rock and heaved it at the witness with telling effect. It struck him on the forehead, breaking the skin and causing an ugly wound. A little lower and an eye might have been destroyed.

The basis for extenuation was the claim by the defendant that he had been unjustly charged with the theft. Over the weeks the injustice had rankled within him and impelled him to seek revenge. I inquired why he had not appealed to the Distad for a hearing and learned that nobody had told him such action was possible. It appeared there was no record of prior trouble. After admonishing the defendant against further violation of the Criminal Code, I suspended most of his six-months' sentence but required him to spend the next thirty days in jail.

A case involving custody of a young girl of thirteen came up for hearing. The dispute was between her father's brother and her mother's clan, represented by the chief, a plump and jovial gentleman obviously used to having his way. The child's natural parents were dead. At the time of her father's death a short time before, she had been living with her two younger brothers in a cottage that had been owned by her father, built on land belonging to his clan. Her father's people wanted her to remain and agreed to support all three children until maturity, but the mother's clan had come for this child and taken her away, so the case was heard as a *habeas corpus* petition, questioning their action and custody.

The clan of the child's father had paid to her mother's clan at the time of her marriage a piece of Palauan shell money which had great value among the natives, for the property which could be acquired with it. In a matriarchy such as Palau, the fruit of a marriage usually goes to the mother's clan, should the marriage be dissolved either by divorce or by death. In this case, however, the mother's clan did not wish to take all the children, but only the girl child. Both sides were apparently qualified to have custody. Both vigorously made claim.

Obviously this situation required resort to native custom. Judge Ringang had been acting as assessor, so I retired into chambers with him and Anthony, the clerk of courts, and submitted the proposition. I was told that Palauan girls are much prized by their clans in the pre-nuptial negotiations. An attractive girl who had proved her fertility, could persuade her prospective mate to solicit substantial gifts from his clan, not to her or to the young couple jointly, but to her clan. Since she would upon marriage leave her clan and go to live among her husband's people, this would seem at first blush the height of foolishness. However, at divorce, which occurred frequently, she would return to her people. The same would usually occur upon the husband's death, so it would be wise for the bride to obtain the best deal for her clan: it would provide a trust fund for her future needs.

In the case before us, the father's clan had paid out this valuable Palauan money which it hoped to recoup ultimately by having available another female to bait the trap. Unless it could have the custody and services of the daughter, it would be money out on the deal. The mother's clan, on the other hand, had received the money and now had the daughter. It was inequitable that it should have both and under native custom it should give up either the money or the daughter. Of course the daughter would have the right to choose when she reached maturity, and quite often would apply her earnings to reimburse the clan paying out the Palauan money, in which event she would be a free agent and could rightfully choose the other clan without any recrimination.

Armed with this knowledge, I resumed court and announced the principles which the assessor had urged for adoption in this case. When neither party showed a disposition to question the authoritative view of the assessor, I awarded the child to the father's clan. This had the beneficial effect of uniting her with her brothers.

The next case was one involving injury with lasting results caused by the accurate throwing arm of Yona, an athletic young Palauan in his late teens, related to one of the chiefly families. The prosecuting witness, Nerangeboi, a man in his forties, came into court wearing a black patch where his eye had been. The case was hotly contested, both sides called numerous witnesses, the decision gave me considerable trouble, as you will see from these facts:

The scene of the dispute was the municipal building of one of the outlying municipalities on Babelthuap, which had just been completed. A celebration was under way. All the important men and women were present, with an assortment of younger members of the clan. In charge of the arrangements was the prosecuting witness, who was also in charge of public order, with authority equivalent to that of a town constable. No other peace officer was present, which is not unusual, as members of the constabulary are stationed not in the towns but in Koror, the district center from which they carry out special assignments in the surrounding islands. So deeply ingrained is the respect for elders that in a normal situation each clan is able to restrain its members without police intervention. This, however, was not a normal situation.

As in all celebrations, native liquor was readily available to all and, as might have been expected, quite a few people became intoxicated, among them the defendant, Yona—and also, to his everlasting regret, the prosecuting witness Nerangeboi.

When the festivities were at their height, Yona started to press through the throng gathered at the entrance door of the new structure. As he was about to enter, a *rubak* came from the inside on his way out and they met in the doorway. Instead of giving way, which was his duty under native custom, Yona pressed forward in his haste and jostled the other man. One of the *rubak's* friends noticed what had happened and reproved Yona, who was, however, not disposed to accept reproof and answered back. An altercation ensued and there soon appeared the unofficial policeman, Nerangeboi, who ordered Yona out of the building.

A few minutes later some one told Nerangeboi that the youth had come into the council chamber through one of the many windows, and he was found sitting on his mat, communing with friends. Once more Nerangeboi approached him, pulled the boy to his feet and forced him to leave. No blows were struck, but as both approached the door, there was some scuffling with Yona striving to hit the older man who used his greater weight to bear Yona down. Both of them being unsteady, they went down outside the building, and were parted by solicitous friends. Yona started away and when he refused to stop the other started after him. It was clear from the evidence that Yona was not too inebriated to get away from the slower, quite intoxicated elder, but after getting a safe lead and while Nerangeboi's attention was momentarily distracted, Yona picked up a sharp piece of concrete and heaved it with deadly aim at his head. It hit him in the eye, and when he woke up in the hospital, Nerangeboi's health was shattered as well as his eye.

What to do under the circumstances? Both parties were wrong, the older man for becoming intoxicated while charged with the duty of keeping order and constantly provoking the younger man when he was causing no trouble; the younger man for not going away as ordered by proper authority and striking a blow when there was no threat to his person. In view of the fact that so far only one of the two had suffered, I imposed a jail sentence on the defendant, after a full review of the evidence and the theories upon which the sentence was based.

It took several days of trial to dispose of the Yona case. When the Public Defender asked for a stay of the sentence so that he could take an appeal, it was granted and the defendant was released on his own bond. Actually, I had no objection to occasional appeals: first, because it gave the appellate division of the court the opportunity to state legal principles as precedents to guide the trial courts of Trust Territory thereafter; second, because nothing gives the native people a stronger feeling of confidence in American justice than to know that any sentence is reviewable by higher authority.

The path is made easy for criminal appeals, which are processed by all courts at nominal cost to the appellant. In every appeal the record of the testimony is written up and the reviewing court reads it and gives the case sincere consideration. The extent to which American courts in Micronesia strive to impress the natives with the fairness of American justice is indicated in the case of a prosecution for grand larceny, involving, of all things, theft of a sawmill alleged to have the value of $1000.00.

The defendant was a young man who had worked some five years for the Administration as foreman of a government sawmill on Babelthuap—one of the projects initiated by Trust Territory Government in the hope that a woodworking industry could be developed among the dexterous natives. The Palauans are very clever with woodcarving and make handsome bowls, trays, tables, and objects of art. It was believed therefore that a lumber mill would be economically feasible, with the substantial amount of timber available on the slopes of Babelthuap. However, after five years it seemed to the authorities on Guam that as a government project it was undesirable. Instructions were given to the Distad of Palau, and through him, to Stan Darby, the head of the agricultural station on Koror in charge of this project, to close up the mill and bring the equipment back to Koror. But when Darby broke the news to the crew which had been operating the mill, they were unwilling to quit. The defendant, pointing to the long hours he had spent breaking in the crew and the faithful service he had rendered during his five years of employment, felt that the government should not close down the mill, but should instead let the natives run it on a cooperative basis. If, therefore, he could acquire the mill, he would take charge of it and keep the crew producing lumber for the diverse needs of the islanders.

Darby seemed to have admitted that the closing of the mill was unfortunate and that the defendant was entitled to generous treatment by the government in recognition of his years of service beyond the call of duty. He offered to go back to Koror and attempt to persuade the Administration to make the defendant a gift of the mill, or if not, then to sell it to him on easy terms.

Without awaiting Darby's return the defendant started dismantling the mill. He took the machinery and tools to his home, told all his fellow employees that he was the owner of the mill and intended to set it up on Koror, and the next day had them transport all of it down to the dock and load it on his chartered boat. The boat left for Koror but when it arrived there it was met by Public Works officials, who seized the cargo and initiated prosecution.

While the prosecutor was making his presentation, there was much whispering between the defendant and a little group composed of public defenders and what appeared to be members of the family. When I called upon Roscoe Edwards to make his opening statement for the defense, he said that the defendant had decided to plead guilty and throw himself on the mercy of the court. I called the defendant up to the bench and interrogated him. It was clear that he understood the consequences of his plea of guilty. I accepted it and sat back to hear what the parties had to say.

The prosecutor's statement presented no new material. He pointed out the defendant's previous good record as well as the government's desire to punish the conversion and theft of its property. In view of the fact that the mill had not been lost and the government had sustained no damage, he recommended a light sentence.

The public defender had in mind a different result and used different tactics. He asked permission to put the defendant on the stand to show mitigating circumstance. As he testified, it was brought out that he was under the impression from Darby's conversation that he was being given the mill in recognition of his past service to the government.

He had taken the mill not surreptitiously at night but openly during the day, and with the unconcealed assistance of his crew. He believed he was within his rights in taking possession of the mill transporting it to the boat and ultimately to Koror.

As this testimony continued I began to have increasing doubts of the guilt of this man under a criminal charge. Yet he had already pleaded guilty. Finally I stopped his counsel, pointing out that it would be improper to hear testimony impugning the guilt of a man who had admitted theft by his guilty plea. Such testimony should more properly have been presented under a not-guilty plea. I felt therefore that the defense should adopt one of these courses: either to withdraw the plea of guilty, which I would permit, or refrain from offering evidence of innocence.

I allowed them some time for conference by adjourning court until the afternoon, when Edwards advised that his client had decided to withdraw his plea of guilty and stake his chances on the trial. The District Attorney made no objection and the taking of testimony started. When the government had put in the testimony of some half-dozen witnesses before resting their case, I held that a sufficient *prima facie* case had been made, and ruled on the defendant to put in his defense, which he proceeded to do.

One unusual bit of evidence later weighed heavily in the verdict: the testimony of Father Edwin McManus, the priest in charge of the Mission School on Koror, a kindly and urbane gentlemen I had met on Yap. He was called as an expert on semantics, because of his long study of the Palauan language. He had lived on Palau some nine years and was on friendly terms with everyone. His long white frock of the Jesuit order, surmounted by a noble brown beard, and deep-set eyes which danced with utmost good humor, gave him an arresting appearance. From the witness chair he proceeded to expound the peculiarities of Palauan syntax, the purpose being to show the understanding conveyed to the defendant by Darby's offer to get the mill for him as a gift from the Administration. Just as the defendant had testified, the words translated into Palauan had meant to him that Darby was actually giving him the mill at the time. This contradicted Darby's testimony that he would give the defendant the mill when he had obtained permission from higher authority. Father McManus then explained that the present tense and future tense are the same in Palauan, so that when you say, "I will give" it may be translated either that way, or as "I give"—a circumstance which, unless great care is exercised in phrasing, can obviously make for confusion.

Other testimony established that the Navy had occasionally indeed given surplus and salvage materials to Palauans as compensation for services or in cases where to move it would have cost more than could be reclaimed upon sale. It was shown also that the defendant's actions were conducted openly and under claim of right. Weighing all the circumstances, I came to the conclusion there was such reasonable doubt on the question of intent to steal that I could not in good conscience hold the defendant guilty of larceny. I pronounced judgment of acquittal, after explaining carefully to the audience a cardinal principle of American justice: that although a person may in fact be guilty of an offense, it is required that the government prove guilt beyond a reasonable doubt. Reasonable doubt persisted in my mind so I was forced to discharge him. If guilty in fact, the defendant was the beneficiary of the tender solicitude of our legal system which was based on the principle that it were better for ten guilty men to go free, than for one innocent to be wrongfully convicted.

As one might imagine, the acquittal was received with

great delight by the defendant and his assembled clan-members. Of course due commendation was given the public defender's staff, and from what I later ascertained, Mr. Edwards could have been elected mayor of Koror. The prosecutor accepted the verdict philosophically, and if the Distad and Trust Territory disapproved, I at least never heard it from them. However, I thought it best to write an explanatory letter to the Attorney General of Trust Territory to rebut any presumption of improper procedure by Stan Darby in the alleged gift of government property. Had the case involved the validity of the alleged gift, I would have had no difficulty deciding for the government; it was quite another matter, however, to hold the defendant guilty of a criminal conversion in view of the doubts cast by the circumstances.

This case and a few others of no particular note finished the criminal call, so I was free to take up one remaining civil trial and approximately forty cases of land claim appeals. The civil trial was one brought by the Ibedul, or principal chief of Koror Island, one Ngoriakl, and a lesser chief, Ngiraked, against Trust Territory Government, to confirm title in Ngoriakl to a parcel of valuable land lying close to the administrative center of Koror Municipality. The chief's title was claimed through a Japanese businessman who had been repatriated to Japan, after the late war. The Government contended that the title inhered in it by international law as property of a national of the former sovereignty defeated in war.

This case developed some interesting and unusual aspects. It was tried for the plaintiff by the public defender whose duties cover cases where native claims require legal assistance in order to obtain justice. The defense was handled by the Government's other trial lawyer, the district attorney. Of course, Palauan assistants sat in at the trial and took part in the strategy on both sides.

The land had been owned during early Japanese times by Ngiraked's brother, now deceased. It was chief's land and therefore could be transferred or leased by the chief without clan approval. Plaintiffs testified that the land had been leased to the Japanese businessman for erection of a store building from which he intended to carry on a trade goods venture. The building was in fact erected on the land, as well as a dwelling, and for some years the business was carried on. Ngiraked's sister-in-law gave testimony to establish collection of periodic rent. An imposing woman of about 65, she was carefully dressed in a dark cotton gown, with bare arms and legs revealing the heavy purple tattoo associated with women of high rank. She knew nothing of any sale of the property to the Japanese merchant, as suggested by the district attorney, but had collected rent until shortly before her husband's death. This of course tended to establish a lease and negate the idea of a sale.

When asked why she had stopped collecting after her husband's death, her reply was that his property was not hers, and under the custom passed to his clan or to his children, if such had been his will. In Palau, the wife does not inherit such property, and upon her husband's death, returns to her own clan who have the duty of maintaining her. This answer also made sense.

Ngiraked testified that he knew that his deceased brother had borrowed heavily from Ngoriakl and before his death desired to pay the debt. He had therefore given the property to Ngiraked with instructions to sell it and pay the debt from the proceeds. This Ngiraked wished to do as soon as the Government's claim was withdrawn.

The testimony of Ngiraked and the confirmation of the

debt by Ngariakl seemed to make a convincing case. The picture appeared consistent with Palauan custom, mindful of the need to conserve ownership of land in clan or lineage members, while permitting foreign nationals to make a present use at a guaranteed rental. However, the Government's defense was devastating.

Its major witness was Sakuo, the ranking native land claims officer in the Palau district, who had held the same position under the Japanese. His familiarity with the Japanese language which he wrote and spoke fluently made his presence as interpreter at Japanese-Palauan transactions an invariable custom. He had attended the parties at the negotiation of this transaction between Ngiraked's brother and the Japanese merchant and was able to supply the details. It was actually a sale of the land; the merchant intended to erect a stone dwelling which could not be justified by a lease only. The purchase price had been paid and the store building, subsequently erected and occupied by the merchant was demolished during the bombing of the islands and the land had not been used since.

The district attorney, realizing of course that he could not rest his case on the uncorroborated testimony of a present government employee, had done a superlative job of combing the woods for other witnesses. He produced several who recalled admissions by the seller that he no longer had an interest in the property after the merchant had taken possession. But the prize witness whose testimony caused complete consternation in the camp of the plaintiff was the major of Koror Municipality, Rudiml, who told of being consulted by the seller about the advisability of making the deal, and being present when the transaction was closed. This testimony by a Palauan magistrate contradicting the story of the leading chief of the southern islands was most unusual. It indicated that the plaintiff's case was infected with fraud. When no counter-evidence developed, I announced a decision in favor of the government. To this there was neither protest nor appeal.

That week we were fortunate in getting access to one of the old jeeps which, once you got it started, ran after a fashion. Roads go all around Koror Island and are quite passable except down in the village where homes and business establishments abound. Native jeeps and other vehicles were on the road, far more than in any other district. We noticed too that many homes did not rely on rain catchment cisterns for household water but enjoyed the same water service as the American colony, through pipes.

We followed the road down to the waterfront and parked in front of the large double store of the Western Carolines Trading Company. The manager, Sid Seid, greeted us and showed us his stock of giant clam shells, strewn around the docks by the score, each weighing over thirty pounds. Seid explained that the shells are brought up by divers who attach a chain around them by which they are hoisted into the fishing boat. It is essential for the diver to keep clear of the shell, as the tremendous muscle closing the shell could never be loosened in time to avoid a tragedy.

He told us of the fearlessness of the hardy Palauan fishermen and his experience with one of them who brought his son, a boy of twelve, on a hunt. The two men had anchored their boat in deep water off the reef and were spear-fishing, when a shark came along. The boy had been swimming nearby and seeing the great fish, swam to the boat in fright. The men surfaced and followed him into the boat and the father upbraided his son for his fear. He would be of no use to his people, he said, if he could not face any peril of the deep. He told the boy that the shark was even less willing to risk an encounter and, faced resolutely, would go off. He then picked up the boy, threw him in the water and dived in after him with his spear-gun cocked. Luckily the shark was no longer in sight.

We brought a pair of the giant clam shells and arranged to have them polished and delivered to the plane for shipment to our home island. We also bought some of the heavy wooden figures handcarved by the natives and known as "monkey men." The dark wood, called *dort,* abounding in these islands is hard and weighty and is dexterously fashioned into salad knife and fork sets, bowls of all kinds, chess men, and even long cocktail tables frequently inlaid with polished shells and indented with figures depicting ancient scenes. We also bought a story board, a rectangular slab of polished wood on which was painted the story of a lover whose woman was desired by the tribal chief. The lover cuts off her head and brings it to the chief in lieu of the rest of her, whereupon the chief's men fling spears at him as he runs away.

We found such items on display as dishes, clothing, tools, toilet articles, soft drinks and even outboard motors. The Palauan youth, quite westernized and aggressive, leave their islands readily, especially if they can settle on Guam and enjoy more of the material comforts available there, and there is a good sized colony of Palauans on Guam where they hire out as domestics. Their good looks and industrious habits make them favorites over other Micronesians. If the islands ever join in a national confederation, I predict the Palauans will lead the others.

That afternoon I visited the laboratory and office of Bob Owen, the district entomologist, and found out why Palau is the only district which enjoys the full-time service of an entomologist. For some years the coconut palms had been ravaged by the beetle whose depredations threatened the major portion of Palau's leading money crop. Research into the life cycle of the beetle in other lands where its threat was of modest proportions revealed that its most effective enemy was the scolia wasp, an intelligent creature that likes nothing better than to find a fat little beetle feeding contentedly on the heart of the palm, paralyze him by a swift stab of its stinger, and lay an egg on his back so that upon hatching the young wasp would have a supply of food. On the theory that the enemies of our enemies are our friends, Owen had developed a fine colony of wasps which he felt would in time decimate the prolific beetles. His pride, as he pointed out the heaps of enriched soil in which the wasps were germinating, was understandable. He had discovered and catalogued other villainous insects which preyed on plant life and trees and had developed methods and means to attack them. Liaison was maintained with the agriculture station where state-side plants were introduced into the native colony, but the major attention was given to developing better strains of the indigenous crops, and samples and cuttings were constantly exchanged between districts. These activities of the government rank among the most important of our services to the Micronesians.

The first week was about over. The time was approaching for the trochus hunt which, with the absence of litigants, interpreters, constabulary and court officials, was expected to close the court for business. However, I had been studying the files of the long pending land claims appeals and was ready with a plan for disposing of them with the help of the district attorney and of the public defender. The plan contemplated our spending the weeks of the trochus holiday drawing pre-trial orders to simplify the issues and, wherever possible, to decide the cases on legal grounds, not on the presentation of evidence. This was possible because the land claims office had in each case filed a report setting forth the facts. If both sides agreed the facts were sufficient the cases could be decided after a hearing of argument on the law to be applied.

Besides, many of the cases had a common background both of fact and of legal principles because they originated in attempts by the land office to declare as public lands hundreds of acres taken by the Japanese from their native owners and used for public purposes. In some cases the clans had accepted the Japanese offer of compensation; in others, they had accepted less than a fair price because of coercion; in still others there had been no compensation at all. Those cases that had been involved in litigation at the outbreak of war and had never been disposed of were obviously entitled to be decided as though they had been instituted against our government as the old sovereign.

There were also numerous cases in which the lands had been taken for inadequate compensation many years earlier —before Japan fortified the islands and excluded foreigners from their boundaries. During this earlier period there was a way to present claims to a Japanese official and have the land restored to the clan, or else to fix fair compensation. The government insisted that such claims arising before March, 1935 could not be considered—under international law which provides that where opportunity for challenge and relief had been available, a new sovereign power is not required to right the wrongs imposed by an earlier power. In such cases, however, the government was prepared to concede that due compensation had not been paid, so no additional evidence was necessary.

As both counsel and I went over each file in the presence of the court reporter, we were able to classify the cases and agree whether there were still any issues on which the parties had the burden of offering evidence. I then undertook to prepare and dictate an appropriate pre-trial order, which after modifications suggested by counsel, was adopted in each case. Since separate detailed orders were needed in every case, the two weeks of the trochus holiday were barely sufficient for preparing the forty orders needed. And the court reporter was kept at work diligently, knocking them out, while the two lawyers commenced accumulating evidence for those cases in which actual trials would be held.

Of the total land cases on the call, in about one-third the lands had been seized for public use prior to 1935 with no effective steps taken in protest. In these, I entered judgment orders applying the harsh rule of international law which I felt obligatory, and confirmed title in the Trust Territory Government.

In another one-third the lands had been taken with no adequate compensation, since the March 1935 cut-off date. These cases broke into several classes: in some there was no compensation, in others the amount received was scanty. As this later group had offered to return the compensation, I considered them to be in the no-compensation class and I entered judgment requiring the government to redeliver the respective lands to the claimants. Among the cases were those involving the ownership of most of Peleliu Island from which the native owners had been evicted in 1938 in order to make possible the construction of an airstrip. Actually this airfield was no longer needed by the government. Indeed it was no longer usable, the concrete runway had cracked and disintegrated and heavy tropical vegetation had taken over. It would be some years before this process would be completed, but at least the clans could now make plans for planting coconut and nipa palms, breadfruit and tapioca.

The last one-third of the cases required trial of issues of fact. Some denied receiving adequate compensation; others claimed that the deals had been consummated by coercion;

in some the government contended that known amounts
paid by the Japanese were fair and reasonable upon the
basis of buying power at the time the money was admittedly received. These cases then, had to be tried, and all
that were ready for trial were in fact concluded and final
judgment orders were entered. Some of the trials were vigorously contested and long drawn-out. It took considerable
determination to follow the testimony attentively in the
heat of the Palauan day and under the perpetual lulling
drone of the ceiling fans overhead. The Sheriff was kind
enough to send a jeep to bring our court party to and from
the hotel for court sessions. I always refused the rides, except at the close of the day when the heat and bickering had
finally worn me down. However, after an hour's sleep and
a refreshing shower, my energies were renewed sufficiently
to enjoy a cocktail or two, a fairly adequate dinner, and a
game of chess or a movie.

Unfortunately, the court reporter, Miss Griffin, suffered a
stroke before the session ended. With no other competent
person to take shorthand notes of the trials, I found it
necessary to take my own notes of the evidence and rulings
in longhand, and on that basis to make decisions and enter
judgment orders. Some of the least complicated orders were
typed by Anthony Polloi, the Clerk of Courts, but most were
prepared for me by staff members on Guam, where I removed the files and worked on my opinions.

It is interesting to note that no appeals from the final
judgments were taken by any of the parties. The government was content to abide by adjudications permitting the
confirmations of title to large tracts of land by the former
owners, who in turn were gratified to have our government
undo some of the injustices of the Japanese. Even defeated
litigants had some consolation, for they could acquire
claimed lands under the homestead procedure, which in

the islands works on a somewhat more liberal basis than in the states. In Micronesia, priority is given to former occupants or owners, and to obtain a land grant no money need be paid to the government. All in all, we passed an instructive, fruitful ten weeks on the most beautiful and progressive Trust Territory islands, and we left with expressions of friendship and esteem by the local judges and municipal officials as well as the Distad and his staff ringing unforgettably in our ears.

Upon our return to Guam, Nat Logan Smith the personnel officer, suggested that we have complete physical examinations to determine whether we had picked up intestinal parasites on our long sojourn in the Western Carolines. We understood that this happened quite often in eating food prepared by natives, many of whom suffer from such ailments. Of course we were certain we had the bugs from descriptions of symptoms given us by kind friends, but after complete checkups from head to foot by the competent Navy doctors at Guam Naval Hospital, nothing worse was found than an inflamed throat. We did thoroughly enjoy our experience in this tremendous and elegant hospital, which impresses those Micronesians fortunate enough to be treated within its walls, with its competence and dignity, infinitely superior to anything available to the people of Trust Territory, both white and native. It is too bad that our government does not realize the loss in prestige it sustains when the perceptive natives compare facilities available to residents of an arm of the United States with those offered to residents of a mere trust territory.

CHAPTER 14

LAST DAYS ON TRUK

I did not return to Truk on the next available plane, but extended my stay on Guam for several weeks in order to complete the opinions in the cases tried on Palau and dictate them into the recording machine. It was also necessary to expand the legal research begun in the modest library at Koror, to take advantage of the well-equipped air-conditioned library in the office of the Attorney General of Guam. Each day a Trust Territory car would transport me the several miles from the territorial headquarters to the government center in Agana, where I spent most of the day in study and drafting.

With the work of transcription undertaken by the Deputy Commissioner's secretary, I was able to leave for the Truk Atoll, but my wife remained on Guam to greet our daughter, Marcia, who was coming out on surface vessel to spend the rest of our stay with us.

They both arrived at Truk some weeks later, and then our little cottage resounded with the conviviality of life with a high-spirited outdoor-loving young female, able not merely to exist but to look attractive on a diet of little food and less sleep. It is safe to say that with a little encouragement Marcia could easily have made the grade as a Class "A" beachcomber.

Shortly after she arrived, her mother received distress-

ing news from home about her mother's serious illness, and
had to make the long journey to Chicago to arrange for
proper nursing care and supervision. This took much longer
than anticipated and when it appeared that my mother-in-
law's illness would be fatal, my wife remained with her until the end. This sad period extended into months and ultimately made it necessary for me to return to the states
and give up my judicial post.

Meanwhile, however, daughter took over the care of the
family household with good spirit and tried to carry on in
her mother's place. Before it was over she became a pretty
good cook and shopper, but you could detect the influence
of France in her cooking, particularly in the ominous addition of wines both French and American to our daily diet.
Daughter made up for this in part by putting us both on a
diet of Slenderella for at least a meal a day. I could never
be sure whether this was due as much to my gain in weight
as to her desire to eliminate one of the meals she had to prepare. Anyway I thrived on this mixed diet, whereas daughter remained what I thought was downright skinny.

Another court session arrived meanwhile, with a division
of work between the Chief Justice and myself. There were
only civil cases, most of them involving use-rights of lands
and fishing rights to the teeming waters inside the reef. In
two of the cases, because certain witnesses whose testimony was considered vital by the litigants lived on Uman,
an island about 15 miles southwest of Truk, and were too
old and feeble to make the trip, the parties begged me to
travel to take the testimony of these witnesses. After I had
all the other available evidence and studied it I concluded
that their testimony might well be controlling. I could have
delegated this task to Ichiro Moses, one of the district
judges, who happened to be the leading chief and magistrate of Uman, for the Code of Laws provided for appoint-

ment of district judges as masters in chancery to take testimony in areas outside the centers. But I felt that so much depended on both their knowledge of facts and their candor, especially under cross-examination, that it was important for me to observe them on the stand. When I announced I would travel to Uman Island and hold court there, the parties professed their appreciation.

Next I checked with "Red" Steele about transportation for the week I had scheduled. This was within his province as assistant distad. There were few boats suitable for the trip: they had to be sturdy enough to withstand the sudden squalls which occasionally came without warning and changed the peaceful character of the lagoon. "Red" informed me he could schedule me on a Higgins boat LCVP if I could take along a team of medical practitioners scheduled to inoculate the children of Uman against an epidemic of measles and mumps which had struck on the Truk Atoll. The court party would consist of five at the most and the boat could comfortably hold forty so I was happy to agree.

When Marcia heard the news that night she refused to give her approval unless I took her along, saying what a fine opportunity it was for her to study the Trukese there—an area where the influence of the American-oriented district center would be minimized. She had even heard that no American girl had ever set foot on Uman (this I am sure is not true) and wished to blaze a historic trail. This, as it turned out, she certainly did, but in a way quite different than intended. After a few lame arguments on my side, easily demolished, I capitulated, particularly as we expected to leave early and finish our work in one day, and I turned over the task of organization to our clerk of courts Misauo, who was to accompany us.

On the day fixed, Marcia was up early and prepared a light lunch to take along in a duffel bag—a few sandwiches, some fruit, and a thermos of iced tea. With this and a hot breakfast, I felt we could easily overcome any dragon of the deep. The pick-up truck came for us and before eight o'clock we were speeding past students on their way to the schools lining the main roads. We stopped at the courthouse, picked up Misauo and the court files and continued on our way to the dock, passing many natives trudging in both directions and exchanging friendly greetings as we drove by. The Trukese invariably seem so happy when they meet you. It is always difficult to reconcile this image with the fierce war clubs on display as an aspect of life in these islands a mere generation ago.

At the waterfront we were met by the crew of our vessel and some of the medical party. In a few minutes the two policemen who were to serve as bailiffs drove up, and later, a few natives from Uman who had received permission to return to their island in a government boat. Most natives travel from island to island either in an outrigger canoe equipped with sails, or in a canoe Western style, sporting an outboard motor. In the comparatively wealthy Palaus and Marshalls, you see many motor-propelled canoes, but only a few in the Truk District so the natives always welcome a ride in a government boat between the islands— permission is given only when public business requires.

While we were waiting on the dock one of the Public Works supervisors, Warren Bacon, whose job it was to see us on our way, sauntered over and called my attention to the white caps riding off shore and the gentle swell in the distance. Looking quizzically at the sky he opined we might have a few waves on our crossing. Fortified with my memory of the dangerous crossing in the Marshalls, I was of course able to accept this conjecture with an indulgent smile, for how could the relatively calm waters of the lagoon compare with the lordly ocean? And of course daughter who had crossed two vast oceans was hardly concerned by any possible discomfort on this hour-and-a-half trip in sight of land at all times.

So we all took our gear on board and made ready for the voyage. The bow and middle section of the boat were without protection from the elements, except by the gunwale which was at least five feet above the hold. The stern of the boat was surmounted by a deck, in front of which was the wheel and behind it an unprotected seat for the helmsman. Below this deck—which had no gear and was bare except for a bench placed across it and able to hold a half dozen persons in comfort—was a shallow hold, containing ropes, chains and anchor, and several compartments stocked with emergency rations and gear.

As honored guests, my daughter and I were handed up to sit on the bench athwart the deck and were joined there by Misauo and several of the medical team. Some sat at our feet, their legs dangling over the hold, and others stood behind us, their feet braced on the wooden deck. That there was no railing around this little deck we did not realize until later.

The captain counted noses and made sure every authorized person was present. Since the boat was assigned to the judiciary department, I, as the senior officer, was technically in command, and so I gave the signal to cast off and get under way. The boat's powerful engines obeyed the command, we backed away from our berth, and the dock and Moen village receded rapidly in the distance.

Passing around the west shore of our island, we saw for the first time its southern shore, which looked quite impassable with heavy timber growth and thick underbrush almost to the water's edge, and we knew why no roads had ever cut along the shore to the south end of the island. The high hill behind our cottage reached down towards the southern shore, and few natives lived on the other side of this hill. Those who did found it advisable to transport their copra in small boats to a central gathering point in Moen Village.

Passing the South end of Moen Island, we entered a channel about a mile wide between Fefan and Dublon, two large well-inhabited islands. The waves were just high enough to be sporting, we were in high spirits at what seemed like a holiday, and as we passed the shelter of the two large islands, the immensity of the lagoon came home to us as we caught our first glimpse of Uman about ten miles off and realized that the bounding reef was many miles beyond Uman. We quickly approached the jetty marking Uman harbor and prepared to swing out to avoid the rocks marking its entrance. As we did so the swarthy Trukese captain pointed down toward the water and, following his finger, we were able to discern in the clear water the masts of a large vessel only a few feet beneath the water's surface. Misauo told me there were numerous other Japanese craft on the lagoon bottom, though the work of reclamation had been going on there for years.

Soon we were in the harbor and in a few minutes scrambling onto the pier where the island chiefs were waiting to greet us. First among them, of course, was Ichiro Moses, leading chief and judge of the Truk District Court, who pumped my hand and my daughter's, saying over and over the only English words in his vocabulary, "Thank you very much." To this, daughter responded in Trukese, "*Kettah pwan i fany*." "You are welcome." In private, daughter would pronounce it "catch him by the fanny!"

Also present was Upuini, another district judge from Tol, one of the largest islands of the Truk District, of which he headed the leading clan. I knew both men well and favorably. We also met another half-dozen dignitaries, officials of local governments and elders of clans. Through the Administration's encouragement most of the large islands now had municipal governments which were taking an increasingly important role in local self-government; and each municipality sends a representative to the annual session of the Congress of each district where legislation is adopted for the entire district. It is hoped that the legislative duties of the High Commissioner will in time be taken over by the district Congresses and ultimately by a territorial Congress for all Micronesia.

Conducted by our hosts, we walked to the main village along the shore, noting the municipal headquarters, with a large meeting hall on the first floor and a small dining room adjoining. A high railing circumscribed this dining area and in its shadow was a pile of green coconuts. One of the party picked up a large nut, whacked the top off with his machete, handed it to me and then performed the same courtesy for Marcia. The liquid was cool and sweet and came just in time to spare me from making the *faux pas* of drinking from our thermos, when we learned that we would be entertained at lunch between court sessions with a native feast. I naturally expressed my pleasure though I had good reason to regard the food with something less than enthusiasm.

As we stood there on the porch conversing through interpreters, I noticed, among the throng following us, young girls pressing quite close to the railing and watching Marcia's antics with complete absorption. She was wearing pedal-pushers which tapered down close to her ankles and a gay handkerchief covered her head. It was when she had finished with the nut and handed it to one of our hosts that she picked up her purse and took out a powder puff with some other beauty aids. The girls pressed closely around as Marcia applied powder and then lip rouge, watching herself carefully in her small hand mirror. When she had finished this repair job, and given her hair a few licks and straightened up, the delight of the maidens bubbled over in squeals and laughter. They pointed toward her face in the greatest glee, having apparently never seen this operation so dear to the hearts of civilized women, though I was sure some of them must have read of it or seen ads in American magazines.

In a short time the meeting hall was converted into a courtroom and court was convened. The old people I had come to see took the witness stand and in a few hours all their essential testimony had been recorded. With the completion of evidence in each case, I was able to announce my decision, giving my reasons and the basic legal theory, as was my custom. The noon recess had now arrived so I discussed with Marcia and later with Misauo the possibility of avoiding the native feast without affronting our friendly hosts, but it was quite clear that it couldn't be done. We could, however, save our sandwiches and tea for the return trip when we would doubtless develop an appetite.

We entered the dining hall. The table was covered with a white cloth, something decidedly unusual, and places were set for six—Judges Upuini and Moses, Misauo, Marcia and myself and the secretary of Uman Municipality. In the center of the table there were three platters, one filled with boiled fish, another with whole boiled chickens, and the third with taro, apparently baked, and then sprinkled with grated coconut. As a concession to Western custom, there were plates, forks and knives for each person, and cups for the coffee which had been heated on a grate outside.

We were each served a whole fish caught that morning and kept wrapped in banana leaves to resist the hot sun. Salt and pepper are not used by the natives, but if you are

hungry enough—a circumstance normal among the Trukese—you can eat the fish without much difficulty. But
Marcia and I merely nibbled at one side, hoping our attempts would not attract too close attention.

After a while, the plate of boiled chickens was passed to
me. Determined not to take any more than I could eat, I
started to cut a chicken in half, but the combination of
tough chicken and dull knife proved unbeatable. I couldn't
make a dent. After a little struggle, and with everyone's
eyes on me, I stopped awhile to reflect on what Emily Post
would approve under the circumstances. Suddenly the decision was taken from me. Judge Upuini, who was seated on
my left, reached over and grabbed the chicken in his hands,
tore it in two and placed one-half on my plate and the other
half on Marcia's. We were each also helped to a large slice
of taro, which we worked at industriously, and after a bit
the meal ended with most of our food still uneaten. Of course
I apologized for our poor appetite and bemoaned the waste
of food which I knew to be in short supply on these islands
away from the district center, but as I stood outside the dining hall I noticed several of the officials picking the uneaten food off each plate and carefully wrapping it in banana leaves. In answer to my question, Misauo advised me
that no food is wasted—what is left from a "feast" is first
offered to the next echelon of dignitaries, then finally to the
waiters and kitchen help.

After lunch it appeared that the parties to a pre-trial conference and their counsel were at hand, so we went to the
courtroom and spent several hours in conference, of which
I took complete notes. When court was adjourned, I sent
Misauo to alert the medical team, and followed him to see
what was going on in the infirmary adjoining the courthouse. I saw a line of women and girls carrying infants and
leading small children to a table outside the building where

the medical men had set up their equipment and in a matter of seconds, each child was lifted onto the table and given a shot in the buttocks. Some cried pitifully, some merely whimpered, others laughed with a bravado designed to conceal pain which they would not betray in public. When the last one had been treated the medical team made ready to pack up and follow us on board ship.

Meanwhile, I started to look for Marcia who had decided to avoid the boresome afternoon session and to explore the island instead. For this purpose she had enlisted a few of the elementary school children who were just beginning to study English. Marcia soon discovered that music was better than speech for developing understanding, so she started to teach the children some of the tunes that stateside children and grown-ups sing at community gatherings. One of the most appreciated was an old favorite of our family group, *Old McDonald Had a Farm!* By the time she had walked the mile or so around the principal village, the children were following her in droves gleefully coming in with the refrain, "Eee-I-ee-I-O!"

I would wager that her action that day was far more effective in painting a picture of American culture than my studious attempt to interpret our conception of justice. The children hated to see us leave and most of the village accompanied us to the dock. We took leave of our hosts with expressions of mutual esteem and boarded our little craft for the trip homeward.

It was four o'clock. All of our party were aboard, except the few passengers who had made the return trip to their home island. In their place the medical team had brought a young mother carrying a sick baby for treatment on Moen, placing her in a protected spot in the hold, with the baby's face covered with a cloth. From the worried expression on the young mother's face it seemed evident that she feared the worst. The trip and what happened later was hardly likely to have contributed to the baby's recovery.

As we cast off and waved goodbye to those on the pier, I noticed the overcast sky and said I thought it was likely to rain. Marcia had forgotten her slicker, but mine was in the duffel bag so I took it out and placed it on my lap when we took our seats on the bench along with Misauo and three members of the medical team. As on the trip over, in front of us, seated on the deck with feet dangling over the hold, were a few other members of the hospital staff and behind us were others standing with bare feet braced on the deck. Perhaps a half dozen others sat or stood along the rail in the bow.

Soon we had made the turn out of the harbor and were just outside the protection of the pier which ran along the north boundary, when the modest swell we had noted in the harbor changed quickly into an angry sea and in minutes gave us real concern for our safety on the perch athwart the unprotected deck. The sea hit us broadside and as we rose to meet the charge I noticed a surprising fact: the bench which had seemed to be a solid part of the deck's construction commenced to slide toward the churning waves. So it was merely furniture, its only protection the weight of those sitting on it and the grasp of those standing behind it! Each time the boat keeled half-over the bench slid closer to the edge, then as the boat righted, it slid back toward the other edge, never quite making the last two feet on either side. At first the humor of it struck us both and we laughed but I finally said to Marcia, "Let's get out of here," and led the way to the hold. A little while later we looked back and saw that some of the Trukese had taken our seats, and those sitting on and those standing behind the bench were using their utmost strength to keep it from plunging into the heaving waters. I could not help being reminded of one of the old Keystone comedies. I thought of the hapless police jumping crazily onto a truck, holding on to the tailgate, the running board or anything else, utterly woebegone and ineffectual.

We were taking a beating. Our skipper, struggling to keep the nose of our sturdy craft lined up with the channel between Dublon and Fefan looming dead ahead, sat up there on his perch on the starboard side of the deck holding grimly to the wheel while the spray broke over him. When the waves were about to hit us broadside he maneuvred skillfully to meet them head-on, then made a quick half turn as they receded and we rode through the trough. This was truly an angry sea, and the savage wind lashed us and the waves with equal fury. Marcia and I stood side by side along the rail above the hold and my thoughts turned to the possibility that our boat might be overwhelmed by the high seas. I thought it wise under the circumstances to warn my daughter, who is an excellent swimmer, against trying to save her father, who swims like a lump of lead. And yet I doubted that any but the very strongest and luckiest could keep afloat in the churning waters and reach the beaches of Dublon which were coming ever closer.

After what seemed an eternity we struggled into the friendly channel and knew at long last that the worst part of the terrifying trip was over. For we had passed through the open sea and now we would be in the shelter of land for all but the short run around Moen Island. As we were relaxing from the intensity of our struggle we saw a pathetic sight coming toward us from the other end of the island channel. As we steamed in its direction, there hove into view a Trukese outrigger with a mast from which a sail hung in shreds. We could see that it was filled with six people, two of them women, and one a lad, and we discovered that it was a family trying to reach home on Uman. They were obviously in great distress, unable to make much headway against the turbulent waters without the help of their sail and able to use only their short oars. They exchanged friendly greetings with our captain, who then advised me through Misauo that the wayfarers had asked for a tow as far as we could go toward Uman. The captain wished to know my directions in the matter. I discussed it with Misauo and the leader of the medical team and we decided to tow them as far as Dublon harbor which offered a safe refuge until the sea would subside. They accepted gratefully and after several attempts one of our seamen finally placed a line over the little craft which they made fast to their mast, and off we went. We had to reverse our direction and run several miles off course, which we were glad to do, and we pulled them right to the entrance of the harbor. With many thanks the Umanese cast off our line and we turned back towards Moen. Chancing to look back later towards Dublon Harbor, I could at first find no trace of the little craft, but then at last I caught sight of it. There it was standing out to sea on its way to Uman after all. I had to admire the plucky spirit of these Trukese who preferred to brave the angry sea we had just left and try to reach home at whatever hour rather than spend the night cold and wet on a neighboring island a few miles away. We heard later that they made Uman late that night.

As for ourselves, we traversed the channel without further incident and with a marked lessening of wave and wind. But as we passed the shelter of the channel, it began to rain and then it poured heavily and relentlessly and for the next hour we took a soaking as unpleasant as you can possibly imagine. It was too wet under the deck to sit, and you couldn't stand there without hitting the ceiling, which, of course, was the floor of the upper deck, so it was necessary to huddle closely at the rail. The rain coursed coldly down my back from my pith helmet. I had taken off my slicker and put it on Marcia despite her protests, for I at least had the protection of my long-sleeved shirt, but we all took a real soaking, and when we finally reached Baker Dock and disembarked the water was still coming out of us in buckets.

Fortunately, a pick-up truck was awaiting us, and in twenty minutes we were snug in our comfortable abode, getting wet clothes off us and drinks of whiskey into us, which renewed vital forces until the warm shower restored us to humanity. That night we arrived at the Gallemore's an hour late for dinner, for which we were forgiven when we told the story of our trip. Of course I had to act blasé and play down the seriousness of the peril through which we had passed, for Roy Gallemore, as an ex-submarine captain, and many of his guests were quite accustomed to the travails of the sea.

I was happy indeed to have completed all my pending cases, and after dictating the last of my opinions to Roy's secretary I was able to close my desk a few weeks later with all assignments satisfied.

Shortly afterwards, I boarded the plane for Guam, where I expected to stay several weeks before rejoining my wife in Chicago. There was some question whether we would return, at least to live on Guam in a different capacity—so when I left Truk it was not necessarily goodbye to Trust Territory. However, when I took leave of the staff and the wives who make it their pleasant duty to meet each plane, my heart sensed I would not return to this fascinating life. I was most deeply aware of the strong emotional bond I had developed with the people in this Micronesian paradise. As we taxied off to our place at the top of the runway and passed the arms waving farewell on our quick take-off, I was unable to resist the hot tears.

CHAPTER 15

HOW ARE WE DOING?

In the day when our dwindling gold supply makes it desirable to re-appraise each international commitment that adds to the flow outward, Trust Territory deserves a few glances. True enough, the cost to the United States is small, no more than about five and one-half millions annually. If the result, however, is merely to fill a few hundred jobs without accomplishing anything of lasting value for either the Micronesians or ourselves, early disengagement from our responsibilities would be very wise—unless of course our commitments under the trusteeship are such that we cannot honorably terminate them until we accomplish some end not yet in sight.

To measure our national obligation, it is helpful to turn to the trusteeship agreement for the terms of our mandate from the United Nations. There we find our aims stated as the development of the peoples of Trust Territory so that they can assume the responsibilities of self-government and become as nearly self-sufficient economically as possible; and to encourage respect for their culture, while affording them an opportunity to take whatever aspects of Western life will enable them to live richer lives.

It is of course true that we never needed to assume trust obligations in these island, for they were ours by right of conquest. A number of alternatives were presented to us at the close of the war with Japan. We could have returned the islands to Japan. This would have been unwise after the blood and treasure we had poured out because others controlled the approaches to Hawaii. It was also important to our security to eliminate any threat to the safety of Guam, our westernmost naval and air base on American soil.

We could have given the islanders the freedom to fend for themselves which they had not enjoyed since the last years of the last century. It would have been morally untenable to do this without first restoring the damage we had caused by shelling and invasion. And of course without benevolent supervision, the islands might have fallen ready prey to any other power wanting a foothold a few thousand miles from Pearl Harbor.

Or we could have followed the course we finally did select, helping to advance these island peoples to a healthier, more meaningful existence.

Sound policy dictated our control over the islands, at least until strategic military considerations need no longer govern; and our honor was pledged to the goal of self-sufficiency and self-government within the framework of native culture, enriched by any elements of Western culture the islanders might find of value.

Consequently we are in the position of a trustee propelled into office by pressing strategic considerations. These considerations will decrease with time and in fact even now may have little validity, yet we have assumed obligations not to be held lightly if we wish to preserve the rank among nations we have earned dearly by high purpose and scrupulous fulfillment of our pledges. We must moreover always adhere to the principle that a trustee's self-interest is subordinate to the needs of the trust beneficiaries.

The question then is whether our performance measures up to our self-imposed obligations, at least in those fields in which government programs are of major importance.

First among these programs is political advancement, a fertile field entirely neglected by the Japanese who preferred complete control by administrators sent from Japan working upon the clans through their chiefs. There was no education in self-government, no participation in government by the islanders.

Under United States trusteeship the trend has been toward the other extreme. We have been prodding the often reluctant inhabitants of those islands with enough population to justify local government, to organize into a municipality, the basic political entity in the islands. One hundred and two had been created in the five years ending June 1957, with twenty more scheduled for chartering the following year. These municipalities are not autonomous but do have large discretion in distributing the burden of taxation, providing for primary school education and construction of schools and local public works. Subject to possible disapproval by the local administrator and by the High Commissioner, the elected councils of these municipalities can adopt ordinances effective within their jurisdictional confines. Each muncipality has its executive officer, the magistrate, and a scribe or treasurer, all officers being elected by popular vote in the districts, (except in four municipalities where the magistracy is hereditary).

In addition to those local units, most of the districts have district-wide Congresses to which each municipality sends at least one representative selected either by popular election or by designation of municipal officers or council. The Congresses act as advisory bodies to the High Commissioner for programs for their districts, and some have local legislative authority also. You have only to attend the district Congresses and listen to the delegates debate to develop a profound respect for the intelligence and capacity of many of the native leaders.

Once a year a territory-wide conference of the leaders of the six districts is held, usually at Trust Territory headquarters on Guam. Problems of a territorial nature are considered, to which the Administration accords due weight. Thus the seeds of a territorial congress have been planted which will take firm root as soon as the Micronesian leaders come to think of themselves in national terms and not solely as representatives of their native communities.

An important duty of the assistant distad and of the education department head in the districts, is to help unorganized areas create municipal governments. Of course, persuasion is often required before traditional leaders willingly accept the restrictions on their authority which a municipal charter tends to impose. There is reason to believe that the aggressive program of the Administration for imposing self-government on certain communities before they are ready for it is caused largely by the constant needling we receive in the United Nations Trusteeship Council at the hands of delegates from Russia, India and the newly created Afro-Asian States. We should resolutely oppose any target date for self-government and rely instead on the demonstrated ability and desire of the island peoples to enjoy greater independence. Surely the spectacle of the Congo ought to serve as an object lesson for those whose antagonism to colonialism blinds them to the dangers of premature emancipation.

Of course, political development has not proceeded at breakneck speed, but it has been steady and demonstrably successful and there is no valid necessity to step up the pace merely to win approval from quasi-dictatorships, whose attention could be better directed toward their own deficiencies in democratic self-government.

In economic affairs, if our major objective is to bring the native people to self-sufficiency, we are far indeed from substantial success, but in appraising accomplishment in this field one must be careful not to judge by Western standards. We have been exposing the natives to the advantages and material comforts of American civilization for a dozen years, with noticeable effect on their promising young students. It is too much to expect that the perceptive youngsters who take over and ably fill jobs vacated by Americans will continue to accept economic returns insufficient to permit a comfortable life according to American standards, though adequate by native. The pressure is already evident and by the rules of logic should intensify over the years.

Administration policies inevitably tend to feed the fire. For one thing the fact that only natives can own land in Micronesia or go into business, along with the limit against immigration by non-Micronesians, effectively blocks the commercial development encouraged by access to markets on equal terms. There is no great incentive for the islanders to engage in business enterprises or develop the skills for commercial success. If they were to engage in such enterprises even on a modest scale, it would be socially unpopular to require cash payment from needy relatives and clan members, and the consequent slow payment on credit sales and inevitable credit losses would bankrupt all but the wealthiest enterprises. This has been the experience with a credit union formed in the Truk District a few years ago, with capital contributed by many families. Nobody was able to compel payment of money borrowed by the members or their families. And the law in Trust Territory making land and necessary possessions immune from seizure for debt mitigates the pressure which might be exerted upon defaulting debtors.

The islands of Micronesia are geared to a subsistence economy and some might even be able to maintain themselves on a subsistence level, if required to live off the land and sea, with supplementary imports for which copra, trochus and handicraft could be exchanged. But that, for most islanders, would mean deprivation of the adjuncts of civilized living to which they are daily becoming more accustomed. For the growing class of educated young people, it would be tragic, throwing them back into the lower ranks of the native hierachy from which their education would elevate them. The major result would doubtless be a decline of the public school system painstakingly erected by the American authorities, and a sharp reduction in the free medical, dental, hospital and public health programs.

There is no doubt that Trust Territory Government is fully committed to the view that the surest bulwark for adequate social programs and the arts of government is in a sound island economy. It has demonstrated its interest in improving the quality of copra, by employing an eminent specialist who travels to the island districts and supervises planting methods. It maintains an experimentation station in each of the island districts, with a particularly extensive operation on Ponape Island, where native plantings are improved and non-indigenous crops studied. And it has advanced substantial sums ($400,000) to Micronesian-owned trading companies to encourage expansion where the public interest appeared to justify it.

There has also been study toward developing a fisheries industry, canneries, a cultured pearl industry, and increasing the market for native handicraft. Some success has been achieved with new crops such as cacao which reach a world market, but mainly it has been in the improvement of copra production and harvesting of trochus.

The slow pace of the Administration in economic development is attributable for one thing to the meager resources in the islands; for another, to the unwillingness of the authorities to encourage outside enterprise, out of fear that it will bring exploitation; and for yet another, to the lack of trained personnel in fields where technical proficiency is essential.

For the public health program the picture is brighter. Each district has a main hospital supervised by a native director with the minimal medical training essential to operate local medical, dental and hospital organizations. By 1958 there were at least 123 small dispensaries scattered through the outlying communities, staffed by health aides and other partially trained personnel. The medics get their training in the medical school at Suva in the Fiji Islands which trains those intending to specialize in island practice. Medical and dental teams visit the islands periodically to inoculate against tetanus and other diseases which occasionally become epidemic. About half of the infants are now born in hospitals in the district centers, or in infirmaries and treatment centers in the outlying islands; the rest are born with the help of local midwives, some of them trained in district hospitals. There is a nurses' training school in the Palau District, with a small student body and an annual graduating class of less than ten.

Dental care is provided free for children of school age and hospital and medical services at slight charge, unless the patient is unable to pay. The fees collected amount to between five and eight per cent of the total cost of public health services, exclusive of construction and maintenance. While the service is good by island standards, the facilities are far below American standards. For this reason American staff members use the medics only for emergency treatment and if further treatment is required, are taken to the United States Naval Hospital on Guam. The laboratory and technician aspects of medical treatment are particularly weak but incomparably better than when our government took over. Worst of all are the poorly maintained structures, often open to insects, and the failure to observe standards of cleanliness and order.

Considering the need for trained staff members in hospitals and training centers in the islands, and for expanding medical, dental and health services throughout the territory, it came as a shock in 1958 when the government budget reduction for services on Truk was applied to the medical department as well as nearly all other branches. This eliminated some six semi-skilled jobs held by Micronesians whereas if anything, more were needed. A similar cut was made in the staff of the education department where more rather than less must be provided, with the larger number of children coming to the schools each year. Even more straitened circumstances resulted in 1962 with the cost of moving Trust Territory headquarters from Guam to Saipan, and the inability to obtain from Congress the necessary supplemental appropriation to cover it. Money had to be drained from the districts to support the move.

At present there are some 168 public and 34 private (religious) schools in the elementary and intermediate grades. The native tongue is the only language taught in the elementary grades (ages 8 to 14); English is added to the curriculum in the intermediate schools which cover grades 7 to 9 inclusive. Besides one public high school with about 200 pupils now at Ponape, there are three private (religious) high schools, one at Truk, one at Palau and one in the Marshalls. In these schools, English is the language of instruction. Attendance through the elementary grades is compulsory, and proof that compulsion is not unpopular is shown by the attendance record which for 1957 showed 8779 school children attending out of a maximum school population of 9949.

Some 15 scholarships are provided annually by the Administration in schools of higher study at Guam and in Honolulu for students of promise; additional scholarships are offered by local trading companies. Some 223 students were studying outside Trust Territory during 1956, with the number expected to increase the following year. All in all, the educational program of the Administration is well organized and administered and in the course of another decade will make a significant contribution to Micronesian life. The Administration's practice of supplying grants-in-aid to local communities equal to half the cost of school construction has had a twofold advantage: providing adequate school plant and encouraging local participation in planning and operating these facilities. Each year the number of native teachers increases and Micronesians acquire greater control of their educational system. The enlightened program of the United States authorities, promoting vocational training in the schools and in practice, and turning over to Micronesians more positions in all branches of the Administration, is worthy of high commendation. It cannot fail to produce in time a corps of elite cadres able to fill the shoes of departing Americans.

However, the lot of the typical American staff member out in the districts does not present so favorable a picture. Life on Guam (now Saipan) itself in government-rented quarters is not too different from the States: goods, services, medical, dental, hospital and recreational facilities, are all available in reasonable number and variety. But Saipan is not typical of the districts where the real work of Trust Territory is accomplished.

Without intending to minimize the necessity of adequate staff in the main office on Saipan, or the logistics involved in maintaining the far-flung territorial organization, it is nevertheless true that the significant achievements are those of the unsung heroes in the comparatively primitive environment of distant domains. Since it is the accomplishments of local staffs on which the Administration's success rises or falls, you would think the authorities would make every possible effort to keep them and their families as comfortable as possible, considering the difficulties of transport and the deterioration of equipment. Yet we must admit the inadequacy: either the funds are not properly allocated towards the needs in the districts or an insufficient amount is appropriated by Congress. As a result pressing rehabilitation programs are cancelled or postponed, and the district staffs disheartened.

As for housing, most of the districts still house their staffs in the old quonset dwellings of Navy days. Originally designed for three years of tropical service, when we left in 1959 most were starting their 13th year. In some districts a start is being made on new houses of concrete block, attractive and serviceable. If and when completed in substantial numbers, they should reduce the excessive cost of repair and maintenance now in the territorial budget. While the obsolete dwellings are being replaced, a first necessity is to solve the water shortage which makes life particularly disagreeable on Yap, in the Marshals, and even on Truk. The Public Works staff on Truk suspect that the underground water pipes have leaks which carry off much of the rain water. Each year they think the problem is solved, but restricted water hours persist none the less, and there is more griping heard about shortage of water, despite oceans all around, than any other deficiency.

Still another major problem is the absence of transportation facilities in a climate where the sweat literally pours off your back at any exertion in the sun. Some districts have jeeps of ancient age and in poor operating condition—not even as good as some owned by natives. Truk District has Chevrolet pick-up trucks which do well in negotiating the hills where staff homes are built, and when half of them were returned to Guam for service, the remainder were incorporated into a temporary, reasonably satisfactory, taxi service. In all the other districts save Rota, whose problems are unfamiliar, the ancient jeeps are disgraceful, constantly representing a poor advertisement for Uncle Sam among the under-privileged peoples of the islands and Asia proper.

As a fitting adjunct to the vehicles, we furnish a pretty awful road system, and it is always in bad shape despite continual upkeep by Public Works. Small wonder that so few staff members have elected to bring private cars into the districts. The rutted roads and the heavy toll taken by the salt air on machinery and metal effectively discourage all but the most reckless from entrusting their machines to this locale. In road building and maintenance, we have never equalled the Japanese whose concrete roads and structures are in certain locations still usable. As a nation whose pride in the performance of an outstanding administration is quite justified, we should bow our heads at the inadequacies of that transportation setup.

Expansion of the road system around the major islands would enable the natives to bring their copra for export into the district centers, without having to depend on water transport. It would also permit American staff members to use the beaches which turn out to be far removed from population centers. The paucity of such other recreational facilities largely explains why families fail to renew contracts for continued service; island life is confining to Americans used to mobility and freedom. Morale is vital. In domestic relations, many problems are created by the continuous close association of family members, neighbors and staff. Not everybody can take that life and continue to perform necessary duties.

It would not be seemly to close this chapter without stressing one phase of our Administration which is deeply humiliating to staff members who serve in the districts. This is our failure to construct public buildings of dignity and beauty, to place them in attractive and harmonious settings, and to maintain them in a style befitting a great conscientious power. The remarkable fact is that members of Congressional committees who visit the district centers periodically, seem never to have noticed the makeshift, nondescript construction which typifies almost all our public buildings, and the poor state of exteriors and grounds. Where is the pride which actuates these persons when they promote a new federal building or post office in their own districts? Here we have a showcase on exhibit to the missions sent every biennium by the United Nations Trusteeship Council and to students returning from world centers to apply their arts in the service of their peoples. Probably just as poor a case as can be imagined is shown in our use of salvage lumber and other materials, and corrugated metal to patch outmoded structures; it shows the United States in the role of a miser, too penurious to pay adequately for his assumed obligations, but willing, which is even worse, to pay the costs only where they show and can properly impress.

This regrettable condition is fairly representative of practically all Administration buildings, all territorial hospitals, and almost all hotels. It is certainly true of all but one courthouse, that on Koror in the Palau District. It is true of warehouses and public works buildings. The psychologically depressing effect of working in substandard structures is manifest in a downgrading of the nature of the service by

staff members, and in occasional snide comments made by
the perceptive natives, many of whom remember the beautiful public buildings, shrines and *torii* gates erected by our
predecessors the Japanese, and destroyed during the bom-
bardment.

This is not to say that we must use marble, or rare and
costly woods and furnishings appropriate to a legislative
chamber in the States. Concrete block and native woods
will serve in these surroundings just as well; harmony of
structure with natural setting can be achieved without unreasonable expense. The important point is that it is beneath our government's tradition to carry on its work in
foreign lands, without full attention to the impression we
create among the peoples we work with, to the dignity and
comfort of those who work for us, in the facilities and services we offer, and the character of those we delegate to
administer them. Here is a place where the present Administration can without great effort chart an improvement in
a small phase of our foreign policy, which has been crying
out for it all during this last decade.

It will not lighten the load of the American taxpayer to
do this and the work will gain slight, if any, credit for its
accomplishment. But credit is of little account when basic
humanity is a true concern. For the living benefit of the
natives who wonder at American parsimony here in painful
contrast with its prodigality elsewhere, and for the staff
which has to blush often in personal discomfort for its country's inconsistency, the time is not past when our present
practices can be corrected and humane considerations genu-
inely served. This is precisely the point at which our interests and our humanity may intersect, and history bear sympathetic witness in the time to come.